Fields of Fire

Fields of Fire

Emancipation and Resistance in Colombia

Louis Edgar Esparza

LEXINGTON BOOKS
Lanham • Boulder • New York • London

Published by Lexington Books
An imprint of The Rowman & Littlefield Publishing Group, Inc.
4501 Forbes Boulevard, Suite 200, Lanham, Maryland 20706
www.rowman.com

86-90 Paul Street, London EC2A 4NE

British Library Cataloguing in Publication Information Available

Library of Congress Cataloging-in-Publication Data

Names: Esparza, Louis Edgar, author.
Title: Fields of fire : emancipation and resistance in Colombia / Louis Edgar Esparza.
Description: Lanham : Lexington, [2023] | Includes bibliographical references and index. | Summary: "This book identifies the concept of the emancipatory network as a coordination of loose, discrete, and differentiated actors to explain how activists surmount overwhelming odds"— Provided by publisher.
Identifiers: LCCN 2023033655 (print) | LCCN 2023033656 (ebook) | ISBN 9781666927023 (cloth) | ISBN 9781666927047 (paperback) | ISBN 9781666927030 (ebook)
Subjects: LCSH: Plantation workers—Colombia—Case studies. | Sugar workers—Colombia—Case studies. | Labor unions—Organizing—Colombia—Case studies. | Human rights workers—Colombia—Case studies.
Classification: LCC HD8039.P4962 C747 2023 (print) | LCC HD8039.P4962 (ebook) | DDC 331.7/6336109861—dc23/eng/20230810
LC record available at https://lccn.loc.gov/2023033655
LC ebook record available at https://lccn.loc.gov/2023033656

And he said to them: The harvest indeed is great, but the labourers are few. Pray ye therefore the Lord of the harvest, that he send labourers into his harvest. Go: Behold I send you as lambs among wolves.

St. Luke 10: 2-3 DRC

Contents

List of Figures

FIGURES

TABLES

Acknowledgments

This book has received extensive feedback over the years. The most significant of this feedback came from Michael Schwartz and Naomi Rosenthal in 2007–2010. These two patiently read and commented on dozens of drafts. That the story is now told in any intelligible fashion owes a great debt to their careful attention. Also deserving credit for providing important feedback that influenced this text are Jeff Goodwin, Gilda Zwerman, Javier Auyero, and Chuck Tilly.

There are many others who have also commented meaningfully. Among those who I should mention are Jim Jasper, John Krinsky, Vince Boudreau, Haider Khan, Alan Gilbert, Sun-chul Kim, Lindsay Green-Barber, Kate Krimmel, Emmy Eklundh, Peter Manning, Lee Ann Banaszak, John McCarthy, Silvia Dominguez, Hwa-ji Shin, Zehra Arat, Judith Blau, Michael Evans, Judy Tanur, Daniel Levy, Dai Nomiya, Tiago Ribeiro Duarte, Emil Sobotka, John Shandra, Paul Bugyi, Diana Baldermann, Liliana Naydan, Jim McAsey, Rachel Walsh, Lauren Joseph, Marina Sitrin, Alwyn Lim, and Eileen Chanza. Others who encouraged and supported me as I completed this text include Wanda Vega, Pat Bremer, Sharon Worksman, Cindy Chang, Mara D'Angelo, Roger Winn, Adam Carlis, Douglass Hansen, Shari Leskowitz, Liz Monnin-Browder, Haley Harvis, Iris & Galia Halpern, Gio Gaynor, Kevin Lewis, Abby Noble, Dan Barry, Nina Maung, Toni Vicari, Olufemi Vaughan, Kathryne Piazzola, Jean Shin, Karina Havrilla, Diane Barthel, Tim Moran, Thet Win, my parents Louis and Shirley, my sister Leah, and my uncle Lacho.

The project went on in various forms over the years. In that time, I received support from Stony Brook University, Cal State LA, the American Sociological Association Minority Fellowship Program, the Tinker Foundation, the Mellon Foundation, the Latin American Studies Association, Oxfam America, the Society for the Study of Social Problems, Sociologists Without Borders, the Luis Ángel Arango Library, the Irmgard Coninx Stiftung

Foundation, Fulbright Brasil, the University of Brasília, and Chuo University. This help often came at crucial moments, helping me find the time to write, to edit, and to share my ideas with others.

The manuscript might have never been published had Courtney Morales at Lexington Books not approached me about it in 2022. I must also thank an anonymous reviewer for constructive feedback that inspired added synthesis. My experience with Lexington has been tremendous.

Dozens of others in Colombia, the United States, and elsewhere have pushed, challenged, and supported me. Their efforts enable me to share with you a story about the dangerous labor of Colombian sugarcane workers and human rights defenders. During my fieldwork, I came across some of the bravest, kindest souls I have ever met. The fearlessness I saw in their eyes forever changed me. May their stories also inspire courage in others.

Introduction

We slept on the cool tiled floor in a two-story building on a dirt road in a town where all the roads were made of dirt. Our room was large enough for four twin mattresses, which we stacked up in the attached garage during the day. The mattresses kept whosever car that was from making contact with the concrete wall and made room for dozens of plastic chairs for meetings that took place all through the day. Cars passed then, raising dust that powdered the big waxy leaves of the trees, which were strange to me, as strange as they would be to any kid from Elmhurst. The kids here were brown too, and the dust. One of the cars with a megaphone on the roof circled each day selling lottery tickets that someone must have bought, since they passed down the road each day. Some 300 miles to the south, a pyramid scheme called "Fast, Easy Money in Cash" (DRFE) would soon collapse.[1]

The second floor was barren so far as I knew; there was a pile of rusty machetes, the plastic hilts bright orange, and beyond the pile was an empty room that was always dark and always behind a locked wrought iron door that was painted black. They were the same kind of machetes that the workers used to cut the sugarcane stalks this time of year, but there was not a lot of that going on now because of the strike. At the plantations, there was plenty of sugarcane, plenty of workers, and plenty of machetes.

Sometimes at the plantations someone would use their machete to carve a ladle or a statuette out of a piece of wood that they had also used their machete to chop from a nearby tree. Usually there were large cane camions, brimming with fresh-cut stalks and sticky with sugar, and slow and billowing dark clouds of diesel exhaust that stuck to the sides of the truck where the sugar had stuck, but there was not a lot of that going on now because of the strike. There were big tractors, too, sometimes on the back of a flatbed truck that got passed by the motorcycles that zipped through on the way to any other place. The cane

Figure 0.1a   Rusty Machetes. *Source*: Photograph taken by the author in 2008.

stalks were everywhere, all the way to the mountains in the east and the city on the other side, for more than an hour, any way you went. The workers were on strike all through that cane, even if you could not see them, and later in the autumn, the cane grew taller since it was not being cut. The weeds grew, too, in the irrigation canals, even though it was hot and hardly rained. The cars spread dust from the road, and the dust got on everything, and the workers were dusty in their uniforms, which on their upper backs read, "Safe & Fast"; their shoes were dusty, and some of them had red cotton bandanas so that they would not breathe in the dust, which they tied around their necks as they stood or sat.

There were luxury cars, on occasion, which drove quickly; usually there was a manager in the passenger seat and others in the back. You could not see very well past the tint of the window and the thickness of the glass, but you could see the whites of their shirts and of their skin, which were the whitest things one would see all day. They came to see how things were going.

There were police, too, and with the police came the violence. But the workers had help, and, in the end, there were only a few dozen injuries, which was an improvement in this country, which is improving for some people in a certain way.

There were many strikes. Plantations extending to the mountains and over to the city and to the north were under siege, and down even into the northern part of Cauca there were worker victories beyond Puerto Tejada, where we did not go very often because the police harassed us enough already, where the fields and the people were the same but the corrugated metal roofs were rustier and had holes in them and there were fewer of them, and there were more trees with big waxy leaves of the kind I could not discern. Détentes with the police were not a mile from home. But the people were simpatico. It was the coffee that was contentious. The sun beat down on us, and the town had been well organized, but the people still gambled, and many were happy about the new supermarket in town because it meant that someone else cared about them, even if the prices were higher. People rambled and there was a hospital and restaurants and cane trucks on the main roads and a couple of dance clubs, and with the end of the summer, the cool nights, the détentes in the fields outside of town, the town square rallies, the slashed tires of trucks on side streets beyond town, the overgrown cane stalks; these with there being union organizers in the town, the politicians passing in bullet proof cars, sometimes with us though often on the phone; all of these with the emptiness of residential streets that had lost their women and children to the strike kitchens, with plastic chairs stacked neatly along cinderblock walls, and the whole thing going on for so long made Palmira very different than it usually was. The plantations were changed too.

The green cane stalks were overgrown. The fields had been cut months before, but now there were weeds and too many leaves, and the snakes were coming back, and one day in October, when I was out where the cane stalks were eight feet tall, I saw a cloud rush over. It was very fast, and the sun faded suddenly, and everything was grey and the sky was covered and the cloud came across the valley, and suddenly we were in it, and it was rain. The rain fell heavy and straight in the heavy air, and the bare ground was covered, the rows of cane stalks projected, there was water on the men and on the paths in the grass going back to the kitchens in the fields. There were no latrines.

Later, back in the town, I watched the rain falling, looking out through the bars in the window of our room, where I sat with the lawyers and five cups, drinking a pot of coffee, and, looking out at the rain falling fast and heavy, we wondered aloud how long the workers would be out there. Up the road, we saw hundreds of police at the plantation; there were hundreds of police at many of the plantations. There had been fighting and injuries. My friend saw a union organizer going by in the street, speaking to a cane worker, and went out to call his attention. The union man looked up. He saw us and returned to his conversation. My friend motioned for them to come in. The union man shook his finger and went on. That night after the *arroz con frijoles* and chicken soup, which everyone ate quickly and seriously, sucking the marrow out of chicken bones, or else not, we helped ourselves to cola from a plastic 3-liter bottle. It sat in the center of the uneven table, and you would grip from the label with greasy hands, and the soda, dark, bubbly, and made with cane sugar, poured out into the greasy cup. After this course, Javier commenced picking on the union man.

The union man was older, spoke quickly, and had been in other movements like the rest of us, but he wore a golf shirt with khaki slacks. Javier would offer doubtful vignettes about people we encountered for my benefit, in order that I might be swayed and that there be no question.

"The union man was recruiting workers today," Javier said looking at Felipe and at me. Adriana shook her head. None of the lawyers liked the union men, Javier the least.

"Not true?" he fished. "Today I saw him at the plantation."

"No," Adriana said. The other lawyers tried to hide their amusement.

"The union man was not at the plantation," Javier parried. "The union men are never at the plantation," he expounded. He pretended to look through his phone for messages, and then held it to his ear while looking at Ariana and I.

"That guy would marry off his daughter to fill a union card." Felipe laughed. Adriana and Josephina did not. Javier nudged me with his elbow and laughed. Adriana offered a resigned sigh.

"The CUT[2] wants these workers to unionize," Felipe said in my direction. "So that it will strengthen the CUT. They would get a lot of money. It is not a good idea."

"Do you know what they do with that money?" Asked Javier. "You will meet those from the Democratic Pole[3]. They have some stories."

"Stop it," said Adriana. "What does this have to do with the strike?"

"It has everything to do with the strike," said Javier. "You think they are here out of the kindness of their hearts?" I smiled at Adriana and she smiled back. "Don't listen to him," she said.

"He will see for himself," said Javier.

"Most of the plantations are not unionized," Felipe said. "We are not anti-union, however."

"The workers are anti-union," Javier said. "They are doing much better on their own." Someone came in and as the door opened, I could see the rain falling.

"It must be hard on them with this rain," I said.

"Of course," Javier said. "But they are prepared."

"It is not as bad as in Cauca," Felipe said. "There by the river there is a lot of flooding, and last year the mudslides."

"You like to eat?" Javier asked me. "Tomorrow we will go down to this little local restaurant where the women make great fried fish." He kissed his fingers, which he curled together as if to make a shadow puppet, "Marvelous!"

"Yeah, you two could use some meat on those bones," Josephina said, picking up my wrist. "Look at this!"

"And then afterward you guys could put on a CUT golf shirt and head down to the plantation," Felipe said, successfully.

"We will go to this place in Cali, too," Javier said.

"When you come back, bring your laptop," Felipe said.

"Oh yes, and your external hard drive with the music," Josephina said.

"I could use some salsa," Adriana said.

"No, not salsa, this is not a discotheque," Felipe said.

"You could use a discotheque," Adriana said. "When we are done here, I should take you around in Bogotá," she said to me. The others were debating something. "There are good places. Though it is cold and it rains there are good places. We could stay with my father. He is getting eye surgery soon. He is retired and used to be a great doctor."

The table broke up.

THE ARGUMENT

Sugarcane workers, human rights activists, union organizers, local politicians, and the communities in which these are embedded comprised an *emancipatory network*—a coordination of loose, discrete, and differentiated actors assembled to confront authorities. I differentiate this from the *catnet* (Tilly 1978, 63; White 2008a; White 2008b [1965]) as a cohesive, tight, and concentrated actor network. The literature on high-risk activism is in disagreement about its determinants. Chapter 1 outlines this problem, and, aided by the intervening empirical chapters, I discuss high-risk activism and its relationship to networks and repression in the Conclusion.

I illustrate one particular arrangement of the *emancipatory network* in chapter 2, where thousands of workers disrupt thousands of tons of production to extract wage concessions from recalcitrant industrialists. After this ethnography, interviews with workers (chapter 3) and human rights activists (chapter 4) reveal the different forms of knowledge that actors bring to a social movement. I weave "traditional" social movement theory into humanistic discussion with the Latin American literature about activist knowledge. Inspired by these threads, I argue that the combination of different forms of activist knowledge bolsters movement resiliency in the face of repression.

Chapter 5 provides a counterfactual (Tilly 1996), illustrating a lack of mobilization where the *emancipatory network* is absent. Drawing from a contrasting set of field site visits and interviews which I conducted in the capital city of Bogotá, this chapter illustrates how international funders disincentivize the kinds of grassroots organizing seen in Valle del Cauca.

The Latin American literature provides some existing basis for the identification of an *emancipatory network*. Specific to the Colombian context, María Teresa Uribe (2004, 82–3) argues:

> For rebellion to take an *emancipatory* form, it is necessary, besides having self-awareness, to have recognition. That is to say, the situation perceived as oppressive, discriminatory, or exclusionary, should express itself in the public sphere, argued reasonably, addressed or narrated to other social actors outside of one's own environment, and from there, it is necessary to develop *autonomous forms of social organization and alternative practices of producing power with which to confront oppressive hegemonic forces.* [emphasis added]

Uribe here identifies some of the prerequisites for these "autonomous forms of social organization," *et seq.* Accumulating the kind of social momentum necessary to confront sclerotic hierarchies can require coordination at scale. Speaking of large Bolivian movements, Raúl Zibechi (2010, 13) offers, "[a]ctions of this magnitude cannot be consummated without the existence of a dense *network* of relationships between people—relationships that are also forms of organization." [emphasis added] While *emancipatory networks* should involve actors, motives, and ties at some scale, their prerogatives must ultimately intersect with the state. Álvaro García Linera (2021, 133) explains that such mobilization occurs "[w]hen an amassed group of individuals, linked by multiple and interdependent ties, decide that their political objectives lie in state normativity, and decide to act upon that understanding."

In Tilly's (1978) collective action model, *catnets* operate in the context of organization. Thus far, the movement literature has largely limited itself to Tilly's interpretation of the *catnet* to explain why some traits become salient for mobilization while others do not. Traits on their own cannot explain contentious organization. Rather, these need to be coupled, at least, with networks. As Tilly (1978, 63) argues, "a set of individuals is a group to the extent that it comprises both a category and a network." Because scholars have held such different views on the matter, it is necessary to proceed with some degree of specificity (Touraine 1985).

Group heterogeneity and bridges between different categories are important for collective action (Oliver et al., 1985). In Diani's (2012, 24) view, the major contribution of White's concept of *catnet* is that it helps to explain the mobilization of organizations: "White introduced the concept of *catnet* to stress that the combination of categorical traits and network ties was essential to the mobilization of a group." The social movement literature has tended to agree with this view (Emirbayer and Goodwin 1994, 1447; Mische 2011; Tarrow 1995). But most approaches to the *catnet* investigate how social movements become coherent. In other words, a *catnet* approach has thus far meant to use White's ideas to explain how a collection of individuals find themselves taking action to redress a grievance. In Tilly's (1978, 63) words, "[t]he more extensive its common identity and internal networks, the more organized the group." This feature of social networks is true even when they embed themselves within large status hierarchies (March and Simon, 1958).

This is true of Tilly's (1978, 62–4) White. But in the context of White's (2008a; 2008b[1965]) ideas about the constituents of social structure, the idea of the *catnet* is also much broader. White insists that networks are local structures operating wholly within a culture. Ethnographic approaches to the study of movements provide an ideal method for such micro-sociological theorizing (Auyero 2001; Burawoy 1991; Zibechi 2010, 112). This can lead to important insights, as social movements are often the source of important sociological theories (de Sousa Santos 2009) and the method by which theories of social justice become popular (Esparza 2023a). But transnational (Keck and Sikkink 1998), as well as Diasporic (Harrison 2012), and exile (Schneider Marques 2017) human rights networks can also be the source of important resources, ideas, and opportunities.

E*mancipatory networks* take advantage of indirect relations (Granovetter 1973) but also mobilize as a unit. Despite the looseness of an *emancipatory network* vis-à-vis the tightness of the *catnet*, there still exists a degree of cohesiveness. This cohesiveness is defined according to White's (2008b [1965]) parameters for the constituent elements of a social structure. The extent to which indirect relations impact a given actor, for instance, depends on the extent to which the actor is familiar with the intermediaries. Differentiated categories of actors bring diverse resources, tactics, and knowledge to bear. White's (2008b [1965]) discussion of the constituents of social structure guides the inductive selection of these actors.

COLOMBIA'S VIOLENT PAST

Two summers before the strike, in the basement of Bogotá's Luís Angel Arango Library, I aimed to find illustrations of Colombia's violent past. I leafed through the fragile pages of *El Espectador* (1960a), the widest-circulation newspaper in the country. I found so many examples that it is no wonder why Colombian scholars founded an entire field called "violentology" (Cartagena 2016). One of these examples was that of the assassination of small-town mayor Luis Ernesto Esquivel. An article titled "The Mayor of Obando was Assassinated in Valle [del Cauca], Last Night" begins with one-eighth of a column of space on the front page.[4] As the mayor lay dying from his mortal wound, a stander-by "pounces" on the murderer in a narrow boarding house hallway.

This sort of political violence was routine in the middle part of twentieth-century Colombia. Elected officials, union activists, and even sociologists

(Fals-Borda and Mora-Osejo 2003, 30) became targets for violence. Violence peaks again at the start of the 1980s. The Marxist guerilla group M-19[5] began to organize armed resistance in Valle del Cauca in 1979. M-19's "America Battalion" began an offensive called "the Path of Vanquishers" in 1985. The number of homicides remained elevated through 1987. Right-wing groups began a counter-campaign of intimidation, which they called a "Social Cleansing."[6] As the M-19 guerilla group itself declined, right-wing homicides against gays, drug addicts, criminals, indigent, poor, left-wing politicians, and union leaders accelerated.

The CUT, its members, and its leadership were major targets of both the state and paramilitary forces, particularly before 1994. Estimates of union members killed in the country since 1986 hover between 3,200[7] and 4,000.[8] Valle del Cauca is second only to Antioquia as the deadliest department for union activists (Guzmán et al., 2012, 6). Some of the names that right-wing paramilitaries gave to their terror campaigns in and around Cali in the 1980's include "Clean Cali" and "Love Cali." One of these campaigns taking place in the town of Palmira is named "Efficient Palmira."[9]

Until their demobilization during the summer of 2016, the Revolutionary Armed Forces of Colombia (FARC) were the largest Marxist guerilla group in the hemisphere. Their Simón Bolívar Guerilla Battalion controlled the westward road from Cali out to the Pacific Ocean beginning in the late 1980s. Lasting for years, this Battalion clashed with right-wing paramilitaries who attempted to undercut FARC popular support by attacking local small farmers.[10] The FARC had been in the region, at least in Buga, since the 1970s. The Cacique Calarcá Front had 400 fighters controlling approximately seven municipalities of Valle del Cauca. Clashes with the rival "Calima Block" led to the deaths of hundreds of people.[11]

Violence has been a dominant characteristic of Colombia's history. While it can be tempting for those immersed in the country's idiosyncrasies to think that this violence is unique to Colombia, political violence is a widespread feature of the twentieth-century Americas. From Pinochet in Chile (Schneider 1995) and the Shining Path in Peru (Marks 1994), to drug cartels in Mexico (Paternostro 1995), state institutions in Honduras (Longtin 2019), and Ted Kaczynski in Oklahoma City (Fleming 2022), political actors have turned to violence to achieve their political objectives. Taking a hemispheric view, Foweraker (2020) also finds "oligarchy" to be a salient pattern across the hemisphere. As it pertains to Bolivian indigenous populations, Linera (2021, 194) argues,

> It is certain that the power of colonial elites endured beyond the founding of the republic. Whenever they had an opportunity to act upon their deep desire for the physical extermination of the indigenous population, they did so. But it has

been their nationalist fervor which has caused the greatest havoc to the material and spiritual development of indigenous collective groups.

But Colombia's violent history does have specific cultural underpinnings, even as comparativists also turn to the Colombian case for lessons on political violence around the world.[12]

El Bogotazo

We may date the roots of extreme partisan division somewhat earlier. United against the Spanish crown, early patriots managed to tame their ambitions in the interest of nation-building. Through the beginning of the twentieth century, however, conservative economic interests began to conspire. Using extortion and fraud to prevent liberal candidates from winning elections, conservative control of the federal government has rarely been meaningfully challenged. This period saw only sporadic clashes between peasant populations and conservative landowners, generally centering on demands for fair treatment for liberal electoral candidates.

Conservative dominance continued through the mid-1930s and 1940s when a young Jorge Eliécer Gaitán captured the imagination of populist-minded Colombians. Gaitán was an upstart lawyer who successfully defeated the conservative political machine to win Bogotá's mayoral election. Riding a populist wave taking place across Latin America at the time, Gaitán gained wild and growing affection from peasants. This incipient mobilization elicited a number of violent reprisals from conservative forces. Still, such episodes remained relatively sporadic for most of the decade.

In the mold of Argentina's Juan Perón and having personally witnessed the speeches of Benito Mussolini in Rome, Gaitán's rhetorical style gained him enough popularity to seek the 1949 Liberal Party nomination for President. This set the stage for a dramatic encounter with an entrenched political operation. As the election drew closer, it became clear that Gaitán was likely to win. Despised by a conservative regime populated by anti-communists and business interests entrenched in government politics for fifty years, these actors grew fearful of the enactment of a populist agenda sure to follow on the heels of a Gaitián victory. That day never came. On April 9, 1948, Gaitián was murdered by an assassin on a Bogotá city street. While historians disagree about the origins of the assassination plot and whether or not the Conservative Party leadership was implicated in the murder,[13] Bogotá's residents did not withhold judgement. The Catholic Church took the side of the conservatives, with one priest using the pulpit to advocate the shooting of looters and arsonists (González Arana and Molinares Guerrero 2013, 190).

News of Gaitán's assassination spread rapidly. Rioters razed the city to the ground, destroying 80 percent of the buildings in what came to be known as the "Bogotázo." The military and militias maintained and paid by large private landowners reacted quickly to put down the insurrection in the city, but decades of political exclusion animated the violence, once sporadic and contained to the countryside but now endemic. This fierce violence continued unabated until a political solution was negotiated in 1958, some ten years later.

Colombians call this dark period "La Violencia" or simply, "The Violence," a name containing mystery and sparking amazement, akin to the Irish "Troubles." The collective memory of the events has been suppressed, as has the violence that engulfed Uruguay in the 1970s (Fried Amilivia 2016) and El Salvador in the 1980s (Wilkinson 2002). It ended in a political solution involving a power-sharing agreement in which the Liberal and Conservative Parties would alternate Presidential authority every four years. This remarkable agreement shut out all third parties and effectively narrowed the scope of political ideas. In consequence, many peasants in the countryside grew increasingly frustrated with what they saw as a pact between elites.

Revolutionaries and Counter-revolutionaries

Only a few years passed before, in 1964, a group of peasants, influenced by Marxist revolutionary movements elsewhere, organized a "people's army," calling themselves the Revolutionary Armed Forces of Colombia (FARC). This army waged war against the state and was successful in acquiring land and recruiting people into the movement. The FARC remained popular in its early years, earning the support of rural peasants who felt unrepresented and politically excluded from the central government. The National Liberation Army (ELN) followed thereafter, until their demobilization in 2010. Other revolutionary organizations also sprang up in this period, most notably Valle del Cauca's M-19, which in 1980 occupied the Embassy of the Dominican Republic, taking dozens of ambassadors hostage for two months (Farer 2020).

Controversy began to emerge in the Catholic Church as Bishop Gerardo Valencia Cano, Father Camilo Torres, and other clergy began to take explicitly revolutionary positions (Torres 1969). Bishop Valencia Cano died in a plane crash just three years after signing the 1968 Declaration of Golcanda, which advocated for the overthrow of the government. (Dussel 1981, 191) Camilo Torres died in battle against the Colombian National Army, inspired by his "studies and contact with *campesino* organizations," which "convinced Torres that the powerful would never vacate their positions and privileges unless they were obligated by a countervailing force" (Levine

2011). Colombian liberation theologians were sometimes inspired by the ideas of Dietrich Bonhoeffer (1995 [1948]) as much as they were by twentieth- century communism (Pérez Prieto 2016). But Valle del Cauca's social movements often continue the tradition of naming their organizations in the style of M-19.

Only some peasants and members of the urban underclass were active revolutionaries. Many others became active in grassroots populist politics. But these two peasant groups would converge in the mid-1980s to form the Unión Patriótica (UP). The Party did quite well, and their first Presidential candidate in 1986 came in third with 350,000 votes (35 percent of the electorate). This strong showing came unexpected to the *de facto* government and renewed conservative fears of socialist policies. Segments of the Colombian military, aided by paramilitary groups, engaged in the open assassination of UP officeholders, leaders, and even innocent citizens whose only crime had been to campaign or express public support. Several UP Senators, dozens of local elected officials, and hundreds of other party members fell victim to political violence.

Internal Displacement

Since 1985, when NGOs filled the need for reliable and independent socioeconomic data, the Colombian conflict has produced over three million internally displaced people (IDPs), most with origins in rural areas (CODHES 2006). Colombian IDPs are *campesinos* that populate grassroots human-rights organizations in Bogotá and elsewhere. Unlike the international or even domestic professional organizations that work with this population, local grassroots human rights organizations have little in the way of extra-national protection (Keck and Sikkink 1998).

Professionalized non-profits have begun to replace social movement groups in Latin America (Foweraker 2001). Sobbotka (2002) resists this replacement, arguing that professional non-profits do not challenge social structures in the same way as twentieth-century social movements. In the U.S. literature, Child and Grønbjerg (2007) find that non-profits that receive government contracts are less likely to use disruptive tactics. Even if professionalized non-profits are not counterproductive, as Jenkins and Eckert (1986, 827) argue, they "cannot compensate for the power of an indigenous movement." But Colombian social movements remain strong, even if repression has at times been stronger (Carroll 2008). This social movement replacement is more pronounced in Bogotá than it is in the rural areas of Valle del Cauca.

Bogotá has seen an immense population boom in recent years due to IDPs fleeing to this popular hub. Bogotá had a population of 7.8 million people in 2005 (DANE 2007). This includes almost 600,000 IDPs (IDMC 2006). The

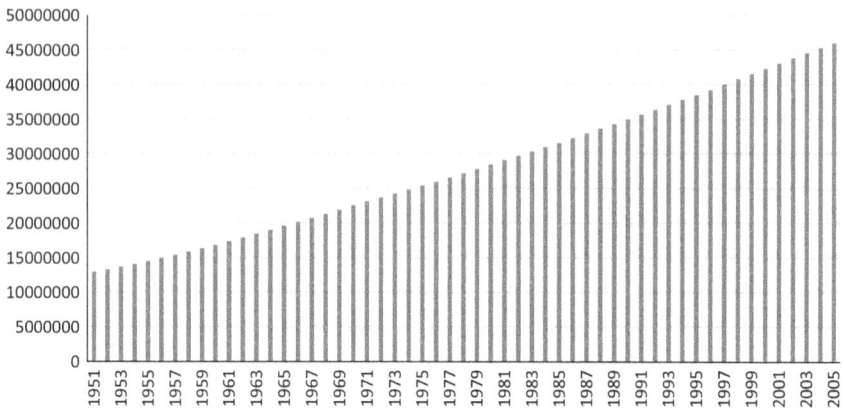

Figure 0.1b Total Population, Colombia 1951–2005. *Source*: Based on National Administrative Department of Statistics (DANE) data.

growth of the city's population has been so dramatic that it has outstripped the city's infrastructure. Still, many displaced persons choose not to leave Bogotá and its surrounding areas. And despite the high levels of country-wide violence, Colombia's population has retained its upward trajectory[14] (see Figure 0.1b).

State Presence in Difficult Terrain

Similar to the constraints of some of its neighbors, Colombia's geography makes it difficult for the central government to maintain the physical presence necessary to secure institutional hegemony throughout the area contained within its borders. Dense jungle forests occupy much of the land south of the Guaviare River—a bit more than one-third of the country. This jungle provides cover from the air, inhibiting aerial surveillance and kinetic contact. The Andes Mountain Range bisects the country, and a lack of infrastructural development here delays ground traffic. The terrain helps to conceal bunkers and cloak rebel movements. Instead, the military must rely on the infiltration of guerilla ranks or other intelligence-gathering mechanisms, short of direct frontal ground engagement.

The terrain also separates the populace, allowing for distinct economic realities and cultural identities to develop. There are many areas where steep mountain passes and choleric jungle forests have yet to be conquered by infrastructure projects. This situation has resulted in a fragmented state presence in many regions of the country and facilitated the formation of guerilla forces and other forms of local revolutionary governance. Carroll (2008, 3–7) characterizes Colombia's rocky democratic process as "violent democratization," containing an admixture of a stable democracy and an elite-captured "weak state." Tilly and Tarrow (2007) argue that such *composite regimes* shape the conditions of protest for populations in Israel, the EU, and elsewhere. Jeff Goodwin (2001) argues that countries with autocratic governments tend to incubate guerilla movements. The birth of a guerilla movement is further developed in places with weak infrastructure, providing a structural advantage to rebels. In the sullen analysis of María Teresa Uribe (2004, 77–8):

> The nature of the armed conflict in Colombia makes one think of the fragility of state sovereignty. It makes one doubt the presence of the state throughout the territory. It calls the indivisibility of the republic into question. It introduces reasonable doubts, in turn, about state power and the capacity to separate citizens from their hostile cycles of violence. It calls into question the state's capacity to provide a peaceful, disarmed society that can invert the conspired [Hobbesian] equation between sovereignty and war.

Landowners and other private interests who feel threatened by guerillas maintain private security to protect themselves and their sometimes-ill-gotten assets. Some elements of the military have not only resisted attempts to disband paramilitaries, but have welcomed their presence. As is the case with private military contractors elsewhere, such as Z Services in Iraq (formerly Blackwater), there is often a high degree of interaction between the paramilitary and the military (Jones 2008). Military personnel at all levels of service often go on to pursue careers in paramilitary organizations. As the conflict between Colombian guerillas and paramilitaries intensified, both sought to supplement their resource streams to feed the war. That search led to the development of an illegal and highly profitable drug economy, primarily in the form of coca cultivation. Paramilitary organizations have reaped substantial profits from the drug trade (Dube and Naidu, 2015). Drug cartels have become a phenomenon unto themselves, with connections to the paramilitary, guerillas, and the state (Felbab-Brown 2006). Guerilla organizations have also profited, though the extent to which this is the case has been an intense matter for debate. The use of drug trade profits for sustaining political aims has led to aberrations in both guerilla and paramilitary ideology. For example, there are in fact instances of guerilla and paramilitary cooperation on some drug operations. Moreover, guerilla use of anti-personnel landmines and child soldiers has drawn stiff criticism.

In the decades straddling the turn of the century, the Colombian state faced increased pressure from their main trading partners and international organizations to dismantle paramilitary structures. In 2005, the Colombian government forced the paramilitary organization Self-Defense Forces of Colombia (AUC) to surrender their weapons and formally disband. However, several reports suggest that subsections of the organization later re-formed as smaller groups of private militias (UNOHCR 2007; OAS 2006; WOLA 2007).

Human rights violations by all parties in the conflict led to a decline in public support for all three armed actors.[15] Guerillas had been criticized for the use of handmade rocket-propelled shoulder grenades, which were inaccurate and often missed their intended military target, injuring many innocent civilians. They were also criticized for attacking military and civilian infrastructure, including planes, bridges, and airports (Human Rights Watch, 2007).

Activism

Activists understand that they may face danger when they oppose authorities. The Colombian National Police have long imprisoned persons who participate in political rallies and marches. Paramilitary organizations, particularly in remote areas, intimidate, harass, deliver death threats, and even maim or kill known activists.[16] Even something considered a very mild form of action in many parts of the world, such as holding membership in a human rights organization, can result in serious reprisals from members of one of Colombia's paramilitary organizations. The occupation of land and factories can be even more dangerous. Despite the risk, there is a long tradition of such occupations in Colombia (LeGrand 1988, 152–65; Neira 2019, 59) and other countries in the region (Sitrin 2006; Zibechi 2007, 87–90).

Colombia's sustained political violence has received particular attention from scholars, drawing the connection between current events and the past.[17] Bogotá's human rights activists work within a historical context rife with violence. The Internal Displacement Monitoring Centre (IDMC 2006, 28) sees the problem thusly:

> Working conditions for many, if not most of the social and human rights organisations are extremely difficult not only because of a lack of resources, but primarily because their work runs counter to the interests of the armed organisations, mirroring in many respects the complexity and nature of the conflict itself. [. . .] Hundreds of leaders of human rights organisations and displaced communities have been assassinated throughout the conflict and attacks and threats remain major obstacles to their work and to their very existence.

Many recent important studies of political violence and contentious politics in Latin America and elsewhere often employ ethnographic approaches to get at processes as they unfold. Moreover, leading scholars in social movement studies argue that the field should focus on micro-level processes[18] and mechanisms.[19] As Tilly (1986, 4) observes, "collective action [is rooted] in the routines and organization of everyday social life, and by its involvement in a continuous process of signaling, negotiation, and struggle with other parties whose interests the collective action touches." A wave of qualitative social movement research accompanies the pronouncement, focusing on cultural differences between and within cases.[20]

Kolben (2010, 451) summarizes why labor movements have turned to the use of human rights frameworks:

> [T]he reasons for the turn to human rights discourse by labor scholars and labor organizations are largely strategic. Fundamentally, they wish to take advantage of the hegemonic status of human rights discourse and the relative effectiveness of some human rights advocacy strategies to help realize several objectives. [. . .] Activists have also used human rights discourse to gain public support in labor rights campaigns and to mobilize workers to take action. Finally, international labor campaigns have increasingly used human rights discourse and methodologies to address labor rights violations in global supply chains.

One illustration of the growth of human rights language, even as it pertains to working-class labor, is that Colombia's two largest labor unions were peripheral to the day-to-day organizing and execution of the 2008 sugarcane worker strike.[21] While CUT has been involved in Colombian labor movements for decades, Colombian labor laws do not permit a strike without first having completed arbitration. Human rights lawyers, therefore, made sure that workers referred to their actions as a "cessation of activities." Unions also generally do not represent children since child labor laws generally prevent their employment. Although I did not personally witness any direct evidence of the use of child labor in Valle del Cauca, the U.S. Department of Labor believes that the sugarcane industry in Colombia has employed children as late as 2013 (Schwarzbach and Richardson 2014, 100). The sugarcane industry in Brazil similarly stems from a colonial past with path dependency from the use of slave labor (Jones 2020).

Recent Progress

Despite this historical context, Colombia is a different place than it was even ten years ago. The election of Gustavo Petro in 2022 signaled a new openness to engaging with progressive ideas under the conditions of "normal" politics. This outcome comes on the heels of large, student-led protests in 2021 against austerity measures (Observatorio-semillero En Movimiento, et al., 2023). Petro, a former guerilla fighter for M-19, is part of a trend of electing formerly imprisoned Marxist guerillas that includes the election of Dilmea Rouseff in Brazil in 2010 and Nelson Mandela in South Africa in 1994. Many of these other elections have resulted in land reform (Vergara-Camus and Kay, 2017). Crime, including homicide and other violence, in the major cities of Medellín, Cali, Cartagena, and Bogotá has dropped considerably. This has facilitated the urban expansion of these cities, including public transit systems and real estate booms. Terrorist attacks have also fallen across the country. Middle-class Colombians had previously had to fly between cities to avoid guerilla or paramilitary checkpoints. Thoroughfares between major cities are no longer a gambit, as the arteries connecting Colombia's urban centers are now secure for all. The sociological impact of these structural changes has improved the collective identity of the nation, not least in urban centers. Recent Presidents Iván Duque Márquez, Manuel Santos Calderón, and Álvaro Uribe Vélez have generally enjoyed approval ratings above 70 percent as a result of these improvements. Most interpret this support as a response to the drastic collapse in the rate of homicide (Guerrero-Velasco et al., 2021) and kidnapping.[22]

But these advances have come at some cost. Explaining the influence of U.S. military aid, a WOLA (2021) report states:

> Since 2000, when it enacted the first "Plan Colombia" aid package, the U.S. government has provided Colombia with about US$12.6 billion in assistance. The United States has been, and continues to be, by far the number-one foreign provider of aid to Colombia. Of aid since 2000, about two-thirds has gone to the country's police and military forces, making Colombia by far the Western Hemisphere's number-one recipient of military and police aid.

Activists throughout Latin America saw Plan Colombia as "part of a greater strategy to control the social movements of Latin America, and the resources of this part of the world" (Zibechi 2005). Drones, for example, are now a regular part of the Colombian National arsenal (Sánchez 2014). Plan Colombia expanded throughout the rest of the region as part of the Andean Regional Initiative, with Colombia as the primary beneficiary (Storrs and Veillette, 2003).

But thousands of middle-class Colombian expats in major cities throughout the world rallied in support of the damage done to FARC rebels.[23] Tourism returned to Colombia with major Caribbean cruise lines adding the colonial port city of Cartagena to their summer schedules in 2009 (Luna-Cortés 2018). Paramilitary violence dropped off, particularly after 2005, due in part to the efforts of Presidents Uribe and Santos to demobilize these groups. While the Colombian security state expanded during this time, this security was "highly selective," routinely killing activists, blacks, and working-class citizens (Jenss 2023). Paramilitary groups still exist as criminal gangs, but do not operate at the same levels as they did previously. Over the past decade, Colombia also has enjoyed an economic boom. Their export commodity industry, driven by coffee, bananas, emeralds, sugar, oil, and flowers, has contributed to one of the most stable GDP growth rates in Latin America over the past three decades.

Human rights groups note that this increase in security and economic development has come at a high cost. During this same period, the level of fatalities, particularly in towns and communities outside of the cities, was still at disturbing levels. Colombia remains one of the most dangerous places in the world for journalists and trade unionists. The number of displaced people in the country rivals that of Sudan and Iraq. Governance under the Uribe administration became more centralized than at any time since the 1991 constitutional reform. For activists, Colombia is still particularly dangerous.

Most Colombians believe that social movements are both necessary to economic development and good to participate in (Latinobarómetro 2009). Colombians also believe by a wide margin that conflict between workers and managers in the country is very strong (Latinobarómetro, 2007; 2008; 2009; 2010; 2017). This conflict can be observed in Colombian public opinion polling, showing a close split between support for the competing values of freedom and equality (Haerpfer et al., 2022).

DRIVING AROUND SUGAR PLANTATIONS

During my fieldwork in 2008, I met Piedad Córdoba, the Colombian Senator who, in that same year, was passed over for the Nobel Peace Prize, ultimately given to Barack Obama. At the time, both figures were overcoming accusations of associating with terrorists.[24] Córdoba sat on a panel hosted by the Universidad del Valle in Cali alongside the leadership of the sugarcane workers movement during what turned out to be the tail-end of a fifty-eight-day strike. It had been less than two months earlier that I had started my near-daily rides in the back of a two-door Renault, traversing sugar plantations, absorbing the anxieties of my human rights activist pilots. I had set out to document Colombian social movements to comment on a rather academic debate about high-risk activism. I had not expected this idiosyncratic curiosity to lead me into the sugarcane fields.[25]

Near the middle of the strike, our vehicle received an upgrade for certain occasions. Accompanied by one of the staff members of a Colombian Senator and their driver, we rode in the Senator's vehicle. On one of these occasions, we stopped at a plantation to deliver food to striking workers. The workers had taken over several plantations and held them under constant siege for about a month. After having made our food delivery, and less than ten minutes after we had left the workers, a police vehicle pulled up behind us and indicated to us to stop. The police interrogated us for over an hour, inspecting our documents and taking notes. They went through the car, including all of my belongings. Noticing that I was from New York, one officer said with apparent awe and with a smile, "You were born in Manhattan! What's it like?" I eased my shoulders, though not too much. They clearly wished that I were elsewhere.

After my exchange with the officer, the Senator's staff member said to me, "Realize this, Louis: This is how they treat the senior staff of a Senator of the Republic—in the presence of an international observer, no less. Imagine how they treat the common worker in this struggle."[26]

Javier followed up, referring to my role as an international researcher, "So, what do you think of repression in Colombia, Louis? The police, the source of our national pride, are here to protect *you*, Louis. And what if we were not with the state? If we were not with a Senator's aids? If we were not in a security car? This is the senator's escort. That is his chauffer. And this SUV belongs to DAS.[27] They are not even supposed to open these cars."

The Senator's driver interrupted to correct him, "No, I am outside of my jurisdiction, otherwise I would have put up a much bigger stink." But the police even had the Senator's driver raise the hood of the car so that they could match the serial number on the vehicle's chassis with the number that was kept on file.

Juana, who had been on her cell phone, joined us and said, "That was my dad. He just found out about the strike on the radio and called me. 'You're involved with this?' he says. Then he goes, 'So, you're going to go live in another country after this or what?'"

I experienced some of the same surveillance that Colombian human rights activists experienced every day. I did intentionally avoid certain areas and events when I suspected that the likelihood for more intense conflict could be higher. I was familiar with Bogotá and the Caribbean coast, but I was new to Valle del Cauca and had only recently been introduced to the people with whom I was trusting my life.[28] Even so, I did manage to fail in staying away from danger at least a couple of times.

Early in the strike, there were severe clashes between workers and police, resulting in dozens of injuries on both sides. In the midst of the fighting, I was in the Renault with a group of human rights activists whom I refer to in this book as "the Doves." One of the Doves, Javier, received a call to his cell phone from a striking worker at the scene of the clash with police. The plantation's private security guards, he was told, were preventing ambulances from responding to reported injuries. We abandoned our agenda and drove, with haste, to the scene.

We arrived at the plantation gates within minutes. The plantation's private security demanded our documents, something that I learned was to become a near- daily routine. We complied but were denied entry, so we drove to another entrance nearby. Looking around us as we pulled into the checkpoint,

Figure 0.2 Private Security at a Colombian Sugarcane Plantation. *Source*: Photograph taken by the author in 2008.

I noticed several private security guards, police officers, and military personnel. Some were armed with rifles and others with machine guns. I elected to remain in the backseat of the car. But the others sprang from their seats, marching right up to these armed men as if to scold a group of children.

After a few weeks of episodes such as this, I became acclimated to perpetual crisis. At one rally, the workers' families gathered to march to one of the plantations. Their husbands and boyfriends, brothers, sons, nephews, uncles, and fathers had been spending their time at the plantations. This march was their opportunity for a visit, and a way to express support. Instead, a dozen or so armed guards stood at the plantation gates, preventing their ingress. Other guards situated themselves nearby. I had a camera with me on that particular day. Standing about 30 feet away from the guards, at the edge of the crowd, I snapped a handful of photographs of the men standing near the gate. Still looking through my camera lens, I watched as an apparently-incensed guard conferred with a colleague and then charged, full speed, directly at me. I lowered my camera, turned around, and ran into the crowd, weaving my way toward the open road at the opposite end. Seeing what was happening and having spent several weeks with me, the people in the crowd tightened around the soldier when he tried to give chase, preventing him from moving. I only caught a few seconds of this before sugarcane workers shoved me into the back of a car that then quickly drove away from the scene. Those who had been my objects of study had now become my accomplices in storytelling. Workers put themselves at risk to protect me and, at times, it was the other way around. My presence, and the presence of my camera and tape recorder, made me the subject of police harassment. But it also made the immediate space around me less dangerous for others. The armed guards did not want to create evidence that might threaten to attract public scrutiny.

But the Doves also felt responsible for my safety. For instance, at the Kuntisuyu plantation on the first day of the strike, the Doves arrived to the plantation and surveyed the scene from the car.[29] After they decided that it was safe enough, we all exited together and stayed on the opposite side of the street from the plantation gates. Javier looked down the street both ways, gravely, as if looking for something specific.[30] I attempted to cross during an opening in the traffic, but he put out his hand to prevent me and admonished me sternly: "Don't go and do whatever you want, Louis. This is a very serious situation. Follow us and stay close. Don't leave my sight. Be very careful."

I was, more-or-less, at the mercy of the Doves for access to the strike. Javier did understand the dynamics of the environment we were about to enter better than I did. But he also played the role of gate keeper, my access to the space itself dependent on his help and cooperation. As the opening vignette of the book illustrates, tensions arose between human rights activists and labor organizers. Working in Valle del Cauca necessitated that I negotiate between the two. Chapter 4 contains Javier's biography, which includes personal experience of being shot at from the road. The early stages of an open conflict can be especially unpredictable, setting the norms and terms of the conflict that have yet to be negotiated and defined. We were already aware of violence having taken place at other plantations. One could not be sure, especially in the Colombian context, that we would not be on the receiving end of some of the same.

I found it impossible to enforce the boundary between researcher and accomplice. Especially in Valle del Cauca, I was immersed in the field site, even sleeping on the floor of the office from which activists coordinated much of the strike, next to the Doves. When I became afraid, lacked food or water, became depressed from bearing witness to the workers' conditions, I thought of the *indomitability* of these activists. Surely if the workers and human rights activists that compose this research could endure sustained political tension for years at a time, then I could bear witness to it for a few months. I tolerated but a fraction of the problems many Colombian families experience in this region. Even so, for years after these events took place, even just the sight of a few packets of sugar at a coffee shop would sometimes be enough to stupefy me.

ETHICS, ETHNOGRAPHY, AND RISK

The topic of research ethics in high-risk activism is worth considering. The data that researchers collect may sometimes be of interest to governments, or others in pursuit of activists. The data that researchers choose to divulge can be used to pursue these individuals. I made decisions over and above what was required of me by institutional review boards to protect the anonymity of activists discussed in this book. Ultimately it is up to activists themselves to decide whether the risks of storytelling are worth the potential consequences. While speaking to activists in Colombia about this it was made clear to me, repeatedly, that it was important to them that I tell this story.

It is important to get this nature of data. Ethnographic approaches are designed to capture and understand social processes as they unfold. They have been employed in many important political ethnographies in Latin America and elsewhere (Arias 2006; Auyero 2003; Auyero 2007; Avruch 2001; Mahmood 2001; Mische 2008; Robben and Nordstrom 1995; Scheper-Hughes 1992; Sluka 1995; Zulaika 1988). Moreover, leading scholars in social movement studies have argued that a focus on micro-level processes and mechanisms captures a deeper level of interaction. (McAdam, Tarrow, and Tilly 2001; Tilly 2008) A wave of qualitative social movement research accompanies this conviction. (Goodwin and Jasper 2004; Goodwin, Jasper, and Polletta 2000; Goodwin and Pfaff 2001; Jasper 1997; Johnston and Klandermans 1995; Polletta 2002; Polletta 2006; Sitrin 2006; Weinstein 2007; White 2007)

Colombian scholarship on the strike tends to take a political-economy approach (Castaño and Castillo-Cubillos 2021; Gómez Nieto, et al., 2016; Jaramillo Ferro 2017; Montoya Duque 2011). These provide helpful context on the organizational impacts of the strike and on the political power of the sugarcane industry in Colombia.[31] Taking their lead, in this chapter I have consciously tried to avoid idealizing the Colombian state as an exemplar of democracy, or pathologizing it as irredeemably corrupt (López-Pedreros 2019, viii).

Aside from fieldnotes, interviews, and audio recordings, I also monitored radio and newspaper reports as well as the fliers, documents, and photographs produced by various actors in the movements that I observed. I also captured hundreds of photographs myself. While the fieldnotes, interviews, and audio recordings were a formal part of my data collection, it was the Doves who asked me to become somewhat of a movement photographer. I shared these photographs with the Doves. On one occasion, the Doves forwarded one of my photographs to a local newspaper, which then published it without my knowledge. After seeing the photograph in print, the CUT asked me to share my photographs with them as well. The Doves requested that I refrain from sharing my photographs with others. I followed the advice of Blee and Taylor (2002), who suggest that "the trick to handling factions and conflicts is to figure out how to remain neutral, because taking sides with one group most assuredly will mean being denied access to the other group." Ultimately, I decided to make a portion of my photographs available to any organization or individual working within the movement that requested them of me during my fieldwork.

I did not interview any sugarcane plantation owners, managers, or repre-sentatives. This follows the convention set by Fantasia (1988). In his study of factory workers, Fantasia decided not to spend time with the management because his research question had little to do with the doings of manage-ment. My questions about activist networks and high-risk activism also had little to do with plantation owners. I also avoided their management so as not to jeopardize my hard-earned relationships with activist coalitions. But this approach also has the benefit of limiting the spiral of "infinite regress," whereby managers complain about owners, owners about the government, the government about the electorate, "until we have studied all of society simul-taneously" (Becker 1967, 247). I did not try to play the role of an authority figure in the field, as some ethnographers recommend. But nor did I make too much of an effort to blend in. I cursed only once and received the same sort of "shocked" response that William Whyte did when he cursed in front of Doc, his primary informant. (Whyte 1993 [1955])

My audio recordings and fieldnotes were another matter completely. While the photographs that I released depicted benign events taking place at large public gatherings, my recordings and notes contained information collected in confidence. Activists take risks when they involve themselves in a strike. If identifiable private comments and notes on their behaviors were to be made public, this could put them in danger. The Doves took this risk most of all. There was virtually no time in the course of a typical day where they were not more than a few steps away from me. Consequently, the authorities knew quite well that the Doves hauled me around on their trips to the plantations.

Maintaining data security, normally a routine process, became urgent as the strike developed. Nearly a month into the strike, six of those whom I observed were arrested, including two members of the Doves and four sugar-cane worker movement leaders. They were charged with six counts, including terrorism, intent to start a riot, and sabotage. Although the terrorism charge was dropped at arraignment, these events led to a local media circus. Because I had witnessed some of the scenes that were described in the prosecution's documents, the defense lawyers and the Doves asked me to provide them with my audio recordings. I rejected this request. Enforcing this boundary some-what strained my relationship with the Doves. I explained that I had collected

Figure 0.3 Security Forces Prevent a Food Delivery. *Source*: Photograph taken by the author in 2008.

the recordings in the context of a controlled research study and that, in my judgement, the risk of breaching the confidentiality of others involved in this research was too great.

But I did side with the movements I accompanied for this book in other ways. Leaving aside the broader debates about value-free sociology, the study of human rights can be analytical without having to be non-normative (Des Forges 1999; Esparza 2012). In contexts of clear norms violations, the researcher must side with those who are deprived of their rights.

This photograph illustrates a scene from the strike detailed in chapter 2. Standing behind the camera lens from this vantage point, I captured armed guards escorting sugarcane workers toward the perimeter of a plantation. These workers had attempted to deliver lunch to others who had been occupying the plantation. The picture's composition implies the role of the armed guards as social isolators. Situated between two groups of workers, armed guards divided unarmed workers and allies. I shared the workers" vantage point, but I only shared some of their emotions (further elaborated in chapter 3). Their faces turned away from the camera, the image can only imply the fear, confusion, wonder, and hope that their words will later reveal. The choices of portraiture, like that of ethnography and creative non-fiction, necessarily remove information in order to reveal prehensible threads.

I was not deported due to my status as a dual citizen.[32] But in the ride home after being pulled over in the Senator's vehicle Felipe said, "I was scared that they were going to take Louis away."

"Me too," Javier responded.

I was able to escape difficult situations due to the wisdom of the activists around me, my technological capacity to record my environment, and my cultural capital as a researcher from the United States My presence allowed workers to "borrow" my cultural capital, as they borrowed that of the Doves.

As advised by Wood (2006), I protected the anonymity and confidentiality of activists by using pseudonyms for all members of the community and organizations in my field notes and in my transcriptions of interviews. I did not record personal identifiers, and all digital interview files were kept double-encrypted during fieldwork. I was the only person with access to the unencrypted data.[33] All participants spoke Castilian (Spanish), and I conducted all interviews in Castilian. I personally transcribed, translated, and hand-coded all interviews and recordings.

I spent time wandering around in the areas where activists gathered in Bogotá and Valle del Cauca, outside of the context of protest. This helped me to gain perspective on how protests change how people interact with each other and insight into police behavior. As is the case in many political ethnographies, my role was not always clear to my contacts. I discovered later that many of the people I met thought that I was a journalist. Some proudly announced to other foreign visitors that a journalist (me) had been in contact with them and was writing about them for a North American newspaper. The Doves would sometimes help to identify me to workers, but usually they lumped anyone there with a camera into the category of "journalist." Felipe, at one rally, announced to a group of gathered workers, "the people who are from the press are with us. They are from the working class," making no effort to distinguish me from journalists. This continued despite my several attempts to correct them.

When I first arrived in Bogotá in 2007 to conduct this research, I had not entered the country in fifteen years. I had been a child then, toted along by my parents to visit my grandparents, aunts, uncles, and cousins spread throughout the Caribbean coast. In the rural areas we traveled by *burro* into the hillside farms. Dirt roads, pocked with holes, flooded during the frequent downpours. Street vendors heckled, balancing giant bowls of tropical fruit on their heads.

I knew nothing, in 1992, of Colombia's political problems. The civil war, bombings, drug cartels, guerilla and paramilitary armies, extreme poverty, mass graves—I was shielded from all of it. Like Wilkinson's (2002) experience in the coffee fields in the Honduran mountains, the silence is deafening and makes the obvious violence ring even louder. Understanding this culture, I intentionally did not interrogate sugarcane workers or their allies about past violent events.[34] These sorts of questions were not part of my research and the results of these kinds of explorations merit their own treatment (Shaw 2007).

In the summer of 2007, I traveled daily to the archives of the Luis Angel Arango Library to better understand Colombia's political violence. Each morning I dug through old newspapers, especially those of *El Espectador* during the time of *La Violencia*. Guided by the work of Fals-Borda (Guzmán Campos, et al., 1962) and Pécaut (1987), I also digested reports and descriptive statistics from national and international organizations and agencies, some of which include Corporación Nuevo Arco Iris; National Administrative Department of Statistics (DANE); Internal Displacement Monitoring Centre; Latinobarómetro; Research and Popular Education Center (CINEP); and the Colombian Sugarcane Growers Association (Asocaña). While guided by this context, this book is no replacement for a full account of Colombia's violent past such as that found in the works cited in this chapter.

In a couple of cases, where aggregated information would clearly identify persons or locations, I intentionally mix information from different plantations to protect further those involved. This is especially important because of the information available in newspaper and journal articles about some of the events discussed here. I took care to make sure that this mixing did not interfere with the analysis. Because of the sensitive nature of the events under discussion, all of the organizations and the people whom I encountered during my fieldwork and whom I mention have been made anonymous, whether they spoke to me under conditions of anonymity or not.[35] This is consistent with the practice of many scholars conducting fieldwork in conflict zones. Some researchers in conflict zones have had interviewees assassinated (Sriram 2009, 59–61). Of the cases that I am aware of, this has to do with the inherently risky nature of the activities that activists are involved in. Nonetheless, it is important to take appropriate precautions. In one recent case, the researcher himself was killed during the course of fieldwork (Nicolato 2022).

Police arrested several activists, including two of my interviewees, during the course of this research. I followed institutional procedures and reported these incidents to university officials without further incident. None of my interviewees were physically harmed during the course of this research. But sugarcane workers continue to be attacked, even to date.[36]

I treated the strike in Valle del Cauca as one event, rather focusing on the several events that took place during the strike. I did this in order to draw out mechanisms at broader units of analysis—namely, a social movement rather than a protest event or movement organization (McAdam, Tarrow, and Tilly 2001).

THE STUDY

I conducted a nine-month ethnographic study of high-risk activism in Colombia, spending six months in Colombia's capital city of Bogotá between 2007 and 2008 and three months in Valle del Cauca, near the country's Pacific coast.

National and international human rights workers in Bogotá, the Colombian capital, receive death threats via mail, email, telephone, and in person. Though the threats are only sometimes acted upon, many activists have gone into exile as a result of credible threats. Death in significant numbers among protesting sugar cane workers is documented back to at least the middle of the twentieth century (Neira 2019, 38). Colombian social protest in general, and it's repression, dates back "almost to the beginning of European colonization" (Archila 2001, 17). Death threats become somewhat of a normal occurrence, complicating traditional notions of what constitutes social movement risk. Movement participants in developed Western democracies often "opt in" to high-risk activism by selecting certain tactics. In Colombia, risk is a thread that runs throughout all forms of human rights activism.

Chapters 2, 3, and 4 on the sugarcane worker strike in Valle del Cauca and chapter 5 on human rights movements in Bogotá illustrate that threats to activism vary within the country. Having weaker ties to international NGOs, Valle del Cauca activists have developed a more refined strategy for lessening their chances of becoming a targets of violence. But the difference between Valle del Cauca and Bogotá is not simply an illustration between "high" and "low" risk activism. Human rights activism in Colombia of any form is inherently high-risk, when compared to the activism found in their more developed Western democratic equivalents.

Research Design

Chapter 1 considers the determinants of high-risk activism. McAdam (1986; 1988) draws attention to the importance of having a comparison group when studying high-risk activism in his studies of Freedom Summer in the United States. McAdam argues that in order to determine the characteristics of high-risk activists, one must know how they differ from non-activists. Because McAdam's study focused on high-risk activism *ex post facto*, he was able to collect data on activists and non-activists using archival data. However, there are serious empirical impediments to implementing that methodology here.

I compare McAdam's study to the Colombian case, not only because it is the most significant study of high-risk activism, but also because the comparison allows us to theorize about high-risk activism across state regime types. Because the data collected in this study captures high-risk activism *in utero*, there is no reliable way to determine when instances of repression will occur or how subjects will respond to repression when it does occur. As such, this variety of sorting is not possible. However, the addition of a second field site with non-ordinal, categorically distinct kinds of high-risk activism provides an exogenous comparison case with which to compare. I strategically selected to study activist organizations so as to allow for a variety of levels of commitment, subject positions, and orientations to activism until this variability appeared to have been exhausted.

There are many differences between the U.S. South in the 1960s and Colombia in 2007–2008. One of the more consequential of these is that repression is much higher in Colombia. The level of non-political risk in Colombia is already great. We can infer, therefore, that high-risk activism in "high-risk societies" is less voluntary than high-risk activism in most Western democracies. In the United States, participants left the relative safety of their homes, mainly located in northern cities, to travel to communities located in unfriendly and uncomfortable districts in Mississippi. In Colombia, everyday life involves risk at the participants" homes, even before they "choose" to engage in political behavior.

Another important difference is that high-risk activism in Colombia is *non-ordinal*. Because baseline risk is higher, differentiating between different *types of risk* contributes more intellectual purchase than differentiating between "risk" and its absence. A more substantive engagement with the literature follows in the next chapter. But ever since the McAdam study, the social movement literature has assumed that high-risk activism is both largely voluntary and measurably "higher" in risk than other forms of activism. While it is clear that some forms of activism within most Western democracies carry a higher level of risk than others, tolerance for human rights activism in Colombia was so low in 2007–2008 that the difference in risk between tactics performed in Colombia that carry "different levels" of risk does not carry the same explanatory value.

NOTES

1. Associated Press (2008). "Colombia police tear-gas pyramid scheme clients." 20 Nov.

2. Centralized Union of Workers, the main federation of trade unions.

3. The main political party of the non-violent Left.

4. El Espectador. 1960. "Fue Asesinado el Alcalde de Obando en el Valle, Anoche." 4 May.

5. The name "M-19" is short for "Movimiento 19 de Abril," or "19 April Movement." Colombia held a Presidential election on this date in 1970, the results of which M-19 founders alleged were illegitimate.

6. Corporación Nuevo Arco Iris. 2007. Bogotá.

7. CUT. 2020. "Informe del Departamento de Derechos Humanos y Solidaridad LXVI (66)."

8. ICLR. 2004. "ICLR Summary and Recommendations." International Commission for Labor Rights, 2.

9. Corporación Nuevo Arco Iris. 2007. Bogotá.

10. Ibid.

11. Ibid.

12. See, for example, Richani's discussion of comparative illustrations including an analysis of Italian mob organizations (2002).

13. Some have even speculated that Gaitan may have been assassinated by a jealous husband. For an authoritative history focusing on these events consult Guzmán Campos, et al., (1962).

14. Unlike genocidal cases, such as mid-nineties Rwanda (Des Forges 1999), which experienced temporary population decline.

15. The Colombian government had a well-documented pattern of publicizing human rights violations committed by the guerillas while downplaying its own. See the rhetoric contained in the "transnational day of action against the FARC" in cities throughout the world as one example (Guerrero 2008).

16. WOLA 2007

17. See for example Dudley 2004; Guzmán Campos, Fals-Borda, and Umaña Luna 1962; Hylton 2006; Molano 2005; Pécaut 1987; Richani 2002; Ruiz 2001; Tate 2007.

18. As described by McAdam, Tarrow, and Tilly (2001), but also for microsociological approaches more brodly.

19. See McAdam, Tarrow, and Tilly 2001; Tilly 2008.

20. For examples, see Goodwin and Jasper 2004; Goodwin, Jasper, and Polletta 2000; Goodwin and Pfaff 2001; Jasper 1997; Johnston and Klandermans 1995; Polletta 2002; Polletta 2006; Sitrin 2006; Weinstein 2007; White 2007.

21. Young (2022, 507) confirms in a Bolivian peasant mobilization that unions do not always serve as an "ignorance-reducing device." Colombian sugarcane cutters and human rights activists performed the lion share of the planning. Union organizations provided important food donations and other service, but their role had little to do with capacity-building.

22. Ministerio de Defensa Nacional 2011, 20.

23. Associated Press (2008) "Colombia bitterly divided on anti-rebel march." 3 Feb.

24. Obama's accuser was Sarah Palin. Córdoba's was Álvaro Uribe Vélez. It has been commonplace to use the term "terrorist" to describe one's political enemies in Colombia, and sometimes in the United States.

25. Rather than designing the study around labor organizations in Cali, I allowed my Bogotá informants to lead me to a developing strike. While this choice was a matter of convenience, I know of no other way of preparing to capture a strike before it is to take place. Choosing a field site after having surveyed several possible field sites can also have its advantages (Barnes 2022). I could have approached a state

agency such as the Ministry of Agriculture. But because of the politically sensitive nature of my fieldwork, I preferred not to draw the attention of the Uribe government. Non-governmental organizations working on similar issues also exist, such as the Organization for Urban and Rural Development (ORDEURCA). My research questions about high-risk activism, informed by the literature reviewed in chapter 1, led me, instead, to populate a network based on key informants.

26. Among the documented incidents, eight unionized workers were "arbitrarily arrested for many hours" and one union leader was "followed by unknown peoples on several occasions in the city of Cali" (ICTUR 2009).

27. DAS was Colombia's National Security Agency until it's dissolution in 2011.

28. My colleague and friend Alwyn Lim wrote to check in on me during fieldwork. In my email response I wrote, "Quite a rollercoaster it is, hanging out with these human rights people—the Left elite in a Right-wing repressive regime. For instance, driving around in the chauffeured vehicle of a high-level political official one minute and then getting thoroughly searched by military dudes with [large weapons] the next. Or being at a cheerful rally of women and children and then a few hours later hearing that the police teargassed them after you and the human rights people leave. It is challenging."

29. I have given pseudonyms to all of the plantations and mixed the location of the strike's events to protect activists.

30. After the first day of the strike, CINEP (2008, 140) reported that "the workers are being 'escorted' by armed men riding motorcycles and wearing ski-masks."

31. There is a rich and important history about how the sugarcane industry was able to accumulate so much land in Cauca and Valle del Cauca (Uribe-Castro 2014). Carroll's (1999) political-economic approach to the study of Colombian palm workers is similarly insightful.

32. According to a report by CINEP (2008, 164) and cross-checked with local activists familiar with the situation, three French citizens were detained, arrested and deported. I reproduce relevant portions of the report here: "DAS agents arbitrarily detained three French citizens. These acts took place in the municipality of Palmira. On 13 October 2008 at approximately 12:45 PM, when they were accompanying sugarcane workers in their place of work, assessing the conditions of the workers [. . .], the three foreign nationals were detained [. . .]. They were obligated to board a grey [. . .] sedan [. . .] and transported to the DAS Cali Branch, without permitting the workers or labor leaders that were with them to accompany them. Those who followed the vehicle to Cali asked to see the three foreign nationals in the presence of a lawyer, but their request was denied and no information was given about them. Nor was any information released to human rights organizations that subsequently arrived." Five days later, on 18 October, President Álvaro Uribe Vélez said of these individuals, "Those gentlemen from abroad should be in jail. We should not have deported them, but we should have instead prosecuted them and put them in jail because they are guilty of stimulating violence" (Correa and Cárdenas Quintero. 2008, 15).

33. After defense lawyers for the Doves asked for my confidential recordings, I transferred my files to an encrypted external hard drive and deleted them from my

laptop. I then handed the encrypted hard drive to a trusted individual who personally flew the hard drive back to the United States.

34. As chapter 3 illustrates, interviewing workers about their experiences of poverty was sensitive enough.

35. I do not conceal the public comments or activities of then-president Álvaro Uribe Vélez, Senator Piedad Córdoba, or other high-ranking officials.

36. Two sugarcane workers were gunned down in February 2023 by unknown assailants in Northern Cauca while working at a plantation, the latest in a string of recent attacks. Activists, as well as sugarcane industry representatives from Asocaña, denounced the attacks (*El País* 2023).

Chapter 1

Risk

Colombian activists are skilled at evading authority; otherwise, they may not last. Loosely organized, decentralized activists are often well-suited for the use of risky tactics against authorities. This chapter examines what scholars know of these types of activists. The first half of the chapter examines decentralized movements. This discussion will aid us later, as subsequent chapters point to the role of networks in such movements. We then turn to the extensive but contradictory literature on high-risk activism. Most studies apply McAdam's (1986) theory to movements in the United States, but the analysis of relevant and specific Latin American case studies complicates our understanding of high-risk activism. Many studies examine the role of tactics when defining high-risk activism. This is useful and correct when sorting between different activists within a specific political context. But when moving across state regime types, as one does when comparing U.S. and Latin American cases, it may be that high-risk activism is better defined by the tolerance of state regimes. At the end of the chapter, I express the juncture at which state authorities respond to activist tactics with violence as the *moment of repression*, when one can be said to be engaging in high-risk activism.

DECENTRALIZED MOVEMENTS

Decentralized movements are more effective at achieving transformational change than their more centralized cousins. Movements cannot be sued, jailed, or fined the way that individuals and organizations can, granting them unique social leverage. For our purposes, we will use a definition of "social movements" that thinks of them as "collectivities acting with some degree of organization and continuity outside of institutional or organizational channels for the purpose of challenging or defending extant authority, whether it is institutionally or culturally based, in the group, organization, society, culture, or world order of which they are a part[1] (Snow, Soule, and Kriesi 2004). Individuals must organize to a degree.[2] Too much organization, however, and movements can become ossified. Less organized social movements can be more effective because they more easily adopt high-risk tactics (Gamson 1975; Piven and Cloward 1977). Less organized movements have been able to execute on these tactics more easily because of the powerful social bonds inherent in small groups. As Cloward and Piven (1984, 588) explain: "The issue of movement organization cannot be separated from the issue of power [. . .] The power of those who are ordinarily powerless does not derive from the valued assets or traits they control; by definition, they control few of these things. It derives from the patterns of interdependence that characterize all of social life, and from the leverage that inheres in these interdependent relations."

Decentralization emerges when activists cannot pursue their goals using extant organizations. Schwartz (1976, 173) explains that "coordinated refusal is dependent upon the creation of workable independent protest groups. These groups cannot be dependent on, or embedded in, the original system, since that system is based on the exercise of routinized power by the dominant group." At the same time, employing such tactics invites repression from government and non-state actors. The relationship between repression and mobilization is complex, especially when compared across cases (Earl 2003, Tilly 2005). For example, repression against rural social movements in Colombia does not necessarily explain movement failure (Carroll 2008, 279). But state repression often creates resource fissures in a movement, starving the movement of energy by diverting resources and attention to the legal battles of its leaders (Zwerman 1994). Indeed, as movement tactics become increasingly radical, so too can the level of repression against movements increase. This is particularly true as movements effectively disrupt more than one authority structure at the same time (della Porta 2006; Schwartz 1976). Because they are usually[3] at a disadvantage regarding resources and do not enjoy easy access to the government or media, these organizations are in constant crisis. In contrast, violence against activists can be more likely when their opponents have access to political operatives promising success (Brass 2005). Put less charitably, Lorde (1984, 53) argued that repression is necessary for the survival of state authorities: "In order to perpetuate itself, every oppression must corrupt or distort those various sources of power within the culture of the oppressed that can provide energy for change."

Decentralization, then, emerges as a necessary movement strategy. In contentious politics terms, tactics are constrained to particular repertoires of contention, molded by both repressive actors and social movement actors themselves (Tilly 1995). Speaking of activists in Argentina, Auyero (2001) notes that activists who have little access to channels of public opinion are anxious to tell their stories to professionals who they think will represent them and their cause to the outside world. Tate (2007), speaking of Colombian activists, came across the "global imaginaries" of those who think that U.S. citizens are connected to a global web of international organizations that can bring them resources and attention. Like William Whyte's key informant, "Doc," activists can act as a research ombudsmen of sorts, providing an essential resource for entering and deciphering their worlds (Whyte 1993 [1955]). Key informants can be particularly important for researchers from Northern countries who venture into unfamiliar neighborhoods in Colombia (Baird 2018, 344–48).

Decentralization operates as a defense against determined state repression. Chilean movements under Pinochet were able to survive as relatively independent agents in the shantytowns of Santiago. A remarkable feat in the face of a state mobilized against them, these less organized groups better evaded repression due to their decentralization. In contrast, it was the NGOs embedded within elite networks that easily succumbed to the *de facto* regime (Schneider 1995). But repression can be significant against all kinds of dissenters. Shantytown protesters, having little to lose, often have had to face severe repression for the most modest of gains. It is not surprising to learn, then, that poor people's movements in Latin America fared worse under regimes that do not respect citizen rights when compared to Western democracies in the United States and Europe (Eckstein 1989).

Activists who are particularly anti-authoritarian, however, sometimes fail to appreciate the ties between public and private organizations. While activists target a company, state authorities can and often do come to their aid. When activists target the state, corporations that benefit from that state also respond. The organizational forms of the modern state and corporation somewhat resemble each other in their hierarchical structures. This allowed hierarchical corporations in the United States to curry the favor of the U.S. government over their more democratically organized competitors (Perrow 2002). It is not surprising, then, to find that some anti-capitalist activists are also anti-state. Tilly (1985) makes this relationship between the state and the defense industry explicit, going so far as to equate state-making with war-making. But political theorists as far back as Thomas Hobbes (2021 [1651]) and sociologists as old as C. Wright Mills (1956) have made similar associations between states and war.

Actually *eliminating* authority from social life is, frankly, not likely. But this has not stopped activists from theorizing life without it. Dussel (2008, 30) conceives of authority, for example, as a "fetishization of power." Murray Bookchin (2007) argues for a sort of libertarian municipalism that practices local democratic decision-making. Even more ambitiously, Kropotkin (1987 [1902]) argued that actually helping one another is at the root of human nature. "Mutual aid," as he puts it, describes how people operate in unison with each other, similar to the symbiosis present between organisms in nature. Lévinas (1998 [1991]), too, argues that helping others is a duty and that the human faculty of reason is itself derived from ethics. Catholic Worker communities in the United States practiced this idea of mutual aid, led by Dorothy Day and others. Day argued that communities operating under mutual aid minimize the kind of hierarchies produced by charitable structures such as the Salvation Army. All parties in a system of mutual aid have the ability to produce an agenda, and the fate of one person is coupled more tightly with the fate of another. Because of the relative organizational flatness that many contemporary prefigurative movements have exhibited, they are able to take advantage of a broad array of creative tactics. Catholic worker communities have sustained oppositional structures that continue to be used as places of prefigurative resistance to this day. Nepstad (2008), for example, illustrates how Catholic Worker communities served as an important base for the transnational Plowshares Movement. Afro-Colombian movements sometimes intentionally withdraw from areas of state presence and into remote areas of the country to protect their cultures from majoritarian influences (Jiménez 2012, 122). These rural Afro-Colombian movements sometimes identify more strongly with their Diaspora than they do with the state (Paschel 2018, 237–8).

The most ambitious, utopian-minded individuals are often driven to start intentional communities in remote or rural areas. Beginning anew, pilgrims to the Plymouth Colony in the seventeenth century believed that they were leaving a world created by Man to find a New World intended by God.[4] Today's American Amish live out their Mennonite values largely undisturbed by the secularist state (Hostetler 1993); Worker co-operatives in northern Spain served as a bulwark against nationalist forces led by Francisco Franco (Molina and Miguez 2008); Industrial workers in the Kibbutz rely on communal socialist ideology and ethnic religious identity to survive rigorous labor (Warhurst 1996); and eco-villages inspired by the Diggers have withdrawn from a "materialist," "wasteful," and "heteronormative" society to till the land on their own (Meijering et al., 2007).

Aside from intentional communities, the New Lefts of the 1960s and 1970s were very much influenced by prefigurative politics (Breines 1980) and non-violent civil rights groups. This was especially true for student movements engaged in high-risk activism (Morris 1986). New Left students, like the Old Left labor movements before them, learned that they often could not win victories without the support of local communities[5] (Gutman 1977). Cohen (2009) details how the Berkeley Free Speech movement thrust itself into national political debates in defiance of mainstream culture. Overtaking buildings to make their point, Mario Savio and other activists pushed the cultural boundaries of acceptable expression. This rebellion created the template used by many contemporary campus movements today. Alinksy's (1971) *Rules for Radicals* is replete with disruptive and prefigurative tactics borrowed from the experience of decentralized movements, and Hoffman's (1971) *Steal This Book* became a popular counter-cultural representation of New Left antipathy for capitalism. Contemporary online cypherpunk activists similarly promote decentralized tactics to avoid the detection of their activities (Anderson 2022).

Revolutionary movements of the twentieth century, often inspired by communist ideologies, attempted to impose dramatic social changes on entire societies using lethal force (Naimark 2006). Replacing old state structures with new ones, this strategy left hierarchy and repression intact, or even magnified the effect of repression on their own citizens.[6] Other twentieth-century conceptions of centralized social authority included world federalism, a liberal cosmopolitanist aspiration for global governance (Marchetti 2006). The turn-of-the-century literature on cosmopolitanism, in particular, introduces vibrant methodological ideas with which to research social, cultural, and political phenomenon independent of the state (Beck 2000; Calhoun 2002; Delanty 2006; Grande 2006; Kaldor 2002; Levy and Sznaider 2006; Turner 2006; Turner 1998). Beck, for instance, argues that social scientists, in order to study globalization, ought to shift from state-centered methodological approaches to more cosmopolitan ones (Beck and Sznaider 2006).

Decentralized movements avoid some of the pitfalls evidenced by twentieth-century revolutions while maintaining equality as an aspirational value. Decentralization allows for internal discussion and the resolution of tension necessary to develop a sense of both agency and belonging. Creating this variety of "buy-in" is difficult, even in consensus organizations. Consensus decision-making structures, though they tend to slow down decision-making, allow all-volunteer movements to generate buy-in for their decisions (Polletta 2002). Gelderloos (2006) points out that having everyone's concerns heard, even if not implemented, facilitates the likelihood that participants will agree to and implement the group's decisions. Colombian student movements often use a version of consensus (Red Revuelta 2008). As Robnett (1996), McAdam (1986; 1988), and others have illustrated in the U.S. civil rights movements of the twentieth century, student activists were categorically predisposed to activism. Like-minded individuals, on-campus and off-campus, find others who share their categorical identities but also find others through their social networks (Snow et al., 1980).

Anthropologists have studied decentralized groups and theorized prefigurative societal arrangements *sui generis* from the economically integrated societies of the contemporary Western world (Graeber 2007a; Graeber 2007b; Mead 1928; Scott 2009). Recently, scholars have applied this growing body of literature on prefigurative movements to small, decentralized groups situated within modern societies (Olesen 2005; Scott 2009; Sitrin 2006). Latin American indigenous groups have asserted autonomous control over their lands since European colonization and continue to make territorial claims today (Holloway and Peláez 1998; Linera 2021; Murillo 2008; Ramos 2008; Warren 1998). Some Marxist revolutions of the twentieth century, including their more grassroots components, would also seize government land from which to challenge state power (Goodwin 2001; Hinton 1983; Skocpol 1979; Tilly 1964; Tilly 1986).

As a final direct commentary on the methodological literature, Desmond's (2007) study of risk-taking among wildland firefighters provides a comprehensive literature review of non-political risk-taking, marshaling Bordieuian habitus against Goffmian and Simmelian theorizing[7] on risk. Desmond argues that not only has social science been under-concerned with risk-taking behavior from the point of view of the participant, but also that those who make the attempt run astray in its theorizing of risk (Desmond 2007, 14–5). Desmond[8] (2007, 8–9) cautions that this epistemological habit proves counterproductive: "Why did sociological theories of risk taking prove insufficient [. . .]? Because current theories are afflicted with an assumption that causes those who come under its spell to overlook crucial contexts. That assumption is that it is legitimate to conceptualize risk taking in a vacuum, divorced from the specific environment and circumstances where it takes place." For instance, one can compare high-risk activism to non-activist risk, as Matthew Desmond does in his study of wildland firefighters (Desmond 2007), or to non-risky activism, as Susan Ostrander does in her study of civic engagement among elite college undergraduate students (Ostrander 2004).

HIGH-RISK ACTIVISM

The empirical basis for the concept of "high-risk activism" relies on studies of the Civil Rights Movement of the 1960s and 1970s in the United States. This section focuses on those theorists who vet high-risk political behavior largely in established Western democratic societies, but is followed by a section of Latin American case studies. For the most part, this literature deals with non-violent movements.[9] Piven (2006, 24) is an important exception, arguing that "[p]rotest movements may or may not engage in violence against property or persons. Students of American social movements have been very timid about this issue. They tend to ignore episodes of violence that do occur, excluding them by fiat from their definitions of social movements." Whereas theorists focusing on the Western democracies consider violence and corruption as largely aberrations, these are normal aspects of everyday life in most of the environments in which high-risk political behavior operates. We will largely sidestep this distinction here. But more often than not, movements are non-violent for strategic rather than moral reasons (Sharp 1973).

Contradictory Findings

Current theories on high-risk behavior in the movements literature do not explain risk-taking behavior in high-risk societies. The contradictory findings across U.S. studies alone provide further reason to reconsider our approach. In their attempt to distance themselves from early sociological theories about crowds (Tarde 1890; Turner and Killian 1957), students of high-risk behavior initially omitted the affective inputs of action and tried to distance themselves from psychological explanations of high-risk behavior (Goodwin, et al., 2000; Jasper 2011). But here, too, we find contradictory results. Peña, et. al., (2023) find the emotional labor involved in Colombian high-risk activism is too much to bear, leading some people to end their movement participation. But Romanos (2014) shows how the Basques practiced emotion work to recharge their "moral batteries" against the Franco regime. Reed (2002), too, finds the resolution of emotional hardship among Nicaraguan Sandanista sympathizers to be important in persistence.

McAdam describes high-"cost" activism as activism requiring high expenditures of "time, money, [and] energy." High-"risk" activism, in contrast, is activism that involves "anticipated danger, whether legal, social, physical, financial, and so forth, of participating in a particular activity" (McAdam 1986, 67). The coupling of these concepts of, risk and cost, has been carried through to even recent studies (Einwohner 2006; Rutten 2000). There is an understanding in this literature that risks and costs constitute two components of the same social phenomenon.

Entering into high-risk activism tends to be a gradual process for individual activists. McAdam (1988) observed this in the dangerous and sometimes life-threatening work of civil rights activism in 1964 Mississippi. In his analysis, McAdam found social networks to be critical in determining whether northern college students who applied to go to Mississippi during the summer of 1964 actually decided to participate. The literatures on friendship, solidarity, and organizational ties are specifically well developed and found to be important characteristics of mobilization (Barnes and Kaase 1979; Fantasia 1988; McAdam 1986; McAdam 1988; Rosenthal, et. al., 1985; Yohanani 2022). However, while scholars accept the importance of social networks as determinants of high-risk activism, there has been considerable debate about how networks facilitate a willingness to confront substantial danger, because recruitment and retention are highly (although variably) dependent on social networks (Loveman 1998; Nepstad and Smith 1999; Viterna 2006; Wiltfang and McAdam 1991). But demographic characteristics cannot explain motivations to activism. The radicalization of activist tactics over time is currently conceived of as a gradual process. As a participant participates in activism over time, radicalization is thought to occur. Munson (2008) agrees that this appears to be a consensus in the literature on this point. It might become increasingly likely, therefore, that the state will respond to more radical tactics with repression.

Schussman and Soule (2005, 1097) find that "individuals who are asked" are more likely to participate. Decidedly non-identitarian approaches to network theory are less developed in the literature (Paul, Mahler, and Schwartz 1997), but Mische's (2008) study of youth activism in Brazil revives the concept of the *catnet* to explain mobilization and Vergara-Camus (2009) also notes the importance of similar political structures in the Brazilian MST movement.

While identity (Álvarez, et. al. 1998; Cohen 1985) can be a motivating factor for activism, McAdam is keen to observe that high-risk activism is not an identity. He observes this, while also drawing attention to the importance of a comparison group (McAdam 1986; 1988). This comparison detaches the activist from the tactic that they employ and also decouples the determinants of activism from factors that do not explain participation.

Goodwin (1997) introduces a secondary set of network variables to this array. He and others find that family and sexual ties, gender, and race are all present in sustained participation in high-risk activism (Goodwin 1997; McAdam and Paulsen 1993; White 2007). This includes affective pressure, whether applied or self-imposed, as well as the maintenance of sexual relations. In Iron's (1998) study of the Mississippi Civil Rights Movement, Irons argues that Black women tended to participate in high-risk activism at higher rates than White women due to personal experiences of oppression. McAdam and Paulsen (1993), however find the opposite effect in the same movement, arguing that the demands made on women's roles in the household precluded participation. A cross-sectional study on the effect of racial discrimination also finds that this is not associated with participation in high-risk activism among blacks (Hope, et. al. 2019). Nepstad finds no significant gender difference in high-risk activism in her study of Nicaraguan social movement participation (Nepstad and Smith 1999).

Despite these competing findings, studies of high-risk activism have advanced our understanding of the demographic characteristics that predispose people to high-risk activism. Goodwin's (2001, 103) cross-national study, for instance, finds that state repression is a cause for grassroots mobilization: "By leaving masses of people 'no other way out' of their various economic and political predicaments, to use Trotsky's phrase, political authorities focused and channeled popular grievances in a revolutionary direction. These authorities unwittingly helped to organize or construct popular revolutionary movements, movements that were able to prosper despite and even because of brutal repression and the contradiction of political space." Studies such as this provide insights into and explanations for cross-national patterns of high-risk behavior. Moreover, even the continued focus on demographic variables helps us identify patterns of high-risk activism. What a focus on the process of becoming an activist adds is an understanding of how this all happens.

Consider Zwerman and Steinhoff's (2005, 86–7) assessment of this literature in their study of radical movements in the United States and Japan: "We know a lot about what the state has done to social movements and very little about how activists resist oppression." Gundelach and Toubøl (2019, 213) offer, "most trajectories that lead to activity combine factors that are associated with each of the theoretical frameworks." But as Viterna (2006) further explains, "if the characteristics that explain activism are shared by activists and nonactivists, then how can these characteristics be the critical causal factors behind popular mobilization?"

Race and gender, though important factors in a variety of settings, do not alone represent the full range of the activist biographical geography (Viterna 2006; Wiltfang and McAdam 1991). To the extent that these demographic variables allow for high-risk participation, McAdam argues that "biographical availability," defined as the absence of personal constraints, is an important determining factor in predicting participation in high-risk behavior (McAdam 1986; McAdam and Paulsen 1993). Even more than cognitive liberation, scholars have pointed to "biographical availability," which encompasses various aspects of the activist biography, to circumvent the analysis of psychosocial motivations at the personal level. However, Nepstad and Smith (1999) remind us that decisions to participate in high-risk activism are highly personal and that analytical categories based on identity cannot fully determine participation. Moreover, these kinds of analyses miss the process of becoming a participant in risk.

One might assume that socioeconomic class grievances might motivate people to take risks on their own behalf. Some sociologists do argue that class interest and class consciousness are predictors of mobilization and of how activists frame their message (McAdam 1989; Paige 1975; Snow and Benford 1988). But in the Argentinian case, Thalhammer (2001, 501) finds the opposite.

Finally, morality, which both Jasper (1997) and Irons (1998) suggest as a factor, fails to predict engagement by appearing in both activists and nonactivists. As Jasper puts it, individual activists face "strategic dilemmas" that they must resolve on their own. It is up to the individual activist to decide whether she will resist authority in any given instance, and if so, in what way she will do it (Jasper 2004).

The studies summarized in table 1.1 have extensively outlined several contributing factors to individual participation in high-risk activism. But some activists, especially those living under local political regimes that are the subject of contention, may not have much choice in the matter (Tilly 1993). As William Hinton notes in his account of the Communist guerilla movement that overtook China, explicit public avowals were not necessary in order for the guerillas to establish broad peasant support in liberated areas (Hinton 1983). Hence, the mobilization of a community for a particular cause may sweep up both the willing and the unwilling.

Andrews (2004) has argued that the African American Civil Rights Movement of the 1960's was effective in certain areas, but not others, as measured by certain institutionalization of parts of the movement. "Success," for Andrews, is institutionalization. But Andrews also acknowledges that social movements have outcomes aside from institutionalization, that some movements do not seek institutionalization, and that there are other factors outside of the movement that impact institutionalization (Schwartz 2007). Piven (2006) especially objects to defining social movement goals as institutionalization, conceptualizing movements instead as social formations that rise up during moments of "lucidity" to flout authority structures.

This literature on high-risk activism is sometimes criticized for being overly deterministic of individual action. Flacks (2004) and Morris (Schwartz 2007) argue that knowledge construction should be agency-centered in addition to being descriptive and analytical about movements. Social movement theory is often critiqued for disempowering actors by attributing causal significance to variables outside of their control. As Flacks (2004, 138) puts it: "What is all this analysis for? In what way does the validation, elaboration, and refinement of concepts provide useable knowledge for those seeking social change? Indeed, does the practice of 'normal Science' actually conflict with the moral dimension of social movement studies?" For analysts, social networks and demographic variables will continue to be of interest for

Table 1.1   Dominant Theories on the Determinants of High-Risk Activism

Biographical availability	McAdam '86 '88 '89
Social networks	Loveman '98, Nepstad & Smith '99
Solidarity	Fantasia '88
Sex	Goodwin '97
Race	Irons '98, McAdam & Paulsen '93
Ideology	Paige '75, Snow & Benford '88
Morality	Jasper '97, Irons '98
Catnets	Tilly '78, Mische '08

understanding determinants of action. For activists, the concern will likely continue to be about achieving social change.

Viterna's (2006) work on women's mobilization in El Salvador largely manages to escape the debates of the literature on high-risk activism by illustrating their non-effect. In her nuanced study, Viterna finds that the identifying characteristics of mobilization were true of both activists and non-activists and therefore could not account for mobilization. Instead, she identifies distinct "paths to mobilization," or patterns in the process of becoming an activist. Arguing for process-based theorizing rather than specific determinants across categories of people, Viterna's approach prioritizes individual biographies in idea-building.

In Wood's (2003) study of *campesinos* supportive of the FMLN in El Salvador, Wood finds that "pleasure in agency" or "the positive affect associated with self-determination, autonomy, self-esteem, efficacy, and pride that comes from the successful assertion of intention," is a more helpful factor in determining and explaining *campesino* participation than were the more traditional variables offered in the high-risk activism literature. Wood offers room to maneuver within the structures that constrain individual action.

In her descriptive account of the 2001 populist movement in Argentina, Sitrin (2006) documents the events taking place after the financial collapse of 2001, leading to the fall of the government and a succession of five Presidents in the wake of protests that demanded, "Throw them all out!" Workers, having lost their jobs, occupied shuttered factories throughout the country, reclaiming and re-opening them as worker-owned co-operatives. These new spaces became places from which to build autonomous organizations, freeing themselves from relying on the state for jobs and self-defense. "Horizontalism," as Sitrin faithfully translates the workers, "begins when people begin to solve problems themselves, without turning to the institutions that caused the problems in the first place" (2006, 38).

Olesen (2005) documents the January 1, 1995, Zapatista uprising against the North American Free Trade Agreement (NAFTA). This movement claimed Mexican land for the indigenous population and asserted a more egalitarian vision for conducting business. Their movement articulated a prefigurative vision for society that created new spaces for equal relationships and self-determination. Rather than mount a mobilization against state policies, Zapatistas sought a divorce from the state. Subcomandante Marcos, when asked what people in the United States could do to help the Zapatista cause, responded, "The best thing that you could do to help us is to help yourselves. Organize yourselves. Make yourselves strong" (Marcos 2001). This communion of the individualist spirit with egalitarian sympathies captures well the ethos of decentralized movements. The same could be said of indigenous and popular movements in Bolivia and Ecuador (Van Cott 2009), radical people's movements in Venezuela (Pappas 2008), and Brazil's youth movements, which shook the country to demand reforms (Mische 2008). Even within elite transnational spaces such as the World Trade Organization, Latin American voices dismantled the 2003 ministerial meetings in Cancun to protest unfair farm subsidies and other trade issues (Esparza 2009).

Jelin (2003) shows how Argentine movements often simply ignore the state. She documents how networks of movements in the region establish disparate centers of policy development. These policies then get implemented by activists themselves, regardless of what the relevant state laws are. Jelin (2003) argues that social movements turn to prefigurative tactics after it becomes clear that the state cannot or will not respond adequately to the movement's concerns.

Malcolm X (1992 [1970], 83) draws a stark distinction between reform- ist protest demonstrations and an action that is more prefigurative, writing, "[A] protest demonstration is an act that is a reaction to what someone else has done. And as long as you're involved in it, you're in someone else's bag. You're reacting to what they've done. And all they have to do to keep you on their string is keep situations developing to keep you reacting, to keep you so busy you never have a chance to sit down and figure out a constructive program of your own that will enable you and me to make the progress that is our due." On the day of the assassination of Malcolm X, he asked the security detail at his speaking engagement to refrain from frisking the community as they poured into the hall (Marable 2011). Malcolm X knew that his speech would be a high-risk activity, but that one could not build trust with the com- munity by arming himself against it.

MOMENT OF REPRESSION

The decentralized approach of activists and the contradictions in the literature suggest that a more networked understanding of how movements organize is appropriate. But it also has implications for how scholars think about high- risk activism. We know that we cannot reduce the motivation for action to demographic characteristics. We also understand that the tactics of those who participate in the activity do not necessarily define risk. What if we con- sider the political regime's tolerance for activist tactics? Figure 1.1 sketches this possibility using a behavioral threshold model. This approach takes the problem of high-risk activism "out of the heads of actors and [. . .] into the dynamics of situations" (Granovetter 1978, 1442).

If authorities, usually nation-states, define high-risk activism according to their response to activist activity, then we can accommodate variation in state responses to similar sets of political pressures. Most studies of high-risk

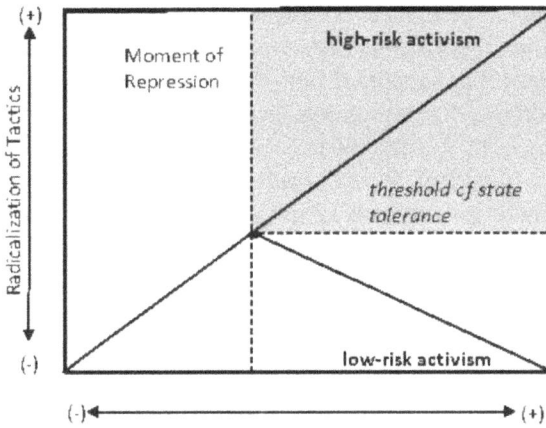

Figure 1.1 Moment of Repression. *Source*: Figure created by author.

activism in Western democratic contexts have left out the effect that context and state formation have on Latin American social movement action (Carroll 2011; Salgado 2018; Wada 2006). But the countries of the Americas are not unique in their varying responses to dissent. Arab Spring nations also saw a similar variance in their tolerance, given a similar set of political pressures (Beissinger et. al., 2015).

Although state tolerance defines high-risk activism, we should consider that this follows sequentially from activist action (Pierson 2000). In other words, the moment at which state tolerance defines high-risk activism is path-dependent on activist action. As activists mount increasing political pressure, it becomes increasingly likely that the state (or other extant authority) will mobilize security forces. Once security forces decide to act upon activists, it can then be said that these individuals are engaged in "high-risk activism." This point at which activists finally provoke a security response, this *moment of repression*, leans on the importance of moments for explaining social phenomenon (Jasper 1997; Lareau & Horvat 1999). Activist tactics matter, too, as increasing pressure tests what a state is willing to tolerate. But because this tolerance varies across states and likely even within states, it is an important factor in defining the riskiness of political action. Anyone who has witnessed the moment when activists persist, even after the tear gas and rubber bullets fly, can attest to the local significance of this event.

Selecting a couple of dramatic examples will further illustrate the point. Speaking of the repression that came with the rise of the Pinochet government on September 11, 1973, Cruz Salas (2019, 112) explains that "[a]fter the first massive *moment of repression* there came a period of selective repression. This time, they aimed at any survivors and small nodes of resistance that managed to endure." [emphasis added] In this case, oligarchic forces in Chile lashed out against the political pressure of the Allende government and the social movements that supported him. Assuming state power, they lowered the state's tolerance for repression and became intolerant of almost any kind of resistance. In the case of rural workers in Nicaragua, Jeffrey Gould (2011) writes, "[i]n 1962, Ruiz Escorcia brought along a 'huge wirecutter' to cut barbed wire as part of a land occupation. He 'personally protected' the campesino leaders in Managua in 1962–1963, a particularly dangerous *moment of repression* in Chinandega" [emphasis added]. Here Gould implies that, in this case, given a similar state of political affairs, state repression can fluctuate over time. But states can sometimes also employ repression in a prolonged and systematic way. Speaking of the 1904 repression of a rebellion of indigenous people in northern Argentina, Greca (2009, 344–6) identifies the "moment of repression" as the motivating force behind indigenous emigration from the area. "We have seen from the analysis of other social movements that questioned the national State in various ways," Greca (2009, 344) continues, "that this was the constant response that was applied systematically to quell resistance." The physicality of repression etches itself onto the body, sometimes pushing people into action (Tyagi 2018, 126) but other times cajoling activists into inaction.

CONCLUSION

As the case of the Colombian sugarcane worker strike in the following chapters will illustrate, workers sometimes decided to calibrate their resistance just below where they thought they might elicit a security response. They did so in order to protect the integrity of the overall strike and militant picket. Having already experienced repression after taking public roads, workers understood the likely consequences of repeating this action. By controlling the opportunities that activists give to the state to repress them, they can also strategically redirect their own efforts.

NOTES

1. This definition manages to ratify the notion of social movements as a "sociology of action" (Touraine 1985, 768). It also avoids the *situational ethics* (Melucci, 1989,160) of definitions of social movements as collectivities that "confront injustice" (Archila 1995, as cited in Archila 2001, 18).

2. Organizations are one vehicle through which individuals collectively express power. While we focus here on decentralized forms, sociologists have explained the important role that organizations play in recruitment and risk, especially through

"multi-organizational fields" (Curtis and Zurcher 1973; Fernandez and McAdam 1988; Klandermans 1992; McAdam 1986; McCarthy and Zald 1977; Snow, Zurcher, and Ekland-Olson 1980).

3. Some disorganized, disruptive movements do receive funding from larger, well-heeled groups. See, for example, the influence of the Open Society Institute in Turkey and Hungary (Ralchev 2018).

4. "The Plymouth tradition was separatistic, having rejected the Anglican Church and withdrawn from it to begin afresh in the proper manner" (Bumstead 1968, 265–6).

5. Successful movement organizations are connected to communities through bridge leaders (Robnett 1997). Gutman (1977) in particular argued that it is not sufficient for workers to withdraw labor from an employer in order to achieve victory, but that community engagement is an important factor to achieve success. Bridge leaders, according to Robnett, engage and organize the community directly, and serve as democratic conduits to the movement organization. They are different from "movement leaders" as defined by Morris and Staggenborg as "strategic decision-makers who inspire and organize others to participate in social movements" (Morris and Staggenborg 2004).

6. See, for example, Kiernan's (2008) treatment of communist brutality in Cambodia in the late 1970s.

7. Goffman (1967) and Simmel attribute high-risk behavior to masculine bravado, thrill seeking, a desire to be perceived as a hero, and other such explanations. Desmond (2007) argues that the categorization of behavior as being high-risk is dependent on who is parsing risky from non-risky behavior. In the eyes of his respondents, firefighting is devoid of risk.

8. This critique is specific to contemporary social movement theory. Historians of colonialism have discussed high-risk political action (c.f. Vlastos 1986).

9. See for instance, the discussion of the division between the social movements and revolutions literatures in Snow, David A., Sarah Anne Soule, and Hanspeter Kriesi (2004).

Chapter 2

Emancipatory Networks

Individuals engage in risky activism not only because of who they are but also because of who they know. When diverse coalitions of these individuals take certain network forms, they may have a good chance at achieving their aims, even against stiff resistance. This chapter illustrates the *emancipatory network* as a coordination of loose, discrete, and differentiated actors assembled to confront authorities. Differentiated from the colloquial use of, say, an "activist network," an *emancipatory network* works as a segmentary kinship network with a high degree of differentiation, involution, and dependence. I distinguish the *emancipatory network* from Harrison White's *catnet* (Mische 2008; White 2008b [1965]; Tilly 1978), which is a cohesive, tight, and concentrated network form. This category/network approach attempts to mitigate the problem of contradictory findings in the literature on high-risk activism. After an examination of a Colombian sugarcane worker strike, I provide a descriptive matrix of demographic and social network arrangements for each of the movement's principal protagonists.

The Andean foothills are fertile, with rich soils that sustain vibrant commodity export economies. It has also long been home to violence and socioeconomic inequality (Gomez Trujillo et al. 2007). 8,500 sugarcane workers went on strike in the Fall of 2008 in Valle del Cauca. I was tipped off a week before the strike was to begin and subsequently left Bogotá to capture what turned out to be a 58-day siege on Colombia's sugarcane plantations. Embedded within a network of human rights leaders, workers, labor organizers, families, and politicians, I illustrate how these actors organized themselves to achieve their aims.

RISK

"So you want to study risk?" Nina asked me at the end of our interview. Nina is a human rights activist and part of a group called the Doves. They fly her around the country to consult with grassroots movement groups that need assistance in organizing, or with legal matters. She is in her early thirties, as are all of the other members of the Doves, and has been doing this work for about eight years.

Nina's question resonated in the boutique downtown Bogotá café that she chose as our meeting location. I allowed the echo to linger into a fade, not having the will to defend myself. I understood how naïve my reason for being there must have sounded to a veteran human rights activist who has spent her entire professional life doing this kind of work. Perhaps sensing my confused sincerity (and, I later learned, an opportunity for recruitment[1]), she broke the silence with persuasive charm, "I will show you risk."

The Doves had been assisting a group of sugarcane workers preparing to strike. On the opposite side of the Andean Mountain Range, the heart of Valle del Cauca is a full day's drive to the West. It had not been possible to drive there just a few years prior. Parts of the highway were intermittently controlled by FARC guerilla checkpoints, making safe travel possible only by air. Still at the café, Nina advised, "If you want to understand political repression in Colombia, you have to leave Bogotá." Nina knew, and I would later discover, that I would only witness a narrow range of expressions of risk with any frequency if I were to stay put. Bogotá, with its density of tourists and international organizations, makes an inconvenient stage for the irregular use of violence. It was not so much the presence of the state, as O'Donnell (1993) has argued, that divided "safe" areas from areas of risk but rather, the realization of a collective need for normalcy and predictability. A variety of keen observers, some sensitive to human rights, restrain authorities from committing egregious offenses by simply being located there.[2]

I joined Nina and two of her co-workers, Felipe and Josephina, on the long drive to the city of Cali—Valle del Cauca's central metropolis. Felipe's work is more specifically focused on human rights law. He is also actively involved in the *Polo Democratico* [Democratic Pole], one of Colombia's left-leaning parties. In addition to his work consulting for the Doves, Felipe is a staff member of a prominent Colombian Senator. Josephina is Felipe's assistant in his governmental role and also a media staff person for the Doves.[3] She writes press releases, secures media interviews, and takes photographs on assignment for the sugarcane worker's movement.

The Doves are a textbook example of a *catnet*—a tight-knit group of human rights activists who have known each other for five to ten years. They have all worked in many areas of the country and have faced difficult challenges that have strengthened their emotional bonds. What had started as a tight professional network had become a tight friendship network as well. Like many such groups, the Doves have had to work through their share of social tensions. Nina felt the need to warn me that she was still getting over Felipe, her ex, "despite all of his flaws." The group's desire to maintain and protect these social bonds was to play a vital role in their effective navigation of the political crisis that they were about to enter.

The four of us and our luggage piled into a small two-door Renault. We snaked up the narrow mountain paths and across the rickety bridges that then-passed for an intercontinental highway. A simple accident in a narrow pass could, and often does, lengthen the trip by hours. Nina and Felipe took turns recounting a government plan to blast a tunnel through the Andes that would cut the travel time. It is one of many ideas that lack both funding and political will in Colombia.

Coming down the other side of the epic cliffs, we began to drive through seemingly limitless acres of tall, green stalks of sugarcane set against an open sky. Felipe began to lecture his small, encaged audience about the region. According to the largest industrial sugarcane trade group in the country, Asocaña (2008), there were 508,207 acres of sugarcane planted in Valle del Cauca in 2008, and sugar is among the country's top export commodities (2009a; 2009b). Together, Peru and Chile buy up 42 percent of Colombia's sugar exports (Asocaña 2020, 11). Asocaña had just entered the lucrative energy market during the 2005 harvest. The inflation-adjusted[4] price of ethanol in the country rose 37 percent between 2006 and 2022 (Asocaña 2023a). Asocaña produced 70 million gallons of ethanol in their first full year of production that following year. Since then, production has grown over by 30 percent (Asocaña 2022). The land was worked by 20,000 sugarcane workers; about 8,500 working as cutters, wielding a machete for sixteen hours a day, alternately sweating in the hot Colombian sun or being drenched by tropical rainstorms.

Cutters were all men, and the vast majority are Afro-Colombian. After Brazil and the United States, Colombia is home to the next largest African Diaspora in the world. At 9.5 million, there are 1 million more African Diasporic peoples in Colombia than in Haiti, and there exist more Afro-Colombians than there are people in Sweden. Most Afro-Colombians live along the coastline, where slaving ships forcibly introduced West Africans to the continent.

Some of those West Africans worked in these same fields for some of the same families. Most sugarcane workers live in plantation housing, that is, housing built on the plantation and owned by the plantation owners. The living conditions are modest. Usually, an entire family will fit itself into a one-bedroom apartment. Everyone in the family—the worker, his wife, and their children—sleeps in the same small room. The floors are often packed with dirt, and generally the kitchen consists of a small sink, two electric burners, and sometimes a small refrigerator. Clothes are washed by hand with soap and water. There is no furniture except beds in the bedroom. Some workers do not have bed frames and place mattresses on the dirt floor.

At some plantations, workers purchase what they need from the plantation store, which is also on plantation property. Because there is no competition, the prices for goods at these stores tend to be higher than those in the small towns in the region. This arrangement is similar to that of late nineteenth- to early twentieth-century farmers in the U.S. South, who did not have easy access to urban goods (Kelley 1990; Schwartz 1976).

Long hours and repetitive motions often left workers injured. Wielding a machete against the thick sugarcane stalks for days at a time can be taxing on the lumbar spine. Tired workers sometimes accidently strike their shins with their own machete. Relatively few plantations have a dedicated ambulance, and according to worker accounts, it could take hours for an injured worker to get proper medical attention. Workers are often limited to seeing

Figure 2.1   Living Conditions of Workers. *Source*: Photograph taken by the author in 2008.

the doctor that has been assigned to them. Workers repeatedly told me that their doctors only prescribe painkillers, usually acetaminophen tablets, and do little to intervene in more serious matters. In these instances, workers must transport themselves to the nearest hospital, which for some can be dozens of miles away. At their rally held in June, the Doves collected the personal testimony of over 100 injured workers who had not received adequate medical treatment for their injuries. This number of testimonies grew twice that size as the Doves travelled between plantations during the strike. Colombian agricultural workers have a poor perception of the health services available to them (Luna 2022) and frequently report "strains, sprains, and contusions to joints, muscles, ligaments and tendons; fractures; concussions; and in severe cases, death" (Polanía et al., 2019, 92–3). A recent study of sugarcane workers in Thailand found musculoskeletal disorders to be widely prevalent (Phajan et al., 2014).

In the distance, Felipe pointed out a plume of black smoke billowing above the horizon of green stalks. "That," he said, "is burning sugarcane." Cut cane is set on fire to accelerate the caramelization of the sugarcane in the process of converting it into sugar. The fires break down the cane's thick fibers, resulting in an ashy carbon that sends smoke up into the atmosphere. It deposits soot, ash, dioxins, and small particulates into the air, which then fall as ash deposits in the surrounding towns where the sugarcane workers and their families live, breathe, work, and play. The workers then enter the ashy landscape to recover the burned cane for processing.

A 2007 study of the health effects of this practice in Valle del Cauca found a positive association between sugarcane burns and the concentration of pollutants in the air. Perhaps more importantly, this same study found a positive relationship between the concentration of these pollutants and the number of daily hospital admissions for acute respiratory distress[5] (Álvarez 2007). The emission of these pollutants increased each year between 1990 and 2007 (Pérez Rincón and Alvarez Roa 2009, 4).

The sugarcane industry in Valle del Cauca has become a powerful regional economic force in recent decades. Agricultural exports and extractive mining have become important contributors to the national economy. Along with coffee, emeralds, oil, flowers, and clothing, sugar is one of Colombia's top exports. The sugarcane industry employed more than 30,000 people in Colombia's Western valleys (WOLA 2010). Today, Asocaña (2020, 5) claims to employ nine times that number across six Colombian departments. Once filled with wetlands, this pastoral landscape is now a vast expanse of monoculture (Delgadillo-Vargas 2016).

Workers at the plantations were initially attracted to the industry by its relatively decent wages and job stability. Many of them had been farmers in Colombia's rural areas before obtaining jobs cutting sugar cane. Others,

Figure 2.2   Burning Sugarcane in Valle del Cauca. *Source*: Photograph taken by the author in 2008.

wanting to get away from or having been forcibly pushed out of coca production by one or more of the various armed groups operating in the country,
preferred the comparatively quiet lifestyle of working the sugar plantations,
even while taking a cut in pay. Indeed, many sugarcane workers earn below
the Colombian minimum wage as independent contractors. But there are few
other work options for them in the region. Large plantations had absorbed
much of the arable land over the course of several decades. Some of this was
through private purchase, but many small landowners lost their property as
a result of paramilitary activity in previous decades. Historians have documented widespread extortion of lands, homicides, and theft that contributed
to the centralization of landholdings in the region (Gomez Trujillo et al.,
2007).

   Sugarcane harvesting dates back to Spanish colonization of the region.
Early sugarcane planters were considered *colonos* for appropriating land for
themselves. Industrialization of sugarcane began at the start of the twentieth
century. This industrialization allowed four Valle del Cauca families—Eder,
Cabal Becerra, Caicedo, and Salcedo -- to dominate the industry. In some
cases, the membership of the corporate boards of the companies that these
families own overlapped by 80 percent or more (Collins 1983). Embedded

within elite networks, these families procured public investments in public roads and highways to better transport their product to market (Sánchez Mejía and Santos Delgado 2014). As late as the 1970's, these four families controlled 75 percent of Colombia's sugarcane industry (Silva Colmenares 2007, cited in Pérez Rincón and Alvarez Roa 2009, 9). With the globalization of the industry, Asocaña has faced increased regional competition for exported sugarcane, particularly from Brazil and Mexico. Perhaps in consequence, Asocaña has dramatically increased its production of ethanol. In 2005, Asocaña produced just 6.2 million gallons of ethanol, while in 2007, this number increased more than ten-fold, to 73.9 million gallons (Asocaña 2009a). This rapid increase in ethanol production has further subjected the industry to global market pressures and, in consequence, raised the ire of anti-biofuel activists in Europe and the United States. Global demand for ethanol and other biofuels has increased in an attempt to relieve pressure from global energy markets.

Because sugarcane is a labor-intensive product to harvest, plantation owners sought to cut the cost of labor, often by violent means. This antagonism has been well documented in the sugarcane industries of Hawaii and Haiti (Jung 2006a; Jung 2006b). In Valle del Cauca, armed private security guards that patrolled the plantation oversaw the workers. Wages had declined over the course of several years, leaving newer workers frustrated at not being able to achieve the quality of life that some of the older workers had maintained. More than half of sugarcane workers surveyed in the nearby department of Risaralda believe that mechanization of their labor displaces workers and creates unemployment (Arias Mendoza 2016, 73).

PRELUDE TO THE STRIKE

Prior to 2004, sugarcane cutters in Colombia were hired directly by the plantations as independent contractors. Because plantation managers hired workers on an individual basis, the terms of employment often varied from one worker to another. This system did benefit some workers—those younger, stronger workers that were able to cut cane at a faster rate. Some of those that benefited from this arrangement supported the independent contractor system, but others did not. Leaving workers with no collective bargaining power to set more reasonable standards that would benefit most workers, the large majority of workers did not support the independent contractor system. If a worker would not agree to work for a given wage or on a given day, the plantation manager could—and often would—just hire someone else. This arrangement led to the depression of wages.

Workers began to form co-operatives that aimed at entering into independent contracts with their respective plantations instead of entering into these agreements individually. Initially, the plantation owners resisted, but when the workers went on strike later that year, owners agreed (in three days) to accept the co-operative system. Unions typically oppose the co-operative system because it is seen as competing with unionization. Locals of the national union, SINALCORTEROS (National Union of Sugarcane Cutters), SINTRAICAÑAZUCOL (National Union of Sugarcane Agricultural Workers), and SINALTRAINAL[6] (National Union of Food Industry Workers), were involved in the strike, but Antisuyu [pseudonym] was the only plantation with a significant number of unionized cutters. It was the largest sugarcane plantation in Colombia, and workers there received the highest wages in the sector. Most of the 8,500 striking workers contracted their labor through co-operatives. This system of Associative Labor Cooperatives (CTAs) remained in place through the course of my fieldwork in Colombia and continues today. Some Colombian scholars correctly point out that the CTA system leaves workers with less pay (Pérez Rincón and Alvarez Roa 2009, 51) and fewer labor protections (Pineda Duque 2005, 120). But workers I spoke with prefer their co-operative for the job stability it provides.[7] The number of these CTAs grew three-fold between 2000 and 2006 (Cuéllar and Vargas 2018, 20), but has been falling since its peak in 2010 (Pineda Duque 2015, 121).

Unlike in Argentina in 2000, where workers commandeered abandoned factories to establish worker-run co-operatives across the country, the workers in Colombian co-operatives did not take control of production. Rather, these co-operatives behave somewhat like worker-run sub-contractors, hired to cut large swaths of sugarcane at a set piecemeal rate. Sugarcane cutters are only involved in the early stages of production, collecting the cane from the field and bringing it to the processing facilities. Factory workers then refine the cane into sugar and molasses or process it into ethanol. Sugarcane cutter co-operatives have significant leverage in that they have the ability to halt production. But unlike Argentine worker-owned co-operatives, they do not have the ability to run production on their own.

Sugarcane cutters saw modest gains in 2004. Wages rose about 1,000 pesos ($0.44 in 2022 USD) per ton of cane cut per worker.[8] Total wages also vary, but estimates are about 5,000 to 8,000 pesos ($2.20 to $3.52 in 2022 USD) per ton. Some work this out to an average of about $4 USD per day (Montoya Duque 2011), while others estimate this to be double that amount[9] (Pérez Rincón and Alvarez Roa 2009, 48). The amount of cane that a worker can cut in a typical day can change depending on weather conditions, whether or not the cane has been burned, and other factors. Workers reported being able to cut about 1.5 to 2 tons on a good day. However, workers saw their rates stagnate against Colombia's high inflation.

The new co-operatives had the effect of generating leaders who began to meet with each other to discuss measures that might be taken to address worker concerns. Elected by workers of their respective co-operatives, these leaders consulted with their constituencies regularly. It became clear that while workers believed that the co-operative system was a step in the right direction, ultimately the new organizations needed to fight to extract further concessions from plantation owners. Conditions had deteriorated to such an extent that many could no longer survive on their wages.

A minority of these workers began to promote the idea of a merger of the co-operatives into a single, unitary co-operative. Many workers did not want to form a formal labor union because this implied that they would have to become a party to the Central Union of Colombian Workers (CUT), the country's largest labor union. Many workers did not trust the hierarchical structure of the CUT, which many of the workers felt was plagued by infighting. A powerful faction of workers from Antisuyu opposed the idea of a unitary co-operative because many of their members were unionized and because they earned somewhat more than workers on other plantations. They feared that if all sugarcane cutters were members of a single co-operative, they would not only be gambling their gains by throwing their lot in with smaller worker co-operatives, but that they would also be gambling their union affiliation.

The co-operative leaders decided to keep the current structure, at least in the short term, but also proposed to coordinate a strike campaign to deal with accumulated grievances. Most workers did not want to join a union, but many of the co-operative leaders hoped to attract other allies, including unions, who might play an influential role in the course of the strike. At the end of 2007, a group of co-operative leaders approached human rights workers, labor unions, and politicians, hoping to shore up support in advance of this action. The labor unions saw it as an opportunity to unionize more sugarcane workers but were stymied by worker ambivalence to unionization. Perhaps seeing that they were not going to see large gains in their membership rolls, labor unions gave passive support to the organizing initiative, forcing the co-operative leaders to organize the strike themselves, with the help of the Doves.

The Doves were enthusiastic about worker plans for a strike and were eager to help. Javier had been instrumental in getting his colleagues involved in the campaign. As a university student, Javier helped to lead a sit-in of the main utility company in the city of Cali. Subsequently, he worked as a human rights activist in Choco, working with Afro-Colombian populations. Later, while in Germany and the UK, Javier was an advocate for Colombian social justice solidarity groups. He singlehandedly convinced the Doves to focus on the sugarcane workers' campaign. That influence helped the striking workers to gain the backing of the *Polo Democratico*, which would prove to be a powerful ally.

During the first half of 2008, Javier and the Doves worked closely with the leaders of the co-operatives as well as with plantation workers themselves, helping to educate them about their rights as workers and to formulate the strike demands. The co-operative leaders representing approximately 8,500 sugarcane workers, in conjunction with the Doves and their labor and political allies, organized a rally in mid-June to sign an "emancipatory" document which outlined their demands. Calling themselves the Huayna Movement [pseudonym] they demanded that Asocaña enter into negotiations. The workers delivered the document to Asocaña with great fanfare and spectacular media coverage but received no response.

THE STRIKE

Ninety days after delivering the document, the sugarcane workers went on strike, but not without first having set-up an elaborate movement infrastructure. In consultation with the Doves, workers embarked on a marketing campaign that included a new logo, press releases in Spanish and English, a website and blog, and thousands of reproductions of their strike demands. These efforts would prove effective not only in educating workers and their communities but also in influencing public opinion. Clifford Bob (2005) argues that the marketing component of rebellious movements located in developing countries is essential to gaining the support of public opinion at home and abroad.

The Doves advised the Huayna Movement to call their action a "work stoppage." As independent contractors, the workers were not legally permitted to strike. Most workers continued to refer to their action as a strike, except those speaking to the media and those directly involved in contract negotiations. The Huayna Movement and the Doves set up a strike center at one of the co-operatives, dubbed "Co-operative One," that served as the primary logistical base for the campaign. The strike center was centrally located in the town of Palmira, located near the center of the valley and a mere thirty-minute drive from Cali. The office was equipped with telephones, fax machines, desks, meeting spaces, computers, printers, a garage, a kitchen, and a stack of mattresses. There was only limited Internet connectivity at the strike center, but a nearby Internet café served as an effective auxiliary. The co-operative took several measures so as not to draw attention to the fact that the Doves were operating the strike out of this location. A large desk, for example, was moved into a back room, away from the window facing the street. This was done so that the curtains facing the street could be drawn open on Sunday. The co-operative staff person particularly insisted that they might draw suspicion from the neighbors if the curtains were drawn closed on a Sunday.

Because of the history of repressive and often violent measures taken against strikers in the region, the Doves and Huayna Movement leadership decided to establish alternative strike centers, in the event that police forcibly evicted them, turned off the utilities, or otherwise were to harass them. These were named "Co-operative Two," located at a local union hall on the other side of town, and "Co-operative Three," at the home of one of the older sugarcane cutters involved in the strike. The Doves provided legal counsel, communications, organizing, training, and important contacts with solidarity groups. Their new branding and association with a human rights group gave the workers an identity apart from the unions, something that most of the Huayna Movement leadership felt was important to achieve.

The Doves were intimately involved with the Huayna Movement leadership in structuring the strike. Worker leadership and the co-operative structure pre-dated the involvement of the Doves. Workers approached the Doves for assistance with organizing the strike. They did so in order to preserve autonomy over their own local decision-making.

On the morning of the strike, workers assembled on the plantation properties and declared a "Permanent Assembly" at each of nine plantations in Valle del Cauca and Northern Cauca. Permanent Assemblies were the tactical equivalent of a militant picket line, with one important difference. Many of the wives and children of the workers established make-shift living quarters

Figure 2.3 Workers Begin to Arrive for a Meeting. *Source*: Photograph taken by the author in 2008.

and kitchens under a collage of tarps and tents. Many of them live on or near plantation property, but some joined the workers in preparing to endure a long battle.

Workers distributed themselves around the main gates at each of nine plantations. Nearly all of the plantations' sugarcane cutters in Valle del Cauca voted to strike, except for two small plantations. Cutters at two large plantations in Northern Cauca also joined the Valle del Cauca strikers. Bus drivers who transport the workers to work every morning from their plantation apartment complexes and surrounding areas parked themselves across plantation gates in several locations. This effectively blockaded the plantations to vehicular traffic. Between two-dozen and several hundred workers guarded each entrance gate at the various plantations to prevent the ingress of police, company vehicles, or private security. Workers communicated with each other via cell phones, some of which had been provided by the Doves and others by the unions. With these phones, workers coordinated their actions in response to developments at other entrances to their plantation and at other plantations.

Plantation owners were not caught by surprise. In the weeks before the strike, according to several workers, plantation managers had been taking individual workers aside and asking them when the strike was going to begin. One plantation fired a dozen workers ahead of the strike in retaliation for their participation in an organizing meeting.[10] Two workers reported receiving harassing phone calls to their homes.[11] Many workers had expressed concern about spies and infiltrators, and—despite efforts on the part of the workers to reveal the date of the strike on a strictly need-to-know basis—the police and plantation owners were forewarned. Police responded swiftly to the militant picket, and plantations immediately began a media blitz. But neither prevented the work stoppage nor the worker occupation of the plantations.

At the Antisuyu plantation, police successfully removed the workers stationed at the main entrance, but only after a sustained battle. The riot control unit of the National Police, called the Mobile Anti-Disturbance Squadron (ESMAD), fired tear gas canisters and rubber bullets, but the front line of workers was not dislodged. The riot police, armed with protective equipment, batons, tear gas, rubber bullets, pepper spray, and backed by water cannon-mounted riot vehicles, then charged. Many workers had brought their work tools, including machetes. Some chose to use them in the mêlée that followed. Police set fire to tarps, tents, and other personal belongings that they could get their hands on. Accounts vary, but about 40 workers and officers were injured. Injuries requiring hospitalization and specialist referrals included "bruises, lacerations, contusions, [and] open scalp wounds.[12] Having lost control of the gates, Antisuyu strikers then retreated into the sugarcane fields. Sugarcane stalks were densely planted and, at this point in the season, grew

Figure 2.4 Workers Occupy a Sugarcane Plantation. *Source*: Photograph taken by the author in 2008.

up to eight feet tall. Police did not dare follow workers into the thick cane fields, where they could be easily outmaneuvered on an unfamiliar pitch. Once in the fields, workers with access to company transport trucks started them up and parked them across the private roads leading from the gates. Workers then disabled the vehicles by slashing their tires, thus preventing the police from advancing further.

At Cuntisuyu, another plantation, a similar engagement between ESMAD and workers took place, resulting in thirteen injuries. There, workers called for an ambulance, but private security and police at the main gates prevented the ambulance from entering the property. Workers called the Doves for counsel. Several Doves travelled with the ambulance to a rear entrance, closest to where the injured workers were and where police presence was least pronounced. However, the ambulance was unable to enter because two private security guards held it at bay until police and additional security reinforcements arrived. Although the Doves pleaded to enter only in order to take the injured to safety, the ambulance was not permitted to enter.

At the Qullasuyu plantation, there was a standoff between the police and the workers. Workers leaned up against the checkpoint bar, just a few feet away from a police line armed with rifles. Just across the street, the police set up a small encampment, so there were police directly in front and in back of them. There were perhaps five hundred workers at the main entrance, with about fifty police behind the main gate and another thirty across the street. Enraged workers raised their machetes in defiance. A few telephoned the Doves, demanding gasoline so that they may block the road with burning tires, construct Molotov cocktails, and set vehicles ablaze.

When Javier got off the phone after this request, he said to everyone in the office, "Imagine that! They are calling us for gasoline! No, no, no, we have to go over there right now to diffuse this before this thing gets out of control. We have to calm them down. Imagine that: Machetes against rifles. They will get massacred, man." The Doves arrived at Qullasuyu and, after surveying the scene from the car for about a minute or so, carefully made their way to the middle of the standoff in order to negotiate with the police captain. Javier made several trips between the Captain and the Huayna Movement plantation representative, eventually proposing that the workers allow the police free access to the plantation. In exchange, the police would permit the workers

Figure 2.5   A Disabled Tractor and Water Truck. *Source*: Photograph taken by the author in 2008.

to block all other traffic, including company and supply vehicles. The police captain agreed, but the strikers, angry and offended that the government had sent riot police to attack them, continued to menace their opponents. Javier then gave an impassioned speech from a megaphone to the workers, imploring them to calm down and to allow police vehicles to enter and exit as they wished. He explained that blocking strike-breaking scabs and company supply vehicles were important pressure points. Javier explained that the police had agreed to leave the workers alone. After some discussion, the workers reluctantly agreed to this deal.

Workers may have engaged in more property destruction and police fighting had the Doves not intervened here. This illustrates the high esteem in which workers held Javier, in particular. Workers had approached the Doves because they sought the help of a human rights organization. Javier was instrumental in selling this relationship to the other Doves. This unique partnership proved to combine important sets of skills.

The Doves similarly intervened at the other plantations to diffuse tensions and negotiate the rules of engagement between workers and police. Although tensions between police and the workers remained high throughout the rest of the week, there was little physical fighting beyond the first day. Instead, workers and police skirmished for control of certain spaces around the plantations. This jostling played out slightly differently at different locations. In general, strikers secured access to the vast majority of the properties, including nearly all of the private roads. Workers maintained a round-the-clock presence at all entrances of each plantation. But workers had also conceded police access to most of the property most of the time. Private security guards, or police, or sometimes both, were stationed at all of the main plantation entrances. At some plantations, there were little more than a few symbolic personnel, sometimes as few as two. At others, particularly at those plantations where there had been heavy fighting, ESMAD maintained a platoon of twenty or more.

At the Cuntisuyu plantation, dozens of riot police protected piles of equipment and several vehicles behind a chain-linked fence. One of these vehicles was a water cannon-mounted anti-riot vehicle. The police occasionally patrolled the private road connecting the main entrance with the fenced-off processing facility, where additional police stood.

Workers at the Antisuyu plantation offered the stiffest resistance. After police shot live rounds into the air, enraged workers struck officers with their machetes and blocked the roads with commandeered cane trucks. Police shot tear gas, but workers here were effective in confining police to the main entrance. Thousands of workers spread themselves across the vast plantation, dotting the private roads with tent encampments. Few workers traveled near the main entrance, where police were concentrated. Instead, workers focused

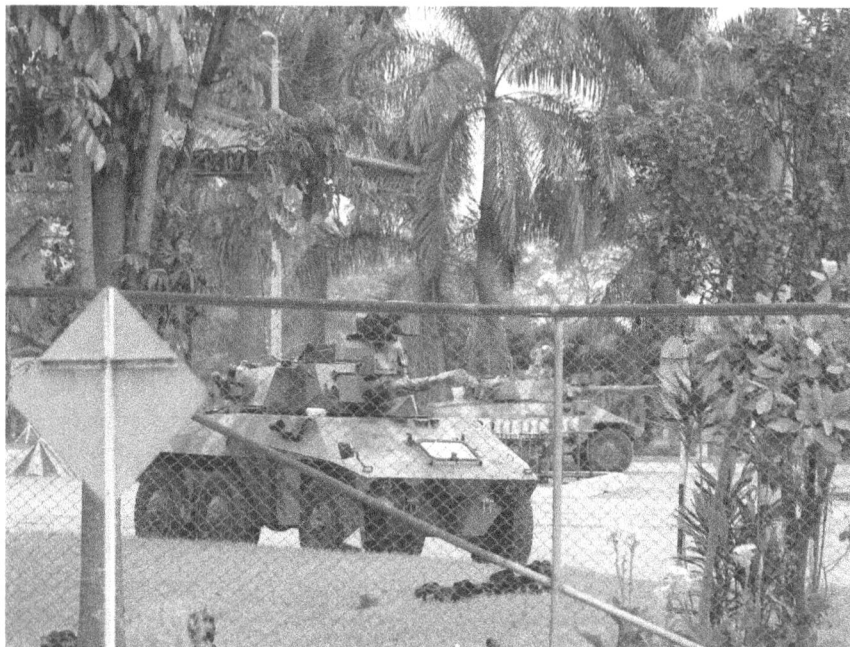

Figure 2.6   Mobile Anti-Disturbance Squadron Tanks at Sugarcane Plantation. *Source*: Photograph taken by the author in 2008.

on guarding the internal roads. In all of my visits to this plantation, I never witnessed police anywhere except at the main gate.

At the end of this long day, Huayna Movement leadership met with the Doves to discuss the clashes with police. Felipe was concerned about the level of repression, offering that perhaps workers should consider moving to the town plazas if this continued. One of the workers replied, "No, we cannot do that. If we do that we will lose. [. . .] If we leave the plantations we will lose." Javier was upset and scolded the Huayna Movement leadership for not doing more to keep workers from physically engaging the police. He urged them to intervene more aggressively to reduce tensions. "We will not win if we fight this on their terms," he told the mostly male crowd at the meeting. The workers largely demurred, but agreed to prevent more police fighting. "You know how people get when they have machetes in their hands," one of them said. A few chuckled. "Do you think that this is a joke?" Javier said, deadpan.

Together, they went over the number of injuries at each location, assessed the needs at each plantation, and determined where to allocate resources. There was hardly any time left to discuss media coverage and the reaction of plantation owners. But Javier later telephoned a *Polo Democratico* member to advise him to pressure the press by asking them if they were in favor of the president's decision to send ESMAD to attack the striking workers.

Workers at the Qullasuyu plantation struck a more conciliatory tone with police. Under the instruction of their representative to the leadership committee and other members of the local community, workers initiated conversations with police about the strike, sharing information and their personal stories. After stiff battles, workers intended to soften rank-and-file police resistance to the strike. Many of the police officers were the sons or brothers of sugarcane workers. Rather than see the police as enemies, these workers began to treat rank-and-file officers, as members of the community.

An equilibrium began to set in after the first week, as workers and police tacitly agreed on the terrain that each was to control. Antagonism continued at a low simmer, with only isolated events of harassment from police or from workers. Once this uneasy truce was established, the workers expected negotiations to begin, but plantation owners maintained that they would not negotiate until the workers ended the strike. Plantation owners communicated this to the workers through the Huayna Movement leadership. Plantation owners took the position that the co-operatives were competitors for contracts from the plantations. They refused to negotiate with the co-operatives as one unit. Workers maintained that the strike would not end until a new contract had been signed that involved all plantations and co-operatives. The plantation owners ended communication with the workers after only a few days of discussions, likely hoping to outlast the strike.

On one occasion at the Kuntisuyu plantation, hundreds of workers crowded around two Doves, Nina and Juana, immediately upon their emerging from their car. The workers complained that the police had just been caught trying to smuggle scabs disguised as police into the plantation to conduct repairs. The workers were able to identify the scabs because they had been their co-workers. Surrounded by workers, the Doves caucused with Huayna Movement leaders for a few minutes. They decided that Nina would ride with a worker on the back of a motorcycle to the scene. Workers quickly endorsed their plan for Nina to document what she could with a camera.

One of the images that Nina took depicts individuals in plain clothes holding police fatigues, semi-stuffed into duffel bags. These individuals are surrounded by a ring of police, who are themselves enveloped by an animated crowd of workers. Workers consistently complained that the police never wore identification and that it was near impossible to track them during the course of documenting human rights violations. Speaking of a worker representing the Kuntisuyu plantation, Juana said at a meeting at Cooperative One later that day, "I saw Don Camilo get red in the face and wave his hand in the air at an armed police man. Man, that is one tough guy!" Nina reported that the police major pleaded with her not to report the incident.

According to Nina, the police major told her that he had permitted this to occur at the request of the plantation owner, who became desperate to fix a machine that, left unrepaired for a couple of days, would have to be replaced at significant cost. In Nina's telling, she insisted that this was a grave violation and informed the police major that the use of Colombian National Police equipment for non-police purposes carries with it a swift penalty. In the end, however, Nina chose not to report the incident, saying to the Doves in the car, "I felt bad for the guy—it would have ruined his career. We scared the crap out of him and we will keep the evidence on file. I don't think that he will be giving us any more trouble."

The others remained silent, perhaps understanding that the leverage that they now had over this police major was more valuable to them than turning him over to the justice system. Because he wanted to protect his career, this police major implicitly agreed to abide by the law in the future, at least as long as the Doves were somehow involved. This "gentlemen's agreement" speaks to the class values that the Doves and the police major share. Nina reported these events to the Huayna Movement leadership later that day, but the workers were not involved in making this decision. Nor were the workers in a position to audit the decision after Nina had made it. The large number of quickly developing incidents that the Huayna Movement leadership had to consider and the extraordinary assistance that the Doves provided likely prevented the Huayna Movement leadership from questioning Nina.

The stalemate with the plantation owners continued for three weeks. The workers were sustained by a strike fund that they had prepared, solidarity funds compiled by the Doves, robust community support, and in-kind food donations from unions. Several local mayors had the fire departments fill the water tanks that workers were using for cooking and drinking every morning. Priests and nuns visited the plantations to conduct mass and to bring food and donations from local parishes. Unions, students, indigenous communities, and the workers' own families visited the plantations to bring food, clothes, cell phones, funds, and to offer their moral support.

A steady drumbeat of negative press was building, however, and the police issued warrants for the arrest of two Doves, Javier and Felipe, and two Huayna Movement leaders. They were charged with sabotage, inciting a riot, and terrorism. The four leaders went into hiding for several days, after which they decided to turn themselves in. This development created a strain on the resources of both the Doves and the Huayna movements, which now had to sustain the strike, a legal battle, and a solidarity movement for the accused.

The most serious charge, terrorism, was dropped at arraignment, but the arrested leaders were charged with sabotage and intent to start a riot. The four spent the night in jail, and their heads were shaved during processing. This was particularly humiliating for Felipe, who had long hair. They were

Figure 2.7a Food Donations Played a Major Role in Sustaining the Strike. *Source*: Photograph taken by the author in 2008.

released the next day, the judge ruling that the leaders were not a threat to society. In an apparent attack against the prosecutor, the judge said, "not only are these people not a threat to society, but a segment of society is a threat to these people." The arrested leaders were legally obligated to stay within the town in which they held residence. But they rarely left their homes for fear of violent reprisals from hired paramilitary groups.

The threat of death, even for the Doves, had not been zero. About a month into the strike, Felipe, Javier, and two members of the Huayna leadership committee received death threats. Fearing that their phone conversations were being intercepted, some of the workers on the leadership committee explained at a meeting that they had begun to communicate in code. Adriana advised workers not to do that but to "just be careful about what you say. For instance, the other day someone called to tell me that they 'have two chickens ready' for me, and I had no idea what they were talking about. Then I called them back, and they said, 'No, it's just that I have two people who need to speak to you.'"

The workers movement began to send delegations of workers to visit them. On one such occasion, the Huayna movement sent a bus full of workers to each of their homes, surprising them with memorable visits. Not expecting visitors, Javier opened his front door slowly and suspiciously before relenting to a jubilant crowd.

But despite their minor victory in the courts, the mood at the plantations became noticeably somber after the arrests. With two of the Doves confined to their homes, and the others more cautious about public exposure, workers saw visits from the Doves much less frequently. Union organizers visited the workers, but became discouraged by their failure to recruit new members.

An accounting of food donations conducted by the Doves during this time of the strike showed that workers had received and distributed over 200 large packages of donated rice, cooking oil, black beans, tuna, sugar, *panela*, coffee, flour, and potatoes. Juana had some concerns that some of the donated food had not reached the strike kitchens. But in the process of tracking down those missing packages, she discovered that plantation workers had decided to divert a small amount of food to families in exceptional need. The strike had hit the plantation owners hard. But as the strike extended well beyond a month, it also hit working families who had little in savings. After accounting for this, the actual number of packages that Juana could not account for was negligible. This near-absence of pilfering and the decision of the Permanent Assemblies to divert food to needy families illustrate the discipline of the workers and the affection that they shared with their communities.

NEGOTIATING THE STRIKE'S END

The Doves turned to then-Governor of Valle del Cauca, Juan Carlos Abadía Campo, to intervene. Knowing that the workers, their families, and their communities represent a large voting bloc, Governor Abadía could not allow himself to be viewed as siding too much with the sugarcane industry. Perhaps wishing to be viewed as playing a constructive role, the governor largely did not comment on the strike. The *Polo Democratico* capitalized on this silence to criticize the governor, and the Doves began to pressure him to arrange a meeting between plantation owners and the Huayna Movement leadership. Plantation owners had important influence with both the governor and the national government. President Uribe and his staff were not under the same local constraints as Governor Abadía and were vocal in their critique of the sugarcane workers from the very beginning. But President Uribe was an early backer of negotiations after the initial confrontation between workers and riot police. The Minister of Social Security, Diego Palacios, stated in the press that he believed there were "dark hands" operating behind the strike.[13] Upon seeing this statement on the television news that evening, Javier elbowed me and said to the room of fellow Doves, "he's talking about us."

More generally, this phrase is used in Colombia to point to subversive, usually left-wing actors who oppose establishment policies or initiatives. But Javier and several other workers also pointed to the racial overtones involved in these comments. Just about all of those using the phrase were white or mestizo, whereas most of the striking workers were black. One reporter asked a worker what he thought of the accusation of there being "dark forces" behind the strike. Jamie Arocha (2008) of *El Espectador* quoted the worker as having replied, "Of course there are! Can't you see that 70% of us are black?"

About six weeks into the strike, the Doves' pressure campaign against the governor paid off. Plantation owners had now agreed to meet with a delegation of two workers, three of the Doves, and Governor Abadía. Several rounds of meetings took place at the governor's office on the top floor of the Palacio de San Francisco in Cali. About half a dozen workers waited outside the office during these meetings, some of which went late into the night. These discussions soon led to formal negotiations. In the meantime, all parties agreed to the following: the workers would continue the strike and militant picket during negotiations, but Asocaña would not represent the owners at the bargaining table. Rather, negotiations would continue with representatives from each of the individual plantations and each of the individual worker co-operatives. This arrangement allowed negotiations to take place, while still allowing each side to "save face," maintaining their initial bargaining positions.

Formal negotiations across all of the plantations lasted between one and two weeks. During this period, Universidad del Valle hosted a solidarity event. In addition to students, faculty, and sugarcane workers, organizers also invited a priest from Germany. The priest, who had once known Camilo Torres, gave an absorbing speech on the global sugarcane industry's ecological and human rights impacts.

After a few more days of uncertainty around contract negotiations, Chinchaysuyu, the third-largest plantation, had settled to a contract. Soon afterward, Qullasuyu, the second-largest plantation, negotiated a settlement. This was followed two days later with the contract settlement at Antisuyu, the largest plantation. The rest followed, all nine settling within the week. The workers ended the strike piecemeal, as each plantation settled. They followed a ritual of holding their militant picket until the negotiating team could reach the plantation and announce the terms to the workers. Workers had decided that the agreements were to be approved by the Permanent Assemblies located at each plantation. But in practice, this was largely *pro forma* and no agreements were rejected or amended by this process.

The workers, on average, won wage rate increases of about 7 percent. They also were able to negotiate additional increases in pay for working on holidays and when cutting raw cane stalks. The new agreements compelled plantations to distribute new work gloves, work uniforms, and machetes at increased intervals.[14] The plantations would also now contribute to a collective housing fund, from which workers could apply for small grants and loans for the purchase of property. Although the workers were not able to resolve all of their concerns, they did achieve significant concessions.

Workers had hit the industry fairly significantly. Sugar production in 2008 was down 17 percent from 2007 and rose 27 percent in 2009. Asocaña, in their twenty-page annual report, made only a single one-line reference to the strike: "The reason [why only 77% of planted sugarcane was harvested] was that at the end of 2008 and for an average of 56 days, a group of cutters blocked the production of 8 mills, which represented 68% of the cane milled, which made the harvest impossible" (Asocaña 2009c). Figure 2.7b illustrates that total domestic sugar production in the year of the strike was the lowest of the past twenty-three years for which I obtained records. But this impact was mediated by the fact that the price of sugar on the international market rose by 22 percent that year (Asocaña 2023c).

Four weeks after the end of the strike, workers held a celebratory rally. They paraded around Palmira in celebration of their gains. Soon afterwards, they began to hold meetings on their prospects for establishing a unitary co-operative. These meetings did not result in the merging of co-operatives. But the strike had established stronger communication networks for workers across plantations and increased their visibility with national and academic publics.

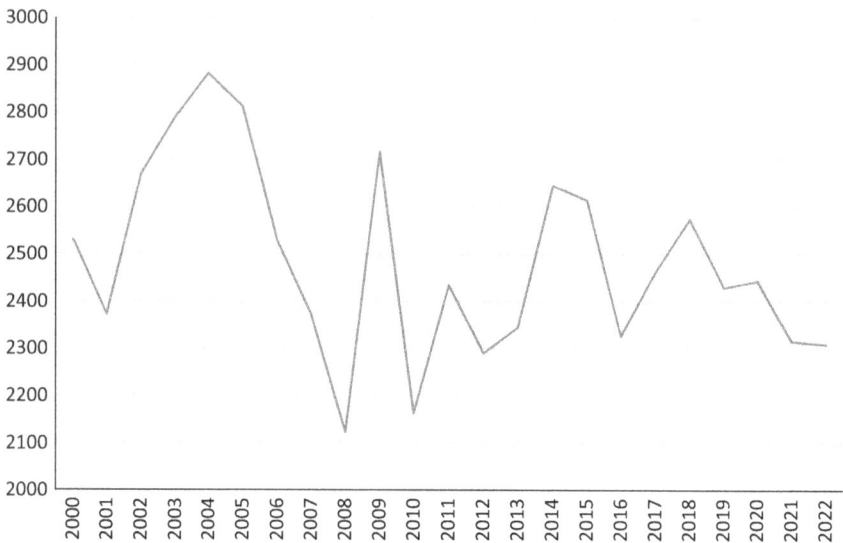

Figure 2.7b   Total Sugar Production (thousands of U.S. short tons per annum). *Source:* Asocaña 2022.

PLAYERS IN THE EMANCIPATORY NETWORK

I now turn to a more detailed analysis of the movement's structure. The following sections take organizational and networked actors individually and detail their role in the strike. I begin with the Huayna Movement itself and how it developed its own oppositional structures. I next discuss the workers' families. They provided important infrastructure that sustained the workers during the strike, providing food and rallying support in the surrounding communities. I then move to discuss the central unions, with which the workers had a complex relationship. Unions helped to sustain worker spirits throughout the strike and also sought to expand their own influence by recruiting workers into their unions. The Left political party *Polo Democratico* also supported the strike and provided important leverage with local governments. The party had good reason to aid the strikers ahead of regional elections. Lastly, I pay lengthy attention to the Doves, who provided legal, media, and logistical support, training, and strategic counsel.

Focusing on each set of actors establishes the field of contention and components of this network of activists. But workers (González Arana and Molinares Guerrero 2013), communities (Archila 2001, 24–8; Dussel 2008, 13; Zibechi 2010, 11), and political parties (Cepeda 2006) in particular have specific historical significance in the literature on Colombian movements (Neira 2019). Micro-level processes exhibited by individual actors within organizations and networks illustrate how deprived workers were able to navigate regional politics to determine events.

Workers

Among the demands that workers presented to Asocaña in June were increases in wage rates, improvements in health care and housing, and more

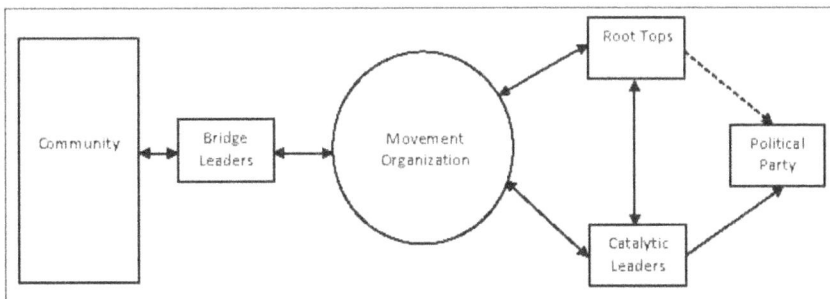

Figure 2.8   Primary Relationships in Emancipatory Networks. *Source*: Figure created by author

flexibility in shift scheduling to be able to take more time off. Asocaña did not respond to these demands when they were presented to them in June. But the workers' rally attracted a large number of workers, families, and civic groups. Media outlets covered the rally extensively. Through the media, this event introduced the Huayna Movement to Colombians around the country. For those living in Valle del Cauca, the event reframed the sugarcane workers as an organized force of independent co-operatives.

Huayna represented workers across nine plantations and drew on these workers to populate its leadership committee. Workers at each plantation elected one representative to the leadership committee. This leadership committee then appointed a tenth member as a spokesperson to represent the movement to media organizations. This movement structure grew out of the already existing co-operative structure that workers had been operating under since 2004. The decision to appoint a spokesperson grew out of meetings between the initial nine Huayna leaders and the Doves. The detail about the spokesperson being detached from representing their particular plantation had been Felipe's idea. Initially referred to as "The Ten," that nomenclature was quickly dropped because of fears that it would be too easy for the media and police to identify, single out, and label the individual leaders. At least one member of the Doves usually accompanied this ten-worker leadership team, acting as legal and strategic counsel. In the early days of the strike, this leadership committee met several times a day. This frequency then decreased to once a day for most of the strike, falling to alternate days only near the very end. When committee members were not at a meeting, they were often at their individual plantations. Each member of the leadership team was charged with traveling to their respective plantation's Permanent Assembly to report on their leadership committee meeting and to inform workers of developing events. There, additional perspectives were gathered and new items were raised to bring back to the leadership committee. All of these meetings were ruled by consensus and sometimes lasted up to six hours. Consensus decision-making structures tend to be slow. But they also allowed the all-volunteer movement to create "buy-in" for those decisions (Polletta 2002). This process increased the likelihood that participants would agree to and implement decisions, having all of their concerns heard and considered, if not implemented (Gelderloos 2006).

There were often problems having to do with a degree of informality to the structure. Often, there would be one or two representatives missing for part or all of the leadership committee meetings. When that happened, the group might solicit feedback from other workers from a plantation whose leader was absent. That sometimes caused conflict, especially when the leadership committee took action based on this feedback. These disagreements were often resolved within hours or, in some cases, after a couple of days.

Workers at the plantations also organized themselves according to the co-operative that they belonged to. Some plantations employed workers from a dozen or more co-operatives with as many as 300 workers in each co-operative. The co-operatives at each plantation would individually caucus to separately address issues specific to their plantation. These caucuses often appointed their own spokespersons to speak to the media. Caucuses were also responsible for staffing the militant picket lines, strike kitchens, procuring water and supplies, and sanitation. Caucuses organized the work into shifts, taking care to ensure that workers rotated among the various responsibilities. Their primary concern was to ensure that there were a sufficient number of workers at the plantation gates.

Leaders of amorphous grassroots organizations, like the Huayna, are able to mobilize people, resources, and information through their personal networks. These leaders might be called *root tops*, as they also represent grassroots activists to the elites with whom they are in conflict. *Root tops* can serve filtering functions by framing movement rhetoric while articulating ideas that filter up from the grassroots. The movement coalition had two sets of leaders. *Bridge leaders* (Robnett 1996) face the community, coordinating movement efforts at each of the plantations. *Root tops* face elite structures. This is somewhat analogous to state Janus-faced structures (Skocpol 1979) that manage internal and external pressures to control citizens. As with any organization of scale, there is a danger that the leaders of large social movements, even of grassroots organizations, may use the movement's internal inequalities produced by its own organizational structure to control activists. The *emancipatory network* mobilized during this strike was too short-lived, however, to manifest an oligarchical (Michels 1915 [1911]) tendency in any consequential manner.

The workers themselves were able to withhold labor from the plantation owners, exerting important economic leverage. Only the workers were uniquely suited to this role since they were employees of the plantation

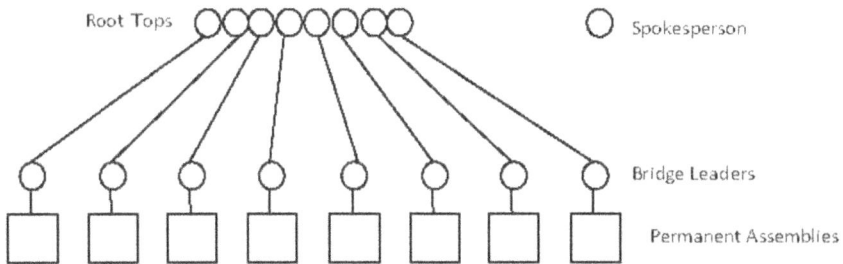

Figure 2.9 **Sugarcane Worker Strike Leadership Structure.** *Source*: Figure created by author.

owners under a wage system. No other actor in the network would have successfully been able to replace striking workers. The plantation owners could have easily ignored protesters indefinitely, so long as sugarcane was being cut. This very scenario took place between June 14, when plantation owners were presented with a list of demands at a large rally of workers, and September 14, the start of the strike. The plantations would have likely continued to ignore the workers past this date had the workers not struck.

But it became obvious when I visited some of the communities that the influence of workers extends beyond the plantation gates. In the worker community just outside of the Antisuyu plantation, workers had set up tents all along the road leading from the front gates to the main building. They had fire pits burning, with pots brewing above the flames. The workers at this plantation were organized with military precision, stationing people at checkpoints all along the roads. Worker escorts always accompanied the Doves during our time in the town and on the plantation. The workers we were with would facilitate our movement through the plantation by letting workers that we encountered know who we were, why we were there, and that they were responsible for our activities there. With that, we were able to get past their checkpoints.[15] The strength of community support for the strike was inescapable.

Wives and Family

Workers would not have been able to sustain the strike for nearly two months without support from family, friends, and community. The wives, girlfriends, sisters, mothers, and older children of the sugarcane workers were the main actors in mobilizing that support. Mostly black and almost exclusively women, their work involved recruiting local residents to populate marches through the town squares, organizing vigils in the evenings, marching through the streets, and traveling to the gates of the plantations. Sometimes they brought their children along, their numbers usually peaking in the low-hundreds. But near the end of the strike, a community rally in Palmira attracted thousands of people and featured the president of the CUT. Several *Polo Democratico* party members and other important Colombians present also helped to attract the large crowd.

These rallies were important places for the families of sugarcane workers to meet others in the community. At one rally, families marched with lit candles through the twilight. Once the march arrived at the town plaza, one woman gave a speech calling Jesus Christ a "revolutionary." A few union organizers with a megaphone off to the side began to compete for the crowd's attention, often speaking over her. I commented to Felipe about how annoying I thought that was, and he smiled in silent recognition. Later in the evening, a band arrived to celebrate a Christian holiday. The crowd was now mixed between the families of sugarcane workers and those who came to celebrate the holiday. The woman who had initially given the speech about Jesus being a revolutionary invited the two groups to introduce themselves to each other.

> "We are not against Catholics," she said. "We are in solidarity with them."
> One woman replied to her, "I am the daughter of a cane worker and I am not ashamed to be here."
> "Don't be ashamed to admit that your husband is a sugarcane worker."

Police largely allowed women to rally and march as they pleased, perhaps fearing the bad publicity associated with harming women and children. But there was one important exception to this general pattern. At one of these marches, several hundred women, along with some children, attempted to enter the Qullasuyu plantation to join with striking sugarcane workers inside. Private security guards prevented them from doing so. Angry at being locked out of the plantation and unable to see their spouses, this group of women

Figure 2.10 Local Politician Speaks to a Crowd in a Town Park in Valle del Cauca.
Source: Photograph taken by the author in 2008.

and children took over the main road across the plantation entrance. Police arrived quickly and tried to intimidate the group into dispersing by yelling and gesturing aggressively with their weapons. After that failed, the police finally managed to break the blockade by firing tear gas into the crowd. Ten children suffered temporary asphyxia as a result of the tear gas.[16] Unlike sugarcane cutters, who only sometimes faced police opposition when commandeering the private roads inside the plantations, the crowd of women and children taking over a public road drew a swift police response. This is despite the fact that tear gas posed a particular danger to children who might easily be affected by noxious gasses, a fact that did not escape local media scrutiny.

Women and families often play a central yet uncelebrated role when men participate in high-risk activism. Staffing strike kitchens, to which they did have access, women relieved striking workers of some of the labor involved in sustaining a long-term militant picket. No matter how much economic leverage workers had against plantation owners, no strike of this magnitude could last beyond a few days without the logistics involved in providing fresh meals to the strikers. The provisioning of these meals was as necessary a condition to a successful strike as the economic leverage of the workers was to its plausibility. Families were the only players in the emancipatory network that were majority women. They, along with the striking workers, were also the only groups in the emancipatory network to be majority black.

In addition to unlocking community resources, cooking, and cleaning, women also provided moral support important to the long-term mental health of striking workers. Women organized kitchens built from makeshift materials. Bamboo or thick sugarcane stalks served as posts to hold up a tarp, or sheets of corrugated metal in some of the more elaborate kitchens. These structures protected the cooking fires from frequent rains. Some kitchens contained wood-fired stoves built from brick and cinder blocks. These would sometimes sit in a pit underneath large aluminum or cast-iron pots. Strike kitchens commonly served soups, bisques, rice, black beans, tamales, and *panela*.[17] Women took turns setting up a schedule at each of these sites to make sure there was always someone available in the kitchen. These kitchens were often short on plates and silverware. Often, workers would eat out of Frisbees or plastic cups. Sometimes workers would simply scoop their calloused hands into the pot and eat hand-to-mouth. Water was also sometimes scarce, often having to be carried in from a tap that could be some distance away. Sometimes the water from the tap was not meant to be potable, so it would have to be boiled before it could be safely used for cooking or drinking.

The provision of food was essential to the strike. Hunger made the workers appear nervous, and its abundance made them seem confident and alert. Local church groups, student groups, political parties, and others would sometimes bring food donations to supplement the efforts of the Doves, unions, and women. These women arranged for the mayors of the local towns to send a fire truck each morning to fill the strike kitchen water tanks used for cooking. This arrangement helped mayors avoid the humanitarian scandal that might emerge, should the public see images of dehydrated and malnourished workers on television. Dehydration and hunger became a threat at the start of the strike, as the details of food and water distribution were yet to be defined.

Women also influenced their husbands, boyfriends, brothers, uncles, and nephews to continue the strike during moments of weakness. Some workers had prepared to strike for only thirty days. Men who expressed doubts about the strike provoked anger in some women. In one interview, one of the wives told me that a plantation had offered her husband double his usual wage rate to scab. Thinking that her husband was planning to accept the offer, she took her husband's machete and work clothes to a nearby friend's home and asked her friend to hide them for her. In the morning, when the husband looked for his work clothes and his machete, he could not find them. She told him what she had done and explained that she had said, "You are not going to break this strike. You are going back to the picket line with your comrades." She explained that he pleaded that they did not have enough money to survive and that seeing his son suffer for lack of medicine broke his heart. She then said that she told him, "We will find a way. But we will never find a solution if you undermine this strike." It was clear that families suffered as a result of the strike. They themselves, however, made intentional efforts to keep the strike going.[18]

Families did not have any leverage over plantation owners. But their involvement was no less crucial to its outcome. The wives of the sugarcane workers trafficked in a *moral economy* (Thompson 1971) that circulated in the townships along the Cauca River. Local shopkeepers and grocery stores extended credit to the wives of sugarcane workers, perhaps understanding that the fate of the workers intertwined with that of their shops. Women were able to translate that goodwill into goods, services, and cash support. The use of this ability is a significant reason for explaining how 8,500 workers, and their families, ate, drank, slept, traveled, and bathed without income for fifty-eight days. Strike campaigns, and protest movements in general, often rely on local communities to secure victory (Gutman 1977).

Unions

The CUT, founded in 1986, draws from a diverse workforce of teachers, government workers, miners, electricians, metallurgists, chemists, agricultural workers, hospital workers, clinicians, oil workers, construction workers, and others. It is a self-described "anti-capitalist" organization and promotes

Figure 2.11   Women Lead Children in a March through a Rural Town in Valle del Cauca.
Source: Photograph taken by the author in 2008.

the labor rights of Colombian workers. The CUT also frequently criticizes international finance institutions such as the World Bank and International Monetary Fund. They are critics of foreign debt, the bilateral relationship between Colombia and the United States, and free trade agreements. The CUT, its members, and its leadership have historically been major targets of both state and paramilitary forces. According to one report, "[s]ince the mid-1980s, approximately 4,000 trade unionists have been murdered in Colombia, more than 2,000 of them since 1991. More trade unionists are killed each year in Colombia than in the rest of the world combined" (Lyle 2006, 11). Killings of union leaders have declined in recent years, but not abated. According to a recent U.S. State Department (2022, 38) *Human Rights Report*, "[t]he [Colombian] Attorney General's Office reported receiving 232 cases of homicides of unionists between January 2011 and January 2021." For these reasons, union organizers in Valle del Cauca were particularly willing to accompany members of the Huayna Movement leadership between meetings, so that they would not have to travel alone.

At the time of the strike, CUT had a strong presence in Valle del Cauca, but represented few sugarcane workers. Less than 2 percent of Colombia's agricultural workers belong to a union, even though they make up one-fifth of all workers in the country (Pineda Duque 2005, 131). Some sugarcane workers, particularly at the Antisuyu plantation, were members of SINALCORTEROS, but only a small fraction were covered by that union. When the majority of non-unionized sugarcane workers formed the Huayna Movement—a separate, non-union, co-operative-based, prefigurative organization—the unions were reluctant to provide support. Although both SINALCORTEROS and CUT contributed to the Huayna strike fund, and visited workers at far-flung plantations, workers expressed resentment at the recruitment campaign opportunistically mounted by both unions during the strike. According to several workers, at least one union organizer had tried to convince workers to join the union by misinforming them that they were obligated to do so.

CUT, representing few sugarcane workers, had little leverage with plantation owners. Nor did they have sufficient community networks to mobilize the moral economy. But CUT did have allied unions distributed throughout the country that were ideologically concerned with promoting worker solidarity in general, and with the sugarcane workers in particular. CUT was able to arrange venues in towns and cities throughout the country for workers to hold solidarity rallies. These rallies were important in shoring up dwindling strike funds. Their union organizers in Palmira and the surrounding towns also helped to communicate statements of solidarity from workers around the country.

Politicians

The *Polo Democratico* is a Democratic-Socialist party which, at the time, had the fifth-largest delegation in the Colombian parliament. The party was formed by the merger of two smaller parties before the national elections in 2006. *Polo Democratico* was seen as the political heirs of the defunct *Union Patriotrica* of the 1980s, which had been the civilian political party formed after a partial demobilization of the FARC. *Union Patriotrica* was dismantled after being decimated by government and paramilitary forces. According to varying estimates, between 2,000 and 5,000 party members were killed (Petras and Veltmeyer 2003). Senators Piedad Córdoba and Alexander López Maya, and Cali City Council member Wilson Arias,[19] all prominent members of the *Polo Democratico*, were involved in public debates about the strike and attended solidarity events in the region. Some of the party's regional representatives and staff maintained constant contact with the sugarcane workers movement. Indeed, there was significant overlap between *Polo Democratico* staff and the Doves. After the end of the strike, a few sugarcane workers who had been members of the Huayna Movement's leadership committee became members of the *Polo Democratico*. Some of them actively worked in election campaigns and even ran for local offices themselves to increase the visibility of sugarcane workers in local government.

Figure 2.12   Two Pots of Cooked Rice and Potatoes at a Make-Shift Kitchen at Sugarcane Plantation. *Source*: Photograph taken by the author in 2008.

Some members of the *Polo Democratico* openly campaigned at the plantations. This became particularly acute near the end of the strike, as regional elections at the end of November drew near. This political campaigning was particularly strong in Cali and Palmira, where banners hung over major arteries and party streamers could be found along local roads. Felipe and Javier also began to split their time between working for the sugarcane workers and campaigning for the party.

Senator López Maya often came to the plantations and delivered speeches to the workers. In the days approaching the election, several party operatives visited the plantations to distribute leaflets and to campaign on his behalf. In appreciation of López Maya's public support for the strike, his defense of the strikers in the media, and his association with the Doves, sugarcane workers came out in force to support him on Election Day.

The Huayna movement gained local leverage by aligning itself with the *Polo Democratico*. As a direct consequence of this linkage, prominent national political leaders publicly defended the strike and assisted solidarity campaigns in raising money for the strike fund. Javier was often on the phone, frequently providing party members with updates from the field for their use in public debates. This worker-party alliance also helped to legitimize workers in the public sphere. Party talking points helped to edu-cate an audience unfamiliar with the details of the working conditions of sugarcane workers. This boost also helped workers to coalesce around an identity separate from the unions. The Huayna leadership was aware that several Doves were also operatives of the *Polo Democratico* and were cog-nizant of what that meant.[20] Although the Huayna leadership would indicate that it was to their benefit to have allies in public office, they never officially endorsed any candidate. But the linkages were clear, strong, and apparent, if not explicitly defined.

Local and national operatives of the *Polo Democratico* amplified the vis-ibility, reach, and impact of the strike. This amplification likely dampened the level of repression that workers experienced, especially when compared to historical levels. It also may have played a role in influencing the decision of the police to allow workers to maintain their militant pickets. The par-ticipation of members of the *Polo Democratico* in public debates in defense of the workers helped to normalize worker grievances in the public sphere. Conservatives often depicted workers as radicals who are influenced by the guerilla. This narrative had now been counterbalanced with statements from legitimate government authorities. Issues that workers had been articulating for years were now being repeated inside of the government.

For instance, Senator López Maya of the *Polo Democratico* was a frequent guest on several television and radio shows to speak on the topic of the strike. Also present at these appearances were often at least one conservative politi-cian, business representative, or economist. From early on in the strike, and on through to the end of it, Senator López Maya enthusiastically combated these detractors before the public. One of these televised events included a national prime time debate between himself and the president of Asocaña, Luis Fernando Londoño Capurro. The high visibility of the strike, and the legitimization of their concerns in the public sphere, protected workers from the most severe forms of repression.

Doves

The Doves formed in 2004 as a registered non-profit human rights orga-nization. Since its inception, the organization has rotated through several issue campaigns, adapting according to political circumstances. A small staff of about ten have worked with internally displaced persons in Bogotá, the families of missing persons in northern Colombia, and—in late 2007—turned their attention to the sugarcane workers in Valle del Cauca. There were six Doves directly involved with the strike, most of them working out of Palmira once the strike began. A couple of others pitched in from Cali and Bogotá. Of the six working out of Palmira, four had significant prior organizing experience and knowledge of domestic human rights and labor law. The remaining two specialized in media and communications. Two of the political organizers were men and the other four Doves were women. Javier was in charge of the regional office and had been personally working with the sugarcane workers for nearly a year. His assistant and girlfriend, Juana, was present for most of that time. The support staff person for the Cali regional office (with whom I only spoke with over the phone) was only involved remotely. A few Doves remained based in Bogotá. Felipe and Nina made occasional short trips from Bogotá to Valle del Cauca before the strike, but were not directly involved until the day before the strike took place. Once there, Felipe did not leave Valle del Cauca until near the very end of the strike. Nina was also there the entirety of the strike, except for two brief weekend trips. One of these was a fundraising trip to Bogotá and the other was to attend to other projects that the Doves involved themselves in.

Nina prepared legal complaints for back wages on behalf of workers who had not been paid by the plantation in a timely manner. Long queues formed to meet with Nina whenever the Doves arrived to visit a plantation. Workers from all over the region also traveled to visit Nina at the strike center in Palmira to prepare these complaints. Juana provided analogous services for the wives of the sugarcane workers, many of whom were internally displaced and were missing identification documents for themselves or for their children. Some of these documents had been lost during the first day of the strike, when police set fire to tents and other items. Juana would shepherd them through Colombia's bureaucracies, including registration for any public assistance they may qualify for. The Doves often provided reimbursements for their trip into town and for the cost of necessary identification photos and document photocopies.

The Doves visited plantations nearly every day, updating workers with the latest strike developments and delivering motivational speeches. These visits often contrasted with the relative monotony that had settled into many plantations after the first week of the occupations. These visits also helped to dispel rumors that developed from the aggressive disinformation campaign that plantation owners waged in the media and through their management. Visits from the Doves were sometimes the primary way by which strikers on one plantation were able to get reliable information about what was happening at each of the other plantations and reliable updates on negotiations with plantation owners. These speeches were effective at conveying and reinforcing important information, even as the workers' representative to the Huayna Movement leadership committee sometimes duplicated this task. The importance of this routine became evident when it was disrupted by the arrest of these orators. The remaining Doves did continue the visits, but with their attention diverted to securing the release of their co-workers, the visits came with less frequency.

The Doves provided leadership, organizing, and communications training to the Huayna Movement's leadership committee. These workers often replicated these trainings with workers at their own plantations. These trainings often focused on the specific language and talking points that workers were to use when speaking with media. The Doves identified, during their regular, long discussions with the Huayna Movement's leadership committee, that there was a need for this content. The Doves then developed this content and developed a plan to push it out to the grassroots.

This effort paid off, with the movement now better able to attract outside support for the strike. Human rights and student organizations that do not usually support agricultural labor strikes now began to come onboard.[21] Noticing this effectiveness, this may have been one reason why plantation owners and their allies began to point to "dark hands" operating behind the strike.

STRATEGY

The players in this strike each brought unique resources to the strike. Table 2.1 organizes these resources alongside the other characteristics that each contributed to the strike. These include each player's mechanisms, motives, risk, leadership, and resources. This is important for understanding how workers and their allies overcame state repression. An *emancipatory network* works as a segmentary kinship network, with a high degree of differentiation, involution and dependence. I examine the network topology's properties, taking each vertex in turn.

Mechanisms. The strength of the strike inhered in the heterogeneity of the organizational types involved. Each exerts a different mechanism by virtue of their relationship to the strike. This organizational and resource diversity made the strike more difficult to defeat. Indeed, one could posit that the movement was not a mere strike but a movement coalition of labor, human rights, and community interests. The workers were in a position to withhold labor, without which the plantations could not function. This structural leverage was a central mechanism in the strike, a necessary but insufficient component for victory. Also important was the community's moral economy, accessed by the sugarcane workers' familial ties. Without this community support, the workers would not have had the food, credit, and favorable public opinion necessary to sustain the strike for fifty-eight days. The political organizing experience that the Doves brought behaved like a *catalyst*, increasing the rate of learning among the others. The Doves transmitted hard-earned lessons in the form of training and speeches, helping workers and their leaders to make

Table 2.1 Emancipatory Network

	Huayna Movement	Families	CUT	Doves	Dem. Pole
Category	Workers	Community	Union	Professionals	Politicians
Mechanism	Structural leverage	Moral economy	Oligarchical	Biographical availability	Clientelism
Motivation	Personal grievance	Community development	Worker power	Ideological/moral	Elections
Risk	High	High	Low	High (voluntaristic)	Low
Leadership	Spokes Council Consensus	Informal network	Electoral hierarchy	Catnet	Electoral hierarchy
Resources	Disruption	Organization	Union solidarity	Framing	Government Leniency

strategic decisions. CUT was able to mobilize the resources of their members in other parts of the country as a result of their hierarchical structure. These union locals provided venues for fundraising events and collected food and resources from their members to support the strike. The *Polo Democratico*, by appealing directly to the governor's voting bloc, played a role in swaying the governor to intervene in the strike. With an election taking place later that Fall, the governor did not want to lose support to a competing party. Any clientelist relationship that local politicians may have had with their communities was under stress from the economic impact of the strike. This, along with Senator López Maya's charm offensive, made some voters vulnerable to *Polo Democratico* suasion.

Motivations. The workers were personally motivated to improve their own labor and living conditions, but this was not necessarily true for others. CUT was primarily interested in expanding their presence among agricultural workers. CUT staff did not themselves have a personal stake in the outcome of the strike. Community members relied on the local economy, which for years has relied on the sugarcane industry. The wives of the sugarcane workers were motivated to improve the income of their households. This led some to forcefully motivate their husbands to continue the strike. It may also be the case that some also persuaded their husbands to abandon the strike for another line of work, although I did not observe this directly. The *Polo Democratico*, like political parties in general, found an electoral strategy that could earn them votes. But they and the Doves also had political ideologies which motivated their lines of work.

Risk. In comparison to the consequences of coetaneous activism in the United States or Europe, all of those involved in supporting the strike could be said to have engaged in activism that is high risk. More meaningful, however, is to judge these behaviors in their own context. But even in the Colombian context, striking workers and their adjutant Doves took significant risks to their personal safety. Armed altercations with police, being imprisoned, and receiving death threats are associated with relative danger in most imaginable contexts. Many of the wives of the sugarcane workers who traveled to or lived on the plantations, or who participated in rallies and marches, also engaged in high-risk activism. Some endured tear gas and had their property destroyed, even though they did not physically engage with security forces. CUT and the *Polo Democratico* mostly did not participate in high-risk activism, conducting their supportive efforts largely from their offices with limited trips to the plantations. But in other contexts and time periods, Colombian labor leaders and Left political party members are a regular target for police, military, and paramilitary violence.

Leadership. CUT and *Polo Democratico* are both hierarchical, membership-based organizations. But sugarcane workers took a different approach.

They used a version of the consensus process, using spokes councils in the form of Permanent Assemblies and various committees. In practice, however, the leadership committee asserted more strategic influence over the strike's development than did other parts of the workers' movement. While the wives of sugarcane workers did organize a few committees to organize shifts at the strike kitchens, they mostly organized themselves through large, informal, loose networks. They mostly organized tasks *ad hoc*, as needs arose. The Doves operated according to a *catnet*, a small network in which all members were also young professionals. Together, this small professional network, mutually engrossed in their personal relationships, defined the involvement of their human rights organization in this coalition of activists.

Resources. The central resource in the *emancipatory network* is the capacity of workers to disrupt the production of sugar. Without this capacity for disruption, the rest of the campaign would not have had the leverage necessary to coerce plantations into addressing worker concerns. As one of the workers had put it, "If we leave the plantations we will lose." But other players in the network had essential resources to prolong and augment the strike's effectiveness. The wives of the sugarcane workers and others in the community leveraged their personal networks to attract food and other support to the striking workers. CUT had access to union locals, which they also used to attract food and resources to the strike. The Doves brought political organizing experience, training, and powerful political connections that enhanced the workers' own abilities, attracted resources from new allies, and forged a kinship with the *Polo Democratico*. The *Polo Democratico*, in turn, legitimized worker concerns in elite media and government spaces. This allowed worker grievances to reach national television in prime time.

SUMMARY

Micro-level processes exhibited by individual actors within organizations and networks illustrate how deprived workers were able to navigate local and national politics to influence events in their favor. This heterogeneous network provided a degree of resilience in the normally repressive Colombian context. Each actor leveraged mechanisms and contributed resources to help sustain the strike. Elements of such *emancipatory networks* may be present in other cases situated in repressive contexts. The relationship between worker movements and labor unions is not necessarily straightforward. Nor is the relationship between the working-class rural poor and human rights organizations always conciliatory. Building and wielding a diverse alliance entails significant and continuous communication between players.

Implications for Social Movement Scholars

The efficacy and utility of the *emancipatory network* may be an observable movement constellation, particularly in repressive contexts. Activists are connected to each other both directly and indirectly. Observing mobilization *in utero* allows researchers to capture these differentiated but networked dynamics, which allow for activists to achieve unlikely objectives in antagonistic environs. Theories of mobilization based on network structures may help us to understand the efficacy of movement forms with heterogeneous demographic characteristics and social relations.

NOTES

1. Not only did I take photographs, but I also translated some of the movement's press releases into English.

2. Antanas Mockus, the celebrated 2010 presidential candidate, brought down the homicide rate in Bogotá by 70 percent during his terms as mayor between 1995 and 2003, illustrating that these kinds of efforts are more easily applied in cities (Mockus 1999).

3. Managing media perceptions would become important in a country with strong overlaps between political and media structures (Arroyave and Barrios 2012). For example, Álvaro Uribe's vice president Francisco Santos comes from a family that had owned the major national newspaper *El Tiempo* for nearly a century. Francisco Santos is cousin to former president Juan Manuel Santos and great-nephew to former president Eduardo Santos Montejo. Francisco Santos later went on to lead the Colombian radio network RCN and serve as Ambassador to the United States.

4. The average annual rate of inflation during this period is 5.48 percent (OECD 2023b).

5. This along with other related risks are an inherent part of sugarcane cutting in Colombia, but also in Brazil (c.f. Pereira Novales 2007). Assuming a Geertzian (1973) position, anthropologists go so far as to privilege the body in their analysis of Brazilian sugarcane work (c.f. Dawsey 2005, 29).

6. SINALTRAINAL is best known in the United States for bringing an alien tort case against Coca-Cola, establishing that U.S. companies could be held liable in U.S. Federal Courts for violating international law. This interpretation was later overruled by the U.S. Supreme Court in *Kiobel v. Royal Dutch Petroleum Co* a few years later (Kearney 2011, 267).

7. A future study might survey workers about this matter, controlling for union membership and age. I did not specifically seek out this variability around this question.

8. Exchange rate calculated using Xe Currency Data API (2023) and adjusted for inflation using OECD (2023b) data.

9. Ibid.

10. CINEP (2008, 140).

11. Ibid.

12. Ibid.

13. *Semana*. 2008. "Que no les piquen más caña." 23 September.

14. Following up with Javier by telephone after the end of my fieldwork revealed that plantations did not fully meet this commitment.

15. By doing this, I closed the door to gaining access to plantation owners, however, gaining access behind these worker-controlled checkpoints is not something that I would have been able to achieve if I maintained neutrality (Esparza 2012a).

16. CINEP (2008, 156).

17. *Panela* is a solid cane sugar made from concentrated sugarcane juice commonly consumed throughout Latin America. This was either donated, purchased, or produced by workers from the abundant sugarcane available.

18. Yet sacrificing family needs for political organizing is a decision that not all members of the family can equally participate in making. Gilian Slovo (1997) wrote about the sacrifices her family made during the South African anti-apartheid struggle while she was a child. Ruth First was often separated from her children, which Slovo resented well into adulthood.

19. Wilson Arias has since also become a Senator.

20. Although it is possible that the strike date was purposefully timed to come before the election, I observed no direct evidence of this.

21. This is not to understate the role that the workers played themselves in deterring repression by engaging the police. Rather, the Doves' role complemented this effort by also working to deter repression through other means.

Chapter 3

Humiliation

This chapter leverages detailed experiences from striking workers to distinguish between different forms of activist knowledge production. After a brief discussion of these different theoretical forms, I draw from worker interviews and fieldnotes to illustrate the forms of leadership and knowledge that workers brought to the strike. Workers came to interpret their experiences as having a similar level of risk to that of their everyday life.

The risk contained in their everyday life was filled with experiences of humiliation. This sustained abasement led people to search for any relief they could find. Many workers had originated in towns replete with violence, travelling to Valle del Cauca and Cauca to find work. They also travelled to find the relative safety and stability of earned wages. Many workers had left behind the informal economies of their remote towns. Some workers reported resorting to working for guerrilla organizations when they could not afford their bills. Tomás is an Afro-Colombian worker from the Kuntisuyu plantation. He explains: "I used to work for the guerrilla picking coca in Huila. In that region, it was not hidden. You could see the coca from the road. It came out from over the tops of the fences along the road. I would pick it and they would bundle it and sell it. I made some money that way . . . I had to leave because it started to get hot. I had a brother here who was in Palmira. So, I called him and he put me up for a little while until I got this job with the sugarcane plantation."

I came across thousands of sugarcane workers during my fieldwork. Every one of them was a man. Those that I spoke with generally came from rural backgrounds. Many had been displaced from their homes, having fled from violence in some other area of the country. Several workers told me that they came to work on the sugarcane fields after having grown coca. Another worker confirmed, "They didn't hide it. It was all along the roads out in the open, just like you see the sugarcane here."

Most of the workers were Afro-Colombian. At the largest plantation, Antisuyu, I came across hundreds of workers. Nearly all were Afro-Colombian. Some had been working on sugarcane plantations for as long as twenty-five years and had direct experience of the depreciating working conditions and wage structure that animated the strike. One worker explained, "It used to be better. Back when I started, the wages were much better. You could raise a family, have a little bit of land. We have some earnings from those days. Now, the people coming in don't have that. It is much harder now." Not all of the workers were part of the Huayna Movement. Some co-operatives chose not to participate in the strike, and a few opted out of the decision-making structure of the Huayna Movement. According to some workers, plantations distributed bonuses or other incentives for working during the strike, for distributing flyers, for rallying in opposition to the strike, or even for just staying home. However, because the striking workers made it difficult to scab, workers reported that most of the men who wanted to continue working found temporary employment elsewhere until the strike was over.

One worker, Tomás, explained that he did not have many options to support his family. When I asked Tomás why he supports the strike, he told me, "Look, I have been struggling all my life. I have been moving all my life. I have been chased all my life. I have been threatened. I have been shot at. At each point, I have run away. We have to start somewhere. We have to stick up for our rights. Someone has to lay the first stone. It might as well be me. It might as well be us."

Confronting armed police in rural Colombia may seem irrational to the outside observer. But the strike served as an opportunity for Tomás to act on his frustrations. In line with his previous experience, Tomás stood on principle against uneven but familiar odds.

Tomás and others may not have perceived a strike as being particularly risky. How much riskier is a smack from a police baton than an untreated spinal injury? What does the momentary sting of tear gas compare to a son's chronic pulmonary disease? Do corporate media lies ring louder than the cries of a malnourished daughter? These personal experiences are important in understanding the perception of current and future risk. Intimate knowledge of risk in everyday life makes tactical political hazards not seem quite as jeopardous.

A strike is not much more of a risk than working through illness. Nor is it much more of a risk than commuting on a bicycle along the highway or eating rotten vegetables every day. The worker may land himself in jail, but he has been there before. Police may beat him, but his body is already leathered. The worker may have to endure days without food, but that is not new to him either.

During the strike, police would often demand that workers spill their water tanks. Workers relied on this collected water for drinking and cooking. Complaining to his fellow workers after one such incident, one worker said, "Here people have filled up water for us and then here, in front of everyone, they made people spill the water. In front of thirsty people!" Another worker responded to the gathering crowd, "Here we are protesting in a peaceful manner. Peacefully! But no, they say 'Get the hell out of here! Lift the strike, I say!' No. No more of that."

Even outside of the context of farm work, Afro-Colombians face active discrimination in Colombia. The mostly mestizo police thought nothing of forcing the mostly black workers to spill their water. Workers complied, even though they knew that they deserved better treatment, to avoid the consequences of betraying police orders.

SABER Y CONOCER

The chapter proposes and illustrates two forms of knowledge production in high-risk activism. It addresses the call posed by Boaventura de Sousa Santos (2009, 56) in *Epistemologias do Sul* [Epistemologies of the South] for a research agenda that answers the question, "what is the perspective from which we can answer different knowledges?" It is an important question for the peripatetic who traverses major cultural, linguistic, and economic boundaries. Borrowing from Bertrand Russell (1997[1912]), who develops a distinction between knowledge "by description" and that "by acquaintance," I distinguish between activist knowledge acquired through analytic study and that stemming from lived experience. This differentiation is perhaps one of the many possible land bridges that can help to address the distinction between "Western and non-Western understandings," as understood by Santos (2009, 56) and other postcolonialists (Gandhi 2019 [1998]). The distinction between these two forms of knowledge is common in Castilian Spanish and other Romance languages. In Castilian, *saber* refers to cerebral knowledge. Activists get this form of knowledge through analytical study and indirect practice. In contrast, the Castilian *conocer* refers to experienced familiarity. This form of activist knowledge is found in the experiential practice of everyday life. Fals-Borda and Mora-Osejo (2003, 36) argue that these varieties of "knowledge summation" can distill diverse patterns of thought into what they call "participatory action."

Stemming from the Latin *cognoscere*, activists get this form of knowledge through lived experience. Luis Villoro (2002 [1982], 197–9) develops this distinction between knowledges as it manifests in the Castilian language.[1] For Villoro (2002 [1982], 207), in order for one to know something by acquaintance, one must be able to apply various past direct experiences of it to new experiences. This is true, even if "[m]any of the things we know by description are based in our own experience, others, in the experience of others" (Villoro 2002 [1982], 215). We trust, for example, that a map of the city of Bogotá might symbolically represent reality accurately enough for it to aid us in navigation. When Tilly (1996, 595) asked his young children to draw him maps of Toronto, he tells us that they "followed conventions of mapmaking they had somehow absorbed from schooling and everyday practice: north to the top, streets horizontal and vertical within that frame, major boundaries defined by waterways and big thoroughfares."

Tilly was concerned with observed behavior and their counterfactuals: *did they take over the road or didn't they? What would have happened if they had made a different decision?* But Villoro's analysis helps us understand how knowledge influences observed behavior: *had they taken over the road before?* Sugarcane workers have long experienced risk in their everyday life. It is not necessary for them to study poverty in a book to grasp the concept, even if such study might contextualize the idiosyncrasies of their own experience. Recalling Desmond's (2007, 8–15) study of wildland firefighters, the judgement of any particular action as "risky" may be contingent on past experiences of similar circumstances. Scholarly knowledge about social movements depends on there being activists who experience them. Scholars who prioritize the presentation of activist experience introduce an important corrective (Sitrin 2006), though much can also be gleaned from scholarly accounts. As Villoro (2002 [1982], 212) puts this, "It is not enough to know that someone is acquainted with something to accept that they know all there is to know about it."

Being acquainted with risk—*riesgo por conocimiento*—is rational and emotional, but also routine, and even banal. Accumulated life experiences routinize risk. Workers such as these may be more likely to take the risks necessary to improve their lives, even if they do not experience it as such. Not everyone has such an intimate familiarity with risk. Those without such familiarity may have a different perception of risk.

SUGARCANE WORKERS

Colombians often use the word *caliente*, or "hot," to describe tense or even violent political situations. Francisco uses the term at a meeting held after the first day of the strike to describe how police treated people at the Collasuyu plantation: "There is one group of soldiers that is very impulsive. Very hot. They even shot [life ammunition] into the air. That got people very angry. They started waving their machetes. We have heard a rumor that the plantations are planning to force cane out of the plantation. So, we need reinforcements tomorrow. At 8:00 AM this morning the soldiers came and confronted the workers. One of them took one worker and threw him to the ground. I told him, 'Why are you doing that? Can't you see that they are here peacefully?'" I followed up with Francisco about this later in the strike. He admitted,

> The first days were very tense, as you well know. They called us "delinquents" because they thought that they could just have their way with us and that we would just roll over and let them push us around. They thought that it was going to be like when they fight with the indigenous and there are injuries mostly only on the indigenous side. But they saw that with us that there were injuries on both sides. The injuries we inflict are more dangerous because we fight with machetes. But they are afraid of that. They are really afraid of that. Imagine if one of those riot police officers gets hit across the face with a machete. Around there, one of them did get slashed in the arm. But those riot police sure are scared of the sugarcane workers.

Earlier Francisco focused on the anger he felt after experiencing police repression. Weeks later, he had developed some distance from this emotion. Francisco articulated a theory of worker power. He was proud that workers resisted police with violent force. He explains that because workers wielded machetes, the police grew fearful of engagement. Workers established a counter-hegemonic violence that police found easier to manage through disengagement.

Francisco was proud that workers stood up to the police. Earlier, Francisco concerned himself with physical abuse. But Francisco later opens up to discussing humiliation and verbal abuse. Workers felt entitled to respond to police abuse in equal measure. This response forced police to change their attitude for fear of injury. It was not necessary for police to recognize workers as equals. Using the threat of violence, workers instead forced police into inaction.

Having experienced a fair dose of fear during fieldwork, I wondered how workers managed. I asked Edgar from the Kuntisuyu plantation if he was afraid of police attacks. Edgar and thousands of others slept overnight on plantation property for eight weeks. He replied with a flat "No."

After waiting for him to continue, he said, "Of being attacked here I am not afraid. What I am afraid of is being ambushed out there somewhere while I am unarmed and being quietly eliminated. But here, fighting for something that I believe in, no. I am not afraid of that. Death will beckon in one way or another. But to die fighting and claiming my rights, may God protect me. Not me. I am not afraid."

Edgar felt safety—even pleasure[2]—while surrounded by others participating in the same cause. He reserved his fear for individual confrontations
rather than collective ones. A worker manipulating the machete he holds in
his hands to reflect a sunbeam into an officer's eyes is not only defiance but
also an expression of agency. This individual expression occurs out in the
open. Standing together while at the plantation, workers seem to feel more
agentic. Faced with the prospect even of death, Edgar's response is, "here,
fighting for something that I believe in, no. I am not afraid of that." Standing
together with others seems to dissipate Edgar's fear. But Edgar sees "quiet
elimination" as a vain death and a more consequential cause for fear.

This fear is situational and also informed by past experience. Facing
adversity at home and at work, workers adapt to accommodate their circumstances. Risk inscribes itself into characters and informs traits. The
consequences of having lived a precarious life inscribe itself into the body.
Whether through poverty or violence, and often both, risk also imbues a
capacity to identify, process, and to relate to other similar experiences. This
form of knowledge helps workers navigate their political environment—an
environment that many outsiders would judge to be replete with interpersonal risk.

Workers receive verbal abuse not only from police and plantation owners but also from the government and media. A few days after the Minister
of Social Security, Diego Palacios, stated in the press that he believed there
were "dark hands" operating behind the strike, Palacios repeated the modi-
fied phrase "dark forces." The President of Asocaña, Luis Fernando Londoño,
continued the trope, using the phrase "foreign forces" (*El Espectador,* 2008).
El Espectador columnist Mario Fernando Prado (2008) preferred the phrase
"dark hands," deploying it in his column of September 25. Several com-
mentators continued to repeat versions of the phrase during the course of
the strike, including *Portafolio* columnist Rosa Maria Cárdenas Lesmes on
October 28[3] (2008). These racial tropes are consistent with historical attitudes
against blacks throughout the Americas (Gates 1986).

Television and radio networks created an image of workers as violent and
irrational. This image was so powerful that a defense lawyer for arrested
workers felt the need to explain in court, "Your honor, there was no con-
spiracy to attack the riot police. The riot police invaded the plantations where
the workers assembled. The riot police took the workers by surprise." Media
narratives bore little resemblance to reality. Often, they reported the opposite
of what workers experienced on the plantations. This admission in court
illustrates the extent of the campaign leveled against workers. Workers faced
injustice from plantations and violence from police, as well as widespread
lies. This denial of worker experiences was as dangerous to the strike as
police violence. Denied their own reality, workers turned to each other for

emotional support. Still, media lies took their toll. Responding incredulously, Orlando explained his situation plainly,

> I have 6,000 pesos ($3 USD) left. What am I going to do? All the money I had saved up is spent. And what am I going to do when that is used up? I have six children. Where am I going to go? Thank God that my wife has scrapped enough together, a little rice here or there, they have gotten by. I am 52 years old. I have been cutting cane for 30 years. I am not doing this for myself, I am doing this for the people who are coming in. If I do not do this now, then what are they going to do to the people coming in? It has always gotten worse. I remember when I first started cutting cane it was good. There was more money. But now, what are people going to do? How are they going to get by? Imagine. We are crying for help. We cannot continue to live like this. We have a group of women that we rely on. They come out at 3am to stop cars on the street to tell people about what is going on. The police went in and they dragged people to jail.[4]

Orlando described how the workers leaned on their wives for strength. The families, already poor, were further impoverished after a lengthy strike. Many workers explained that they saw an opportunity to improve their quality of life and that of less experienced workers. Orlando and others understood the

Figure 3.1 Wife Leans on Sugarcane Worker While Attending a Strike Rally. *Source*: Photograph taken by the author in 2008.

emotions that men suffer in private. This motivated them to intervene in the immiseration of their conditions. Yuri was particularly expressive:

> Here, I tell you my young friend, they say that men do not cry. But I tell you that there are grown men here that cry. Because for every worker that can afford to buy a new outfit for their kids—maybe two or three for each of their kids for Christmas—there are just as many who do not have enough and cannot afford to do that. Or sometimes, if we buy something for the kids, then we cannot afford to buy anything for our wife. Some people say, well, I will buy something for the kids and I will buy something for my wife and I will forego gifts. So, they say to their wife, here is a little something, go buy yourself something nice and they say, 'No, and you? No, you're not going to have anything? Well then don't buy me anything either.' So, in this way, she feels that, why is she going to buy herself a new dress if you don't have enough money to buy yourself something nice enough to take her out in. So sometimes that affects you and you sit down and you begin to cry, thinking about how it is possible for you to be so poor in this country. And all this in spite of the fact that you may have all the strength in the world to work and come out ahead, you not being able to liberate yourself and say that you live well because you are able to provide for your children; educate your children. So that, for us, hurts to be in this situation.

This intractable suffering formed the building blocks of resilience and tenacity. These qualities are essential for anyone who dares square up to violent authorities. But they are also qualities born of suffering. If there are any "dark hands" that operate here, they belong to the plantation owners that intervene in political and security structures to immiserate the lives of their own workers. They impoverish the quality of worker marriages, their health, their diets, their clothing, and what little leisure time they are able to bogart. This impact is not contained to workers themselves but extends to their children. Plantation owners made the attempt to define a worker's very relationship with society.

I reproduce here, at some length, a portion of an interview with Jaime where he breaks down in tears, speaking of these themes:

Louis: Is it difficult to be here?

Jaime: Sometimes it rains and the family asks you what you are doing. Why you are [going out to the plantation in the rain]. We wait for others to come and tell us news of workers who were around. Or friends at other plantations. We've always been run over by the people who have the money. We are trying to survive. The family is suffering because there is no money. My brother is the one who helps me. But this has been going on for almost two months. He is getting tired of it. Every time I go to visit him now he says, "so when are you going to end that strike? I don't have money to keep helping you anymore." And that sort of hurts me and offends me. They are family and have some sort of responsibility to help out. We are getting older. My brother is getting tired of helping me. I find people who will lend me money, but since I don't have anything with which to pay them back, they won't lend me any more until I pay them back. I say, lend me just 20,000 [pesos ($10 USD in 2008)] and they say "no, I don't have any more to lend you." They say, "you don't have any money and you don't know when that strike is going to be resolved." So that is what has been happening. The negotiations are going badly. They [plantation owners] keep saying "we'll negotiate, but you have to end this strike."

Louis: How long have you been working at Kuntisuyu?

Jaime: I've been working here for maybe twenty-five years. Back then we used to earn more money. If we worked, we earned money, if we didn't work, we didn't get money. But then things changed. We would ask for a Sunday off and they wouldn't give it to us. And they took and took until we found ourselves in the situation that we find ourselves right now.

Louis: How do you support the strike?

Jaime: What I have done to support the strike is to accompany them here. If I leave here and they resolve this, and if I am at home, or looking for other work, that doesn't look good while the workers are here struggling to fix this without me contributing. They say that they are going to fix this and we are all here for that. Some people are out there looking for work or at home and here they say, 'well, then let them stay there!' So that is why I am here.

Louis: What challenges do you see in your support of the strike?

Jaime: In the first days there was a lot of tension with the police. And we cannot eat too much because there is not much to go around and we have to make it last. But people aren't getting enough food and they are getting tired. I am going home now, but that is so that I can take a shower and decompress, but I have to come back. Because as I said, if I stay over there then there are problems, so I'll be there for two or three hours and come back. Because here they say too, 'oh that one is going, then I am going too.' And so, if everyone goes then this thing unravels, abandoned. This is a real struggle.

Louis: How does your family feel about you being on strike?

Jaime: My family supports me. Once we get into this, we have to continue. The only thing we have is each other. We have to find the strength to go on. I know that they are suffering too, but if I attend to them, then it turns out worse because they need me here. So, I have to turn my face into the wind and keep going.

Louis: What is your role here?

Jaime: Sometimes lentils are running low, or we run out, so I go get some more. Sometimes when we get water, I get to cooking. Or sometimes there are dishes to be done after meals and I wash the dishes. Little things like that. If the entrance here gets dirty, then I grab a broom and sweep it. Little things like that. That is my role.

Louis: Does anyone come by to visit?

Jaime: The evangelicals come to give us energy. Sometimes people come to give us speeches.

Louis: Do the women come?

Jaime: The women come too. Some women stay and some go back. My wife [sobbing], doesn't come because she does not have anything with which to come. She does not have enough for the fare.

Louis: And is it far from here? Is there a bus?[5]

Jaime: No, it's not far, but I don't have enough for the fare [sobbing]. This is crazy. I'm going now.

These accumulated indignities take an emotional toll, but workers expressed those feelings in different ways. For Jaime, having to ask his brother for money was humiliating. Repeated requests lead to a strain in their relationship. The families and communities that surround the workers are important to them. But their coffers are not endless, and neither is their goodwill. Approaching the boundaries beyond which friends and family are willing to support place a strain on these relationships.

Jaime also points to the slow process of immiseration of working conditions that took place over years. As their lives became more precarious, workers began to organize. Had plantations maintained more acceptable conditions, they may have averted a strike. Several workers lamented this "slow" decline, citing this fact as one reason to strike. But Jaime also implied that he wanted to keep appearances, or what he referred to as "solidarity." It "doesn't look good," Jaime explains, "while the workers are here struggling to fix this without me contributing." Jaime did not seem enthusiastic about his responsibilities. Yet he recognized that fulfilling those responsibilities was important to a successful strike. The movement allowed for flexibility in individual worker roles, as radical movements often do, to keep members involved (Tyagi 2018, 141). If Jaime were to leave the picket for any extended period, it would be difficult to ask others to fulfill their roles.

Thinking about this another way, Arturo compared sugarcane workers to prize fighters. Explaining their life-long struggles and their intimate acquaintance with risk (*riesgo por conocimiento*), he says,

A government representative is not going to come here and tell me how to pick up a machete and how to cut cane. The only one who knows how to do that is me. And no one is going to tell me that so-and-so is going to get tired in this way and that I am going to get tired in that. What being tired is. What excessive work feels like. So we are fighters. We are like those prize fighters that you might see on television, that one does not allow himself to be knocked down by the other. That is exactly how we are. We do not allow ourselves to be knocked down by the bigger fighter. The other one, because they are bigger, think that they are going to coldcock us, so we are going to put up a fight. We are not going to allow ourselves to be laid out. We know that they can win, but we are not going to take it. Everyone is here with the same instincts. Because everyone here, from when they were very little, have been survivors. That is how it works. You know that a prizefighter needs a sponsor. And once they have a sponsor or a manager, then they fight with whomever they have to fight next. And that is how it is. That sponsor or manager on our side has been public opinion. Our community which has sponsored us and supported us. Those people have given us food and all that.

Arturo's vivid imagery of an underdog prizefighter is familiar to workers, who admire boxers and dissect their matches. Arturo emphasizes that the workers endure risk throughout their entire lives. Striking alongside others with a shared experience keeps workers motivated. With community and public support, workers also understand that they do not fight alone. Arturo compares the local community to a fight sponsor and manager. Workers are aware that their success depends on community support. It is even the community, not workers alone, who select appropriate struggles to wage. Arturo continued, this time describing how he sees worker motivation in this strike:

If you are living poorly and precariously, and you see that you are living in such a way, that you will die and your children will live on in the same manner. And so, what happens? So, when things are this way, when there is no dialogue, one must enter into these extremes. Playing with one's life as they say. You go and play cards and you have played it out. You have lost all your money, so you go for broke. I will recuperate my money, or I will be left with nothing. And so, that is why we are here. We did this to find a way to live. We want a way of life that allows us to survive, or we will be left worse than how we were. But we must find some sort of solution, from somewhere. And this is the last option that was left to us. We are treated as if we do not matter. What could be done to improve our situation?

Several workers expressed that plantation owners left them with no other options. Similar to certain revolutionary situations, activists sometimes feel that they are forced to the extremes and that there is "no other way out" (Goodwin 2001). Risk, over extended periods, becomes a normal part of everyday life. This is so much so that workers do not seem to experience it as a risk any longer. Workers do not seem to react to the new political risk; rather, they seem to be motivated by an opportunity to smite hard against a familiar humiliation. It is this humiliation stemming from their economic precarity that motivated workers to intervene in their lives in this manner.

LEADERSHIP

The sugarcane workers movement did not have decision-makers separate from the workers themselves. A team of ten, one from each of nine striking plantations plus a media spokesperson, led the bulk of the workers movement.

The nine workers hailing from plantations were accountable to those workers attending Permanent Assemblies at each of their home plantations.

When these nine were not at a leadership committee meeting, they were often at their individual plantations. These meetings operated by consensus and often lasted up to six hours. Consensus tends to slow down decision-making time. But in volunteer movements such as this, consensus can generate good will (Polletta 2002). Once decided, it is more likely that activists will follow through on their commitments. This is despite the fact that having concerns heard and considered takes time (Gelderloos 2006). Each representative communicated with co-workers from their respective plantations. While at the plantation, they gathered perspectives to voice at the meeting. The next day, the committee would share views from across all plantations.

Workers chose this process with intent, but it also flowed naturally from their co-operative structures. This organizational model also fit well with that of the relatively flat *catnet* of the Doves. CUT, in contrast, is more hierarchical, something that did not appeal to most workers. It was by no means inevitable that a horizontal organizational model alone would be sufficient to carry the strike to victory. Consensus was a major point of differentiation between the workers movement and the CUT. Some workers opposed any semblance of authority. Lifelong experiences of humiliation from plantation owners and other authorities may have bred what became a general mistrust. But this orientation was by no means universal. Some workers were, in fact, unionized. Others stayed home during the strike. And plantation owners allegedly recruited still others to counter-protest. Even so, participation in consensus decision-making was by far the dominant orientation.

Workers decided against unionization because they wanted control over the strike campaign. One worker said during a meeting of the Cuntisuyu plantation workers: "We are not affiliated with any union, so the President is not able to force us to settle." Had workers unionized, they would have faced pressure from their union headquarters. On their own, workers were free to choose their own allies and to develop their own human rights frame. Unencumbered by bureaucracy, grassroots activists were free to make their own decisions. Had workers unionized, the government could have gained leverage over the large, sprawling CUT organization by hurting the union elsewhere, or promising gains elsewhere. In such an instance, union leaders may have forced workers to accede.

With all of the impediments that a democratic structure entails, it also allowed workers to bring the surrounding community into the movement. Co-operatives rotated workers among the various tasks. These included acquiring water, cooking meals, clean-up, and grocery shopping. But family members or others in the community also sometimes completed these tasks. This relationship had also influenced the strike demands to include improved funding for housing and schooling. The interdependent relationship, similar to mutual aid,[6] expanded the strike beyond a contest around a labor relationship. The broad support of community groups, churches, university students, indigenous groups, elected officials, union locals, and local families was essential in sustaining the strike over the eight weeks.

Nearby indigenous communities likely influenced this mutual self-reliance and skepticism of the state and centralized unions. Indigenous groups also likely influenced the workers' search for extra-commonwealth solutions. During the strike, a coalition of indigenous communities had marched from their communal lands to Cali. While there, indigenous people clamored to add human rights language to the Constitution that would benefit their communities. Especially the CRIC (Cauca Regional Indigenous Council), indigenous people have resorted to defending their historical land claims from the Colombian government and private ranchers. Like the Brazilian Landless Workers Movement (MST), this sometimes takes the form of the direct occupation of land. Sugarcane workers, while maintaining important differences with these indigenous movements, are also influenced by their proximity and common target.

SUGARCANE WORKER KNOWLEDGE

A delegation of sugarcane workers accompanied indigenous activists along their journey to Cali. Mario described the effect that this interaction had on him in reflecting on his own struggle:

> We need to move forward because there is no other way. Someone has to lay the first stone in the foundation. I might not see the work completed, but maybe my children will see it. I am doing this so that my children will not have to cut sugarcane like I do, because you do not advance yourself by working on the land. I tell them to go find work doing something else. Looking at the indigenous was an inspiration. They are so much more organized than we are. We have to learn from them. This movement cannot end with the end of the strike. We have to continue to organize like the indigenous people. Of course, there are many differences. They are autonomous and we depend on a salary. But we can still advance. Some people are egotistical and envious and that prevents us from advancing. We need to get rid of that. Our town used to be in a much better situation. People had food. Everyone had his little farm. If you ran out of yucca, the neighbor would go to his farm and give you some and you would give him some of your corn. If you got drunk the night before and did not make it to your farm, your neighbors would look out for your cattle. Then the sugarcane owners came and starting buying up the land. And if you would not sell they would divert the stream that went to your farm so that you had no water and had to sell. They did anything to make you sell.

And if you did not sell, they would have you killed. And the narcotraffickers were a problem. They would buy up the land too. They would give 30, 40, 50 million pesos (15, 20, 25 thousand USD) for a small plot of land. And if you did not sell, they would give you 100 or 150 so that you would leave. It was crazy. But those *campesinos* when they arrived to town and their money ran out, then what did they do? They turned to drugs or they became poor. It was a big problem. The politicians support this. The local politicians receive contributions to their campaigns from the plantations. So, they turn their backs to us now. They do not help. And the government created policies to allow all this to happen to us. No, we need to organize and stop it. There was a big river that people used to go to all the time. Now it is completely taken up by two plantations. I will take you sometime so that you get to know it. No one can go to it now.

These experiences inspired Mario to create a future vision for workers. This vision involved helping workers overcome their differences, to help develop people to become better individuals, and to overcome government and private corruption. Mario was a movement leader representing Kuntisuyu. Lácides was his deputy representative at the plantation while Mario was away. A more reluctant leader, Lácides explains his movement experience:

Lácides: I do interviews with visitors and I make sure that the resources are used correctly. I was elected by the [general] assembly. I was elected Human Rights Advocate before that and they asked me to assume this role. In 2005 I was a negotiator and was at the negotiating table. I took that role by the same process then, by election in general assembly.

Louis: Why did you choose to become a leader in the structure of the strikes of 2005 and 2008.

Lácides: I was elected by the same people.

Louis: No, but why did you choose to assume the role?

Lácides: that is what I am saying, I did not want to do it, I was chosen by others. I was told, 'You know how to express yourself with the press. You are the one who will do this.' Before that, I was not interested in doing this. Because I had that experience before, they asked me to do this in 2008. After assuming the role, I studied the demands so that I can be informed and explain it and defend it. It is only now that I realize how risky it is that the plantation owners are looking for false confessions to bring charges against people. I did see threats in 2005, but only now in 2008 did they go after people legally. In 2005, I did see people be threatened.

Lácides does not see himself as having agency outside of the organization. The threats that he alleges against plantation owners seemed to soften his resolve. But this did not deter his participation. Speaking of risk in his leadership role, he continued:

> People are calling me a "guerrilla." My weapon is the machete and it is what I work with. That is all I have. The only evidence they have is that we are meeting and they accuse us of having meetings with FARC. You have been to our meetings and you see what we are doing. We are not guerrilla or *paracos* [paramilitary] or nothing like that. We are fighting for our rights. Our families are also suffering. Psychologically, they have to deal with all this. The family of the people in jail are suffering. Because they can't see their father. My family supports me, one-hundred percent. I bring home all the sustenance. This has affected everything. Thank God that they have not gone to bed hungry yet. These two struggles are the only ones I have been in.

Louis: Why don't you leave and take up another career?

Lácides: Because I have to think of other workers and other families that have put their trust in me. They believe in me as a person who can help them in getting out of this situation. If it were up to me, I would have left by now. But in my conscious, I cannot find the strength to do that. First, let's resolve this problem for the benefit of everyone. I do not seek personal benefit, but benefit for everyone.

Here Lácides explains not only the risk but also his personal limits. Lácides thanks God that his family has not had to go to bed hungry, adding the ominous modifier, "yet." Lácides and his family have experienced hardship before. He admits that there may be a point at which the personal costs of striking may push him out. Lácides is able to sustain participation beacuse of his earned tenacity. But he stays on strike out of a perceived commitment to others. Community support was vital in supporting this commitment and stemming attrition.

After asking him why he doesn't change careers, Lácides insists that it is not up to him. Even if it would result in a personal benefit for him and his family, Lácides replies, "I do not seek personal benefit, but benefit for everyone." Many of the striking workers expressed similar collectivist sentiments, which also informed their movement's strategy.

Workers made some decisions on the plantations at Permanent Assemblies. Collecting those workers who happened to be there, they sometimes engaged in impromptu debates about tactics. The plantation representative would often facilitate the discussion if he was available. Otherwise, workers improvised. Workers at the Kuntisuyu plantation debated whether to block the road. In rapid-fire succession, four workers interjected:

Worker 1: Tell the indigenous to come here!

Worker 2: At least for an hour, we can block the road.

Worker 3: The riot police are afraid of us. They won't mess with us.

Worker 4: In Tawantinsuyu, they just handed two months of struggle away overnight. Here we are gambling with our lives and with the lives of our families.
We cannot just throw it away like that.

The last worker's appeal resonated with the majority of workers. They felt
that blocking the road would compromise the main goal of the militant picket
line. It would not be the first time—they had blocked the public road before.
The police would respond to the blocking of a public road with swift force.
In the aftermath, workers would be no closer to meeting their strike demands.
Seeking to avoid another confrontation with police, some workers defended
their opposition. "Our lives" and "the lives of our families" are at stake, a
few rejoined.

Risk inhered in many such decisions. There was risk of police violence
with some options. But there was also a risk of losing the strike if workers
did not apply enough pressure. If they fail, the hardship that they and their
families endure every day would continue. Some workers felt it was riskier
to not block the road and engage the police. This course of action would con-
centrate workers on the militant picket line. This was the pressure point from
which their leverage emanated.

These workers were aware of the novelty of their reading of the situation.
Noel is the worker representative from the Antisuyu plantation. During the
worker rally after the signing of the new contract, he said,

> Give yourselves a round of applause for your fortitude and dignity in this
> struggle. This strike has broken all the norms. It has changed the balance of
> power. This movement can change things. And it has changed things. It goes
> beyond the list of individual demands. It is the solidarity that we have built. It
> is the international visibility of the sugarcane workers that we have built. And
> *compañeros*, this does not end here. Tonight, we will go home to our families.
> And tomorrow we enter our labor. But this struggle goes on. The workers of
> Cauca and Valle del Cauca, united, can change the face of this country. We are
> going to do it because we now have the capacity and the tools to do so. Thank
> you so much for your heart. We will achieve and be able to taste all our goals.
> We have not lost anything. We have won. And the plantations, too. They have
> gained something and learned something here, too. They have learned that when
> they take a step, they will have to deal with us if they do not follow all parts of
> this contract. We have won. Long live the sugarcane cutters!

Another worker at the rally at the Cuntisuyu plantation,

> It is true that we did not achieve all the objectives of the work stoppage. But
> we did achieve our main goal. Because with this glorious stoppage, Cuntisuyu,
> with seven other plantations, breaks in two the story of the sugarcane workers

in Valle del Cauca. It breaks it in two because from now on, this will change the way that the plantations treat you. Because you have organized yourselves in a civil manner and shown, not just the plantations, but the entirety of Colombia that you have broken the chains of slavery from the sugarcane industry.

The workers themselves see their strike campaign as not only about wages. For some, the strike is also about transforming their relationship with the plantations. The worker at this last planation frames the strike as being significant. It "breaks in two," he says, worker-plantation relations. The strike may have slowed down the mechanization of their industry and the expansion into ethanol production. The majority of sugarcane is still harvested by machete. It remains to be seen how future labor disputes will resolve themselves.

THE WILL TO RISK

The experience of risk creates a form of activist knowledge that workers use to navigate the dangers of their personal and work lives. The economic and social desperation that plantation owners place workers in creates experiences of humiliation. These varied, prolonged, repeated, and polymorphous experiences of humiliation accustom a person to the risks of everyday life. This warped process makes political risk-taking seem normal. This normalization of risk creates worker willingness to risk their lives and livelihood for a chance to act upon the humiliation and risk of their everyday life.

This mechanism operates in the background of many of the workers actions during the strike. Experiences of humiliation motivate workers to respond to their situations. Their personal experiences give them the capacity to witness, process, and understand the risk and humiliation in the lives of other workers. Their willingness to help other workers motivates their response to humiliation. This altruism does not play a significant role in explaining risk-taking itself. But altruism will play a role in explaining why the Doves undertake these activities. The next chapter elaborates on that idea, relying on the biographies of three Doves. The Doves also reflect here on their activities during the strike.

NOTES

1. José Ortega y Gasset (1952 [1934]) develops a similar distinction between beliefs and ideas. For Ortega y Gasset, beliefs are an essentialized versions of ideas that form part of our identity. In his words, "We have ideas; we exist in our beliefs. [. . .] [B]eliefs are ideas which we are." Boaventura de Sousa Santos (2009, 46–7) claims that Ortega y Gasset captures the work of the Enlightenment in creating this

cleavage. But our distinction between *saber* and *conocer* is better understood as a project to address what Iberophone sociologists fear as an Americanization of Castilian and Portuguese-language sociology (Moncada 1995).

2. Wood (2003) found that activists in El Salvador took pleasure in expressing themselves through their activism.

3. While the phrase is usually levied against Colombia's Left, President Manuel Santos used the phrase against the Colombian military during the course of peace negotiations with the FARC (*AFP* 2014).

4. I could not verify this particular incident with the police.

5. I chose to leave this, and a few other examples of failed moments in my emotion work, in the text (Hochschild 1983).

6. Kropotkin (1987 [1902]) theorizes similar dynamics as "mutual aid."

Chapter 4

Leadership

In contrast to workers, the Doves arrived in Palmira with middle-class credentials. While the previous chapter detailed the experiences of sugarcane workers, here I depict the biographies of three Colombian human rights activists. Interviewed near the end of the strike, their stories illustrate instances of acute repression by Colombian state and non-state forces. Their stories illustrate the accumulation of activist knowledge borne of varied experience.

Environments rife with political violence pose an inherent threat to would-be activists. These threats can sometimes "shock" people into action (Jasper 1997). But this motivation can also be strong when activists attach themselves to land (Jasper 1997, 129), such as in the use of radical pickets or in the occupation of plantations. Biographies help us to understand motives in that they tell a story in the form of a series of interactions over time (Collins 2004; Goffman 1967). Demographic variables can be insufficient for explaining participation (Nepstad and Smith 1999; Viterna 2006). But unlike demographic characteristics, individual "moments" (Lareau and Horvat 1999) hidden in a person's individual story can in themselves contain explanatory value. The decision to enter into high-risk activism is often a personal one, even if it is not always cognitive (Munson 2008).

BIOGRAPHY

It is common for social movement scholars to collect and read activist biographies (Goodwin and Jasper 2003). South African biographies became popular after the fall of apartheid (c.f. Slovo 1997; Mandela 1994). Latin American *testimonios* and biographies also began to grow in the 1980s and 1990s (Menchu 1984; Marcos 2001; Auyero 2003). There are many such firsthand *testimonios* from Colombians who had survived a kidnapping (Romero Leal, 2017). Social movement scholars also read biographical and ethnographic studies of non-activists (Desmond 2007; Esparza 2013). These help us to contextualize the stories and patterns observed in the stories of activists.

Three activist biographies follow below. These detail the trajectories of key members of the Doves. The three members—Javier, Felipe, and Nina—provided legal and organizational support to the striking workers. "The Doves," as such, are a small, technical organization made up of professionals trained in law, political organizing, communications, and operations support. A patchwork of foreign foundations and trusts provide funding for this organization. Javier received international training in Europe, and all three had previous political organizing experience.

As outsiders to Palmira, the Doves played a role not dissimilar from the role that the Highlander Folk School played in the U.S. Civil Rights movement of the 1950s and early 1960s (Esparza 2011; Kelley 1990, 15; Ling 1995; Glen 1988; Horton, Kohl, and Kohl 1990). Both the Doves and the leaders of the Highlander Folk School worked in small groups that provided technical help and training. Both organized and educated movement leaders to work in a target community. Both brought experiences from previous campaigns to their capacity-building efforts with movement leaders. Both worked with grassroots movements.[1]

But more than illustrating their influence on the sugarcane workers' movement, these personal stories unravel biographical mechanisms involved in activism. The experiences of the Doves help us to understand high-risk action writ-large. These stories provide commentary on common concepts that social movement scholars think about. The stories reveal that some of our analytical concepts seem to work for the Doves, while others do not.

JAVIER

Javier attended the Universidad del Valle (UniValle) in Cali. As an undergraduate, he took part in a social movement against a large energy company. ColPoder [pseudonym] had been bilking its customers in the region as part of broad cost-saving measures. ColPoder introduced spikes in the price of electricity while also depressing worker wages at the same time. These price increases personally harmed Javier and his family. Already strained, their household budget could not accommodate these price hikes. Javier saw that he was not the only one in this situation. Along with his friend Felipe, Javier formed a group that would protest ColPoder's price hikes. This group would later plan the occupation of ColPoder's central downtown office building.

Their campaign managed to draw intense local media attention. Their actions also cost the company tens of thousands of dollars in lost revenue. Javier became the subject of media criticism and later left the university to escape the pressures that had accumulated around him.

Javier absconded to Choco, an Afro-Colombian region on Colombia's Pacific Coast immediately north of Valle del Cauca. Javier had read about the history of Afro-Colombians during his coursework at Universidad del Valle. He had long wanted to immerse himself in Choco to see it firsthand. Javier described to me his experience of traveling into Utría National Park. "The forest was so thick," he recounted, that "it was dark even at midday." Javier used a flashlight to be able to see along the overgrown paths. The Emberá indigenous people blazed these trails hundreds of years earlier and continue to protect their land by managing the influence of state development projects. (Acosta García and Farrell 2019) Javier went into long detail, explaining how he relied on local groups to guide him. "It was very easy to get lost along the unmarked trails in the deep forest," he explained.

Javier interrupted this story to reach for his laptop. He wanted to share some of the local music that had a lasting impact on him. Among them, "¿Porque me pega?" (Why do you hit me?) is about a daughter who implores her mother about why she must beat her (Maldonado, 2002). Many of the songs that Javier shared with me were about similar social problems. They all recounted everyday stories in Choco communities.

While in Choco, Javier helped to build houses and taught people how to read. He told me, "The people are the nicest people you will ever meet. Humble people are always the nicest. The people with the least are the most willing to give you everything they have. It was touching. That is a lesson I take with me always and I never forget that. It is inspiring. You must go some day."

There were several international[2] human rights groups present in the area. Javier interacted with these organizations, sometimes working side-by-side with their volunteers. One of these international organizations designed a research project with locals. They would produce a report on the quality of life in Choco. Javier stopped our interview again to stand up. He walked me over to the bookshelf in his bedroom and pulled the bound report from the shelf. Javier showed me the list of agencies involved in the collaboration. Turning to the acknowledgements page, he found and pointed to his name. Javier stored pictures from his time there in-between the book's leaves. He walked me through the personalities of the agencies that he worked with. Javier beamed, making it clear to me that this experience had been a source of pride.

During one period in Choco, Javier travelled with three Swedish photographers and a few guides. "[The Swedes] were smelly and had poor hygiene,"

Javier would tell me. He continued, "They would hike for eight hours, and then dunk themselves in a river to cool off. Meanwhile, they would string up rope across the room and air out their dirty clothes. This is nothing against foreigners, but it was the foulest stench I ever experienced. In my experience, foreigners have terrible hygiene. [. . .] That stuff smelled like shit. I told them to take that shit down. That was the only time I yelled at them." Javier also reveled in telling me of his adventurous travels by canoe. The lack of communications infrastructure had been hard on him. Javier could not reach his friends and family. Everyday life in Choco had been very different from his life in Cali. "No one came to visit me," he told me. But his friend-in-arms, Felipe, did send him the complete works of V. I. Lenin to pass the time. It was the only set of books that Javier had in the time he spent in Choco, and he "devoured" them. Javier told me about reciting Lenin to the people in Choco, commenting, "Imagine that! I was reading Lenin from a tree stump to poor, illiterate Afro-Colombian peasants in Choco. It was like a dream. It was moving for me."[3]

Mestizo activists in Colombia, like whites in the United States, may sometimes idealize black populations (c.f. Esparza 2023b; Rajah 2000). But Javier's passion was sincere. Javier had planned to stay only a couple of months. But he was so moved, he said, that he stayed for over a year. "I fell in love with the place and I wanted to stay. That was my calling." He contemplated beginning a campaign of popular political education. Javier dreamt that this might be a path to autonomous development and "a true revolution." Javier criticized the FARC, the CUT, and the government for reproducing "oligarchic" structures. He wants nothing to do with them, he insisted. Javier left Choco to complete his university degree and to realize his vision.

Back in Cali, Javier received a hair-raising welcome. Several death threats came related to his activities against the utility company ColPoder. According to Javier, someone had hired paramilitaries to assassinate him. His involvement in the campaign against ColPoder made him a high-profile target. The campaign against ColPoder had cost the utility tens of thousands of dollars. Javier described an attempt on his life: "One day, I was getting off of the bus, and it was letting me off in the middle of the road, because, well, you know how the busses are here. I turned to my right and saw a motorcycle without plates peeling towards me and the guy was wearing a black leather jacket and he took out a gun. I didn't see anything else; I just jumped in the open window of a taxi that happened to be right there and ducked. Somehow, I survived that."

After that incident, Javier escaped Cali yet again. Going even further away, this time he lands in Germany. Javier had learned about a program to shelter political exiles. His international connections made in Choco put him in touch with PaxDeutsche (pseudonym). This German peace organization offered to house him for one year as part of the program.

It was the first time that Javier had seen snow. "The snow would come down and it would be up to my waist sometimes," Javier insisted. He lived in an apartment with other Germans who worked for the same organization. Javier had traded chaotic Cali bus routes for serene bicycle paths. Leaping from his chair again, Javier produced pictures showing him partying with his roommates. Shuffling the photographs with glee, he finally discovered pictures of his political work with PaxDeutsche. Javier had helped them to organize a peace march and had also walked in the march with them. "It was funny," he said with broken laughter. "Because they were all little old white German ladies and here I am, this young Colombian guy."[4]

At home, Javier had commandeered a city building, recited Lenin in the deep forest, and cheated a mounted assassin from his bounty. By comparison, his marching in a European villa with "all little old white German ladies" brings him to laughter. Even if, by chance, police had arrested Javier, he could have confidence in a robust legal process. He would have powerful advocates. He would have a strong appeals process at his disposal. And there is no risk of being ambushed by anonymous motorcycle assassins. Except, of course, by any who may have followed him from Colombia.

"They took good care of me and mentored me and they learned a lot from me as well," Javier explained. He described workshops on navigating the world of international organizations. PaxDeuche also educated Javier about similar human rights violations happening in other countries. Javier explained that PaxDeutsche would organize forums on human rights in Colombia. Javier became a mainstay of their speaker bureau. "One time," Javier said with a smile on his face, "I was on a panel with someone from the [Colombian] foreign ministry. The Foreign Minister was not happy to see me," his smile turning sardonic. Javier continued: "I rebutted everything she said. And told of my experiences in Choco and Cauca and *el Valle*. She tried the best she could, but it was embarrassing for her."

The event was so successful, Javier told, that PaxDeutsche flew him to Scotland. Javier again engaged the same Colombian Foreign Minister at an event in Edinburgh. "She was not happy," he said with that same smile, "Not happy at all." Forced exile can have unexpected benefits for activists, such as creating new political opportunities that might not have been possible at home (Schneider Marques 2017). Javier was deepening relationships with European peace organizations that would support his later work.

But European activism turned out to be distinct from Javier's Colombian experience. PaxDeutsche leveraged him as an expert in policy circles in Germany and the UK. These kinds of face-offs usually do not happen. Colombian activists rarely share spaces with domestic officials. This is especially rare in foreign contexts. Javier, not two years prior, had trouble paying his utility bill in Cali. Now he was sharing a stage with a cabinet minister in Edinburgh. Activists in developing countries are often blocked from accessing domestic officials. This forces them to seek leverage from international groups (Keck and Sikkink 1998).

For their part, the Colombian government had been seeking to renew the Plan Colombia spending bill in the United States. To improve their chances of success, they intervened to rehabilitate their international reputation as a dangerous country. The government began an aggressive marketing campaign in 2005. "Colombia is Passion" would share Colombia's artisans, coffee, and culture with global audiences (Echeverri et al., 2010). This campaign was meant to counter Western anti-drug advertising campaigns that continued to reference Pablo Escobar.[5] The "Colombia is Passion" marketing campaign increased tourism to the country as marketers began to learn more about U.S. tourists (Luna-Cortés 2018).

Javier made lasting connections in Germany. But the experience also changed how he viewed his own role. Javier improved his ability to contextualize human rights violations in a broader schema. This proved to be an effective rhetorical device at rallies and in meetings in Valle del Cauca. Javier had started this political evolution by reacting to unfair utility bills, crossing my path after he had already embedded himself into a sugarcane worker strike. Along the way, Javier had integrated his varied experience into effective leadership.

Months before the strike was to occur, Javier had been living in Cali. He made frequent visits to outlying sugarcane co-ops and plantations. Javier was with workers as they planned their meetings and designed their strike campaign. Javier also attended the rally at which the workers presented their strike demands in June. Javier briefed the Doves about this work until the rest of them joined Javier on the eve of the strike.

Felipe

One of Javier's most enduring relationships is his friendship with Felipe. The pair met in college at a meeting of organizing ColPoder workers. It was in this living laboratory that Javier and Felipe gained essential political organizing skills. It was here, too, that they rubbed elbows with a young Wilson Arias, later to become a member of the Cali City council during the sugarcane worker strike. But just as important was that Felipe and Javier formed strong personal bonds over the many ColPoder meetings that were to come.

Rising utility prices squeezed the finances of many families in the region. But affluent families, like the one that Felipe grew up in, remained insulated from the worst effects of the price hikes. Felipe lived in his mother's home.

Fine art and classic literature decorated the main rooms of the expansive house. Felipe's father is an architect who designed buildings throughout the country. But despite Felipe's affluence, he insisted that "the workers had to be helped" and "the people have to pay enough already." Javier and Felipe would both emerge as leaders in the ColPoder campaign, but little could make them more different.

Javier had entered the fray out of a personal grievance. But Felipe had experienced something closer to a moral shock (Jasper 1997). Nonetheless, they became leaders in the occupation of the ColPoder office building together. Police arrested them both together, and the two also spent time in jail together. Their two families became close during this time—especially the two mothers. Both sets of parents had divorced. Javier and Felipe remained unmarried and without children. They became active in the *Polo Democratico* and went on to form the Doves.

Felipe wears his economic class on his sleeve—literally. A Rolex dangles precariously from his wrist. Felipe drives a small white Renault, tucks a neat Polo into his khakis, and makes sure to consult his watch on a regular basis. His hair was long and silky, maintained with regular visits to a local salon. Felipe is an exquisite orator, and his speeches were popular with striking sugarcane workers. How much this popularity had to do with his class was hard to judge, but it would involve some effort not to notice this detail about Felipe. Activists often clue in to class markers, including clothing and jewelry. (c.f. Leondar-Wright 2014) Workers would often trip over each other to get close to him during a speech. Javier joked that Felipe returned the favor, behaving "as if he were Jesus Christ."

Two sugarcane workers admitted that they respected Felipe more because of his economic class. Oftentimes, people of Felipe's economic class will avoid having to associate with working-class Colombians. Even fewer fight alongside them in a political campaign. During an informal moment, these two workers admitted feeling "unworthy" of Felipe's help. This discussion took place hours after a visit to Felipe's home, where they had witnessed the comfort in which he lives. This reverence may be a product of Colombia's stark economic and cultural divides that have persisted since the colonial period. Only Brazil and Suriname have higher levels of income inequality in the hemisphere (World Bank 2022).

But Felipe also made himself affable, often teasing the workers. One of his favorite sources of material was soccer, a sport popular with Latin American men. Originally from the capital city of Bogotá, Felipe would lay it on thick whenever his team beat Cali. This habit elicited fraternal ire from just about everyone around him.

Felipe and Javier traveled, often together, from one plantation to another. They spread news and updates about how the strike was going. Workers were often appreciative since they could not rely on mainstream news sources for support. It was particularly difficult for them to get accurate information about neighboring plantations. Social media was in its infancy in the region in 2008. Smartphones and internet access were expensive and rare in rural Colombia at the time. Moreover, many sugarcane workers were functionally illiterate. But Felipe's and Javier's updates boosted morale. They combated mainstream media disinformation[6], and reminded workers of their goals and sacrifices. It was the workers who were on strike, and the Doves were their advisors. But workers leaned on Felipe and Javier for inspiration and information.

This was evident as Javier and Felipe received warm greetings at every plantation. As soon as workers would spot the white Renault ambling along the road, dozens and sometimes hundreds would jockey around the car. This affinity made workers receptive to Dove interventions—even when they had initially taken the opposite position.

Javier and Felipe attended strike meetings on a daily basis. Attending several meetings per day was a frequent occurrence. They often entered into prolonged monologues about strategy. Workers sometimes strayed into tactics that the Doves thought were too aggressive. But Javier and Felipe also intervened when they saw too much infighting at meetings. They especially interceded when they observed workers expressing that they wanted to end the strike.

One of the most consequential of these interventions occurred on the first day of the strike. Police had succeeded in preventing striking workers from entering the Cuntisuyu plantation. Workers then began a physical confrontation with the police. The workers' plantation representative and leadership committee chose not to stop them. The Doves were not present, but the plantation worker representative called Javier on the phone. He had not called Javier for advice about how to resolve the conflict. Instead, he wanted Javier to bring gasoline so that workers could set tires ablaze to block the roads.

I was with the Doves at the office when Javier received this call. Javier replied in low, even tones, and then hung up. Immediately upon hanging up the phone, Javier exploded in anger. We all turned to him as he unloaded his disbelief at what he thought was an audacious request. It did not take long for him to convince us to drive immediately to the Cuntisuyu plantation. The altercation had subsided by the time we arrived. But this did not stop Javier from admonishing workers. He pleaded that it was important that workers restrain themselves and turn their attention to maintaining the militant picket line.

That Felipe and Javier were men may have played a role in the workers being receptive to calmer tactics. Felipe's messaging drew brawny analogies

Figure 4.1   Disabled Trucks Overflowing with Sugarcane. *Source*: Photograph taken by the author in 2008.

to war. Felipe stood before a crowd of rallying workers at the Cuntisuyu plantation and said:

> This is a battle between the powerful and the vulnerable. Both sides make mistakes but if we make mistakes, it is much more impactful. If the powerful make mistakes, sure, it can cost them a few million pesos. But when we make a mistake—look we are enduring hunger, we are broke, no, it is much worse for us. We have risked what we were going to risk. We have done what we were going to do. In a war, we cannot use up all the ships. Because if we come out of the battle having used all the ships, then we have nothing for the next battle, for the next war. We need to come out of this having preserved the structures that we have created. We cannot go from fame to obscurity. You need to play a role in the long-term. You need to keep meeting like this. You need to keep organizing. You need to keep these habits up. One of the goals of the plantations is to destroy the movement. They don't want you to have labor power. They don't want you to have social power. They don't want you to have political power.

Felipe is communicating a strategic lesson in this war analogy. He pleaded with workers to preserve their movement structures. This would be necessary to survive inevitable periods of *abeyance* (Taylor 1989) between movement campaigns. This lesson is something that Felipe has understood from his study of revolutionary movements. But this strike is the most significant movement campaign that many of the workers have likely engaged in. The workers know more than Felipe about the particularities of their experience. But workers would not have necessarily learned about preserving movement structures from their experiences alone.

Differences between Javier and Felipe

Felipe and Javier, while they shared a great many ideas, sometimes held different views. They differed, for example, on the role of power and on the origins of the strength of the movement. One flashpoint occurred in a meeting after Felipe complained about media coverage. Javier responded, "We cannot win by complaining about the fact that the media are not paying attention. Everyone knows that and they are not just not paying attention to us, but they are not paying attention to anyone on our side, you idiot. What we have to do is command attention by building a base." Felipe had lamented that the media was not being objective. News channels were favoring the plantation owners with airtime and sympathetic analysis. But Javier's view of the media was more cynical. The media, in his view, excludes all persons who would sympathize with the strike. Javier did not want to depend on the media for the strike to succeed. Rather, Javier preferred a strategy that laid the burden on the organizers and on the workers. Building strong grassroots support without help from the media was his preferred strategy.

Felipe and Javier also disagreed on the role of leaders. It is worth replicating Felipe's view at some length. Near the middle of the 58-day strike, he spoke before a crowd of workers. Again using a soccer analogy, Felipe's most clear and complete statement on this topic came:

> We need to preserve leaders. We need to preserve the processes that the leaders have produced. In soccer, they say, 'The young people win the games, but the older players win the tournaments.' Here we say, 'The grassroots win the battles.' What do the grassroots do? They march. Without the grassroots, there is no march. Without the grassroots, there is no work stoppage. Without the grassroots, there is no zero hour. It is the grassroots that win the battles. 'But the leaders win the movement.' The leaders create the movement. If you do not preserve the leaders, you lose the movement. If the leaders are burnt up now, it will take new leaders to start from scratch. And they will start and you will have lost everything that you have built and start from scratch. You need to preserve your leaders. To build leadership, you need to develop trust. If the grassroots does not trust someone, that person can never lead them. It does not serve us to have leaders in jail. We need to keep the leaders out of jail. We need to keep the leaders by the sides of the grassroots. The leaders need to preserve themselves.

It could be that tomorrow there is a strike. It could be that that tomorrow there is a battle. But the leaders must be preserved. The leaders produce victories.

Using another muscular—and perhaps Leninist—analogy, Felipe is further extolling the virtues of movement structures. He focuses on their maintenance but turns his attention to the role of leadership. Understanding leadership as *relational* (Uhl-Bien and Ospina 2012), Felipe compares workers at the plantations to rookie soccer players. Youth here are referring to movement experience. Leaders in the analogy are, in contrast, veteran players. In soccer, the captain of the team is often more experienced but not always the most skilled. Here Felipe draws on a familiar analogy for most workers and for most Colombian men. Before the strike is even over, Felipe foreshadows future campaigns and leadership roles. This anchoring (Tversky and Kahneman 1974) motivates and focuses workers to complete the task currently at hand. Felipe implies that workers form part of a team that is greater than they are as individuals. Felipe is pushing workers to treat leaders as valuable assets to be renewed in perpetuity.

Javier appreciated the role of leaders, but he placed greater emphasis on the grassroots than did Felipe. Javier illustrated this during one of his visits to a plantation. He led an activity with workers to illustrate their power. Javier asked for two dozen volunteers, separating them into two groups. A smaller group would represent plantation owners and a larger group represented workers. Javier laid two sticks parallel to each other on the ground, about ten feet apart. Each of the two groups then lined up behind the sticks, opposite each other. Javier then instructed the 'plantation owners' to try and grab a few workers. As they did so, the 'workers' routed, fleeing from their assigned position.

After some laughter and teasing, Javier had the workers line up again. This time he instructed the workers" to hold on to the shoulders of the worker in front of them. They then formed a circle, the worker in the front of the line circling around to hold on to the shoulders of the worker in the rear. The unorganized line of individuals had now become one organized unit. This time, when 'the plantation owners' tried to pick them off, it was much more difficult to do so. Before, workers had run in different directions. Now, workers ran around in a circle, spurning attempts to sequester any one of them.

Javier's view is that worker strength lies in organization and trust. It is up to workers to deny plantation owners the opportunity to unravel their movement. For Javier, that opportunity only comes when workers break discipline.

NINA

The Doves were more than mere political consultants. The Doves became personal advisors to many of these men. Of all the Doves, Nina served the role of personal counselor in the workers' private lives more than any other. During the strike, Colombian news organizations reported on a collapsed pyramid scheme. This high-profile scheme left hundreds of Colombians destitute (Hofstetter et al., 2018). The Doves discovered that Alver had invested in this fraudulent company. Alver was a sugarcane worker and member of the strike leadership team. He had lost ten years' worth of his family's savings—about USD $18,750. He confided this to Nina, who admonished him, "How could you do this, Alver? You gambled your family's future away! You are a smart man; you of all people should have known better. How could you think that you could short-circuit the system and that it would work out? You knew that these people were shady. No, no, no, I cannot believe it. How could you have done this?"

This passionate chiding was typical of Nina's behavior during the strike and drew workers closer to her. They felt that she cared about their lives, and they soon began to confide personal matters to her. A few workers admitted to not always being able to admit their vulnerabilities to their co-workers. I did not observe workers admitting personal matters to Javier or Felipe that did not specifically concern their role in the strike.

I first met Nina in Bogotá while attending a UN-sponsored human rights workshop. She facilitated the meeting, designed to aid a coalition of internally displaced persons. Nina is an alumnus of a prestigious Colombian university and became knowledgeable in human rights law. Although based in Bogotá, Nina has traveled throughout the country. She works for a law group that consults for many organizations around the country. Nina developed a reputation among the Doves for being both a spirited orator and a political radical.

Nina met Felipe in Bogotá, and she joined the Doves thereafter. Soon after my having met Nina in Bogotá, the Doves flew her to Monteria, in the department of Cordoba. Nina advised families to work with the government to unearth a mass grave. These families sought to have their missing relatives identified. But local paramilitary organizations threatened their lives if they went ahead. Paramilitaries feared that evidence from the mass grave could incriminate them. Nina served as an advocate for these families in legal proceedings.

In Valle del Cauca, Nina was also tasked with the legal issues that workers faced. Nina's role became especially important during contract negotiations. Nina emphasized that plantation owners should agree to clear workers of criminal wrongdoing. She also implored them for a commitment from plantation owners to not to sue for lost revenue. Nina said to a group of gathered workers at the Pichichi plantation:

> We all know that the work stoppage was illegal. And that might put us into jeopardy if we do not protect ourselves from these charges. The charges I am talking about are not of the trumped-up kind. They have already initiated those kinds of

charges, as we all know. With these charges, there is nothing else to do except to fight it. When the prosecutor is told that there is some violation of the law, the prosecutor is required to investigate. That is done. But that is not the only kind of charges that they can bring. They can also bring civil charges against you. These civil charges might imply that the business can sue the cooperatives or the workers for breach of contract. And for the loss of all the business that they suffered during this work stoppage. We are talking about millions of pesos [thousands of U.S. dollars]. If you do not protect yourselves against this, you can negotiate the price of cane that you want and you can form your unitary cooperative. But then they sue you for lost income and you will be in debt for the rest of your lives. We cannot pay for the revenue that the plantations have lost up until now. Or they could annul the cooperative contracts completely. So what we mean by "no reprisals," we are saying that there cannot be any lawsuits or charges against us for anything that occurred during the work stoppage.

The vast majority agreed with Nina's concern. But not everyone was as adamant about this demand. Some of the Doves and worker advocates were willing to drop it during negotiations. Nina travelled from plantation to plantation to beseech the workers: "Not all of your advocates are lawyers. And not all of them understand all of the nuances of this. So even if your advocates do not support this or are willing to negotiate it away, do not let up on this point!" Nina's aggressive appeal to the base stiffened the spines of the negotiating teams. Some plantation owners resisted for days, lengthening the initial progress of the negotiation. But plantation owners relented. The negotiating teams were able to have these clauses worked into the final contract agreements.

This may not have happened were it not for Nina. Acting as an outside catalyst, her involvement improved the contract gains that workers achieved. The negotiating team may not have held out for as long as they did without the campaign that Nina waged. The leadership team received pressure from their workers to protect them from reprisals. This kind of "mutual influence" between grassroots movements and their leaders is often found in poor areas (Souza et al., 2021, 120). Nina did not see this point as idiosyncratic. Rather, Nina's view of the power that workers wield when they are on strike informed her actions. At a meeting of the worker leadership team, Nina defended her position:

We are simply asking the plantations to sign a document that states that the workers were involved in a peaceful action with no violent activities. Right now, the plantation owners depend on you and it is the only time that they will depend on you. As soon as you negotiate, you will depend on them. You should not go in there, into the negotiating room acting like there is no strike out there. You have the power. You have the plantation owners in your hands. I know it is difficult because all your lives you are accustomed to depending on them for your work and this is a different way of interacting with them. But remember that if you negotiate this without the language of 'no reprisals' and for only a modicum of advances, then you will be giving up all that you have struggled for.

The Doves also leveraged their international labor and human rights contacts. The major material benefit of this leverage came in the form of food aid. But it also resulted in visits from international observers. One group that the Doves contacted was the International Labor Organization (ILO). The ILO chose not to send a representative, but they did request regular updates. The Doves were also in contact with a prominent Washington-based organization that advised many Democrats on Latin American foreign policy. Among the visitors who came to the plantations was a German priest. He had been a longtime activist on human rights issues, especially in Colombia. He was present at a fundraising event for the workers at the Universidad del Valle. Here he gave a speech to a large crowd mixed with workers and students. The cleric glowed about Camilo Torres:

> It was over 55 years ago that I came to Colombia. At that time, they already were discussing social inequality. They were already talking about labor exploitation. And they were already advocating for uniting the workers. When Camilo Torres was in seminary, I was invited to come to Colombia. And Camilo invited me to give a talk to sociology students. Later, I came with him to struggles all over Colombia. He had the instruments to analyze society as a sociologist. He was not only seeing poverty. He was able to see that the structures needed to be changed. As a Colombian and as a member of this society, he felt a responsibility to change the society. And as a priest—as a Christian—he was committed to the struggles of the poor and the struggle of the workers. He did not see a contradiction between a radical analysis and Christianity.

The strength of these international networks raised the visibility of the movement, and with that, the cost of violent reprisals against workers. The Colombian government, aware of its poor human rights image, may be unwilling to create a reason for further scrutiny. Washington politicians opposed to Plan Colombia often cited human rights violations as a major reason to withhold support. Colombian labor strikes have a particularly violent history in the country. Hundreds, and in one case, over a thousand, workers have died in previous strikes.[7] But the sugarcane strike of 2008 recorded no deaths by comparison.

DOVE KNOWLEDGE

Akin to Russell's (1997 [1912]) "knowledge by acquaintance" and Villoro's (2002 [1982]) *conocer*, Colombians use the Castilian verb *conocer* to describe having spent time with a person or a place. They also use it to describe having spent time studying a topic, as in the phrase "to know ethnography." Hispanophones reserve *conocer* for knowledge gained from experience. To "know" abstract facts independent of personal experience is handled instead with the verb *saber*. The Spanish *saber* refers to cerebral knowledge. Workers experienced different forms of risk and used *conocer* when speaking of risk.

In contrast, the Doves experienced risk mainly through political action. Javier, Felipe, Nina, and other Doves had a relationship to risk during the strike that was a larger break from their everyday life. Their reactions to non-political risks are thus more expressive. *Conocer* and *saber*, or "to experience" and "to know," touch on classic debates about perception. They recall the Latin phrases *a posteriori* and *a priori*, or "after experience" and "before experience." But *conocer* and *saber* are more specific to ontological and sociological realities. *Conocer* and *saber*, or Russell's (1997 [1912]) knowledge "by description" and that "by acquaintance," allow us to conceive of the temporal dimension of knowledge. This is knowledge as experienced by imperfect sociological agents bound by ontological realities. The Doves know risk, for example, but do not experience it as a sugarcane worker. This *riesgo por saberdura*, or risk relying on description, is a 'calculated' and voluntary risk based on absorbed and assimilated descriptions of similar situations elsewhere. This process is quite different from that of workers, and it is also quite different from the risks of their everyday lives. This form of political action relies on the previous political action of others in the same way that description relies on the previous experience of others.

The Doves did not sleep in the Dickensian conditions of the workers, even during the strike. Even if they had, this acquired experience is incongruous with their everyday life. While workers would benefit from learning from comparative cases of poverty and political action, it is not necessary for workers to do so in order to grasp the concept of what it means to be engaged in 'high-risk activism.' This is not true of Felipe, Javier, and Nina, who do not experience this everyday risk. But rather than being a detriment, this incongruence is the source of the organizational heterogeneity that produced a resilient strike campaign.

CATALYTIC LEADERSHIP

The Doves were close advisors to the striking workers. This was so much the case that the Doves received thinly veiled accusations from government officials and media personalities of orchestrating the strike outright. It is an overstatement to say that the Doves organized the strike—they did not. Sugarcane workers had struck before and had begun to organize their subsequent strike before reaching out to allies. But if a counterfactual were available that did not contain involvement from the Doves, it is likely that the strike would have been shorter and less effective. The Doves helped to orient the worker leadership committee toward effective strategies. Such interventions led to new strategic possibilities. The Doves often steered debates away from in-fighting and toward productive conflict. They dissuaded workers from violence and introduced more nuanced avenues of attack.

But although the Doves had no direct leadership of the movement, they did diffuse themselves throughout the plantations to make direct appeals to striking workers. This involved an enormous commitment of time as the strike contained thousands of workers spread over a 45-mile stretch of the Cauca River. Outsiders may have perceived the Doves to be in control because the Doves were so often able to persuade workers and their leaders. But this persuasion relied on interpersonal trust built over time rather than a command structure. The Doves circulated throughout each of the plantations with ferocious regularity. Worker leaders, in contrast, focused on coordinating efforts at their individual plantations and on communicating those efforts with others at leadership committee meetings in Palmira. But it cannot be plausibly said that five or six individual Doves directed this entire area containing 8,500 workers. While their efforts were intentional, their impact was diluted. This impact, and perhaps also their conspicuousness, was made evident with the arrest of Felipe and Javier. Had the Doves been in direct control of the movement, the arrest of two of their principal operators in the strike would have decapitated the strike. As it was, Colombian authorities dealt a blow by hampering an effective movement *catalyst*. But workers continued their radical picket of plantation properties and the worker leadership committee continued to meet. The Doves were made targets perhaps not because they led the movement but Because there were so few of them, it was easy to turn them into targets.

Despite their numbers, the Doves were effective in reducing the amount of risk that workers exposed themselves to. Labor strikes in Colombia have a history of violent confrontations that both workers and the Doves were aware of. They are also aware that not all of these acts of repression, even in recent history, are well-publicized, or even well-documented. The Doves had convinced workers to cede space to the police on the plantations. Workers, instead, had intended and prepared for physical altercations. This intervention by the Doves, alone, might have prevented wider political violence. But the Doves also helped families navigate government bureaucracies to access needed resources. This resulted in health care services and food for needy workers and their families.

Some sugarcane workers, though a much smaller proportion, did spend time in jail. But workers exposed themselves to physical injury when engaging police at the plantations in a way that the Doves never did. The Doves, nonetheless, were targets for frequent police harassment when traveling between plantations. Workers, instead, dealt with the risk of living in proximity to security forces 24-hours a day during the strike. At the end of the strike, workers and their leaders remain living in the same area. But *catalytic leaders*[8] like the Doves move on to their next assignment. Should they continue in their work, they apply their gained experience to a subsequent movement. Most workers, in contrast, continue to live in the same environment where the strike took place. Even though Javier had twice been run of out of Cali for his political activities, the likelihood of the Doves facing social or political repercussions is likely not as high as that of similarly active workers.

Not all attempts to relate to workers were effective. The Doves often carried romantic notions of what it meant to be a sugarcane worker. On several occasions they the blared music of local artist Yuri Buenaventura from their car speakers. Although they did this for the benefit of workers, it did not seem to have much effect. This was despite the fact that Buenaventura wrote sympathetic lyrics. The first stanza of his song "Estan Quemando La Caña" (They're burning the cane) provides the representative sentiment (Bedoya 2000):

Los carros cañeros pasan llevando la caña brava
Y el campesino en bicicleta llorando, 'penas avanza

[*The sugarcane cars pass carrying the raw cane*
And the farmer on a bicycle crying, har'ly moving]

But the artist's musical style was different from the kind of music that these workers listen to. Traditionally, rural musical tastes in Latin America had been a "diverse repertoire of guitar-based music shared by rural musicians" (Pacini 1995, 11). In contrast, Buenaventura's *Nuyorican*-influenced salsa is more commonly associated with Cali's urban dance halls. Workers, also, do not own cars or sound systems from which to blare music. Such a display might seem abrasive to a rural working-class culture with Biblical values that include meekness and humility. The Doves and Buenaventura were also all mestizo or white. While well-meaning, such *afrophilic* (Gayles 2019, 2101) dynamics had the effect of accentuating differences between workers and the Doves. Buenaventura's song provides such an example (Bedoya 2000):

Color de piel bien negra y me da, el, la azúcar blanca
Cuida 'o que la vida es dura para el humilde que corta caña

[*Dark, black colored skin and, he, gives me white sugar*
B'ware, for life is hard for the meek who cut the cane]

The Doves were often deliberate about thinking through the consequences of their actions. But certain cultural differences prevented them from seeing the ineffectiveness of some behaviors. While actions like this fell flat, the Doves had generated enough goodwill among workers for them to willingly overlook such sentimentality. As outsiders, *catalytic* leaders may not be suited to lead incipient mobilizations outright. But grassroots leaders, through experience and training, can also serve as *catalysts* in other movements. As the strike progressed, sugarcane worker leaders adopted the skills that they learned from the Doves. Over the course of dozens of interactions, workers and the Doves became socially close.

CATALYTIC LEADERS

Leaders, formal or informal, are a necessary component of any movement's structure. Catalysts are not. But they do permit efficient expenditure of movement resources. The removal of leadership can often mean a precipitous end for a movement campaign. But this is not so for catalysts. Catalysts are expendable in the display of high-risk activism. The Doves did not introduce the idea of a strike to workers. Workers would have commanded the roads and engaged police with or without the Doves. But catalytic leaders can contextualize and capitalize on the leverage that high-risk activism provides. Nonetheless, they are not its fountainhead.

We may observe catalytic leadership in both social movements and revolutionary organizations. Javier and Felipe may have been inspired by reading about pre-revolutionary Bolsheviks travelling from one group of workers to another. These catalysts spread information and strategies from workers throughout Russia. The Bolsheviks transformed already-existing and isolated worker movements into a unified effort. But catalytic leaders need not articulate a revolutionary ideology. Ella Baker traveled to advise several local mobilizations during the U.S. Civil Rights Movement of the 1960s. Baker accumulated successful organizing skills through her active involvement in the NAACP for many years. By the time she arrived at SNCC, Baker had become a resourceful *catalyst*. Baker, like other catalysts, tended to be an outsider who was not herself a member of the local communities with which she served as an organizer.[9] Like other catalysts, Baker did not start movements—she improved their effectiveness.

Catalytic leaders are persons who have integrated disparate social movement knowledge and can apply it elsewhere. Grassroots movements invite them to assist with communities that they may not be familiar with. *Catalytic leaders* circulate movement knowledge among and between movements. They embed themselves into networks where their role can be impactful and in places where their skillset is not already present. *Catalytic leaders* are visitors and will usually leave after their role has ended. Catalytic leaders are connected to important actors in the field in which the incipient movement operates in or wishes to operate in. Catalytic leaders provide organizations with exogenous technical knowledge.

By borrowing expertise, the use of a catalyst is one way that a movement can increase its chances. The workers would have struck with or without the Doves. Tilly's (1996, 595–6) preference for a counterfactual is not available for the strike. But Tilly's preference is partially satisfied in the following chapter. Returning to the concept of the *emancipatory network*, I compare activist network arrangements in Valle del Cauca with those found in Bogotá. The comparison also illustrates the difference between knowledge by description and that by acquaintance.

The lack of an emancipatory network in Bogotá leads to uncoordinated action. To read about turn-of-the-century anti-globalization protests in Seattle and Washington, D.C. does not equate to the experience of mounted police charging in one's direction amidst a cloud of tear gas and expletives. Reading about Spanish *indignados* is not the same as hearing screams of terror echo down narrow passages.[10]

"Knowledge by description can be shared. No one, in turn, can know by acquaintance through a third party. Each person must acquaint themselves on their own account." (Villoro 2002 [1982], 211) Put simply, one can say that there is "general knowledge." But there is no such thing as "general acquaintance."

NOTES

1. An analogy might also be drawn to Gene Sharp's (1973) Albert Einstein Institution.

2. International Pan-Africanist groups, too, have been in in Choco, Cauca, and Valle del Cauca for decades (Ochoa 2019).

3. In fact, transmitting Marxist literature to rural agrarian populations is a long-standing tradition in Latin America (Linera 2021, 23). The student-influenced M-19 guerilla group is situated in the area around Cali (Carroll 2008, 12; Palacios 2012, 103), so such readings may not be unusual.

4. This is consistent with other depictions of the contemporary German anti-war movement (Leistner 2022).

5. At least a half-dozen different ad spots ran in the UK featuring "Pablo the Drug Mule Dog," beginning in 2008. Scussolini (2011, 50–1) analyzed the ads for their aesthetics and marketing effectiveness, noting the thinly-veiled reference to Colombia's Escobar. The campaign's Facebook page received "around 200,000 fan connections" before being deleted in 2010 (Rooksby and Sommerville 2012, 406). The campaign

won national awards in the UK and had been funded by agencies of the British government to the tune of £1 million, according to reporting from the *Independent* (2011) of London.

6. Mainstream media disinformation promotes the interests of capital, becoming a major problem for grassroots social movements whose interests may not align (Esparza 2022).

7. The sugarcane worker strike of 2008 took place on the eightiethanniversary of the "Banana Massacre" of 1928. Commemorations serve "not only to remember, but also to forge and strengthen political identities" (Díaz Jaramillo 2019). The United Fruit Company had refused to negotiate with striking workers. The Colombian military resolved the conflict by killing at least one-thousand workers (U.S. Embassy 1928, as cited in Farnsworth-Alvear, et al., 2017, 470).

8. This is different from Gramscian (1971 [1935]) organic intellectuals or Leninist (1988 [1902]) cadre groups. Organic intellectuals are those persons who arise from within the movement to provide intellectual fodder. They are intellectuals that arise from the working class, rather than those that trickle from or flirt with elites. Catalytic leaders by contrast, are not a part of the movement's grassroots. Cadre groups are professional revolutionaries, something that catalytic leaders need not be. Catalytic leaders are also different from bridge leaders (Robnett 1996). Bridge leaders are internal to the movement structure and are defined by what they do. In contrast, catalytic leaders are created by their biographical experiences.

9. There were many imparters of movement knowledge and creators of catalytic leaders in the U.S. Civil Rights Movement. The Southern Conference Educational Fund, for example, raised money to end segregation. Another, the Highlander Folk School trained important labor and civil rights leaders including both Rosa Parks and Dr. King (c.f. Andrews 2004).

10. Esparza, Louis Edgar. 2012. "Time to Strike: Cross-Europe Solidarity Forging a Path Out of Austerity." *In These Times*. 16 November.

Chapter 5

Bogotá

This chapter explores human rights activism in Bogotá. I contrast the organizational models and tactics used in Valle del Cauca with those of Bogotá activists. *Emancipatory networks* can be difficult to achieve and appeared to be absent in Bogotá. Activists of the capital city have some of the same necessary ingredients to form such a network—leaders, grassroots movement organizations, and local communities. But grassroots movements in Bogotá chose to engage in rent-seeking rather than challenging oligarchical structures. Some of Bogotá's movement structures illustrate a dependent relationship because their activities are contingent on the approval of external funders. As a result, these movements become concerned with securing funding to provide direct services rather than organizing communities to secure more ambitious aims. Nonetheless, rent-seeking organizations can face dire consequences for engaging in human rights work. Even office work is a high-risk activity, and death threats are commonplace for the staff of Colombian human rights organizations. I detail the stories of activists who received such death threats and share the text of two such threats that I received myself during the course of fieldwork in Bogotá.

I describe BOGDES (pseudonym), a coalition of grassroots organizations working with internally displaced people. I also identify and describe domestic and international human rights networks in the city. Lastly, I discuss the work of the Markhor Center (pseudonym), an anarchist organization that operates as a home to the Bogotá anarchist community. This anarchist organization serves as an example of the small, radical, and disconnected organizations that exist in Bogotá's movement ecosystem. With this comparative case, I am able to illustrate the efficacy of certain networked organizational forms, even while maintaining similar organizational components.

No less important, the chapter illustrates the risks that human rights organizations take during the course of their everyday work. I discuss Bogotá's international human rights community, with specific attention to domestic groups. One of these groups is the Coalition for Social Justice (CSJ) (pseudonym). With the assistance of strong international networks, this large national coalition of human rights organizations lobbies the Colombian government to pass legislative reforms. I illustrate how this coalition works with local civil society and grassroots movements to achieve its aims. Not surprising is that larger, more professionalized organizations in the coalition experience different kinds of challenges and risks than do the smaller grassroots groups. Organizational size influences organizational goals, tactics, and forms of expression. This comparison illustrates how dependent funding networks moderate tactics and goals.

Entering this world of human rights organizations in Bogotá was not straightforward. Activists sometimes display a healthy suspicion of eager newcomers. Particularly in high-risk contexts, the fear which undergirds this suspicion can be well-founded. Informants, moles, and provocateurs are common counter-movement strategies throughout the Americas (Cunningham 2003; Davenport 2007; Marx 1974). But this suspicion can sometimes cross into paranoia among activists (Becker 2021; Cunningham & Noakes 2008) and also among state agents (Mignone et. al., 1984). For activists, this error can occur when "giving too much credence to irrelevant cognitive cues" (Jasper 1998, 403). Gaining trust usually involves some amount of time and a degree of embeddedness in activist networks. I became the subject of a closed-door meeting about my admission into their spaces. I describe this experience of reaching a point where activists felt comfortable enough to share their spaces and their stories with me. I did not speak to persons with active relationships with guerrilla groups. I made it known to participants that I did not wish to have contact with individuals of this type. The United States designated the FARC as a foreign terrorist organization at the time of this study. This designation remained in place until the end of November 2021 (U.S. State Department 2021).

In previous chapters, I described an *emancipatory network* as a collection of people with varied resources that make a movement difficult to defeat. Such an arrangement speaks to the strength of movements to overcome great odds. But Bogotá's movement network arrangement prevented activists from coordinating in this specific manner. The presence of international funding distracts grassroots movements from such prefigurative goals. This funding creates incentives for grassroots groups to provide services rather than to organize. This incentivization, and resulting moderation in approach, stunts the ability of grassroots groups to organize their communities. Bogotá's communities of internally displaced people connect themselves to their community leaders. Local movement organizations that do exist in these communities are smaller and tend to be more radicalized. The community's leadership tends not to connect itself to these small, radical groups. They instead connect themselves to domestic and international human rights organizations that can provide resources. This is a significant detail, as great need exists among internally displaced people living in these communities. Human rights organizations directly employ some of the community's leaders and hire others to perform short-term projects. Community leaders, in turn, help human rights groups with distributing goods and services to internally displaced people.

Catalytic leaders are present and intervene where they can. They do so with community leaders because of their embeddedness in the communities. Community leaders bridge the gap between human rights groups and internally displaced people. These community leaders are overrun with administrative tasks. These duties distract them from being able to spend time developing prefigurative strategies. Catalytic leaders also cannot fulfil this role, despite their external connections. Catalytic leaders depend on community leaders for their community networks.

Nina, of the Doves, reappears in this chapter to work with Bogotá's internally displaced people. Radical anarchist movements attempt to make inroads parallel to these efforts. But these smaller, more radical groups attracted the most amount of police violence. Acting as a radical flank (McAdam 1996) against more moderate groups, their presence may have softened government resistance against the work of more moderate human rights organizations. But internally displaced activists from smaller organizations remained frustrated by the community's dependence on external resources. This dependency may dissuade community members from supporting actions that they may perceive as jeopardizing those resources.

MULTI-ORGANIZATIONAL FIELDS

I conducted semi-structured interviews and observations with various human rights groups in Bogotá.[1] These data inform a schema distinguishing between three broad and multi-organizational fields: international NGOs, local NGOs, and grassroots organizations. Some activists belonged to organizations sponsored by Colombian state agencies, United Nations agencies, or other international groups. Local organizations included both professional and grassroots groups (see Table 5.1).

Organizations with government or UN sponsorship included groups that collect data on the internal displacement of Colombians. These groups are the producers and gatekeepers of most Colombian human rights statistics.

Table 5.1   Characteristics of Different Types of NGOs in Bogotá

	Tactical Risk	*Organizational Capacity*	*Resources*
State/INGOs	Low	High	High
Professional NGOs	Medium	Medium	Medium
Grassroots	High	Low	Low

They publish many of the documents and reports on political violence in Colombia. The daily activities of activists at these organizations involved office work. They organize and clean data, draft reports, and organize events. They also respond to controversies in the news cycle through the issuing of press releases. Some of these externally funded groups also provided training to former guerilla and paramilitary fighters, aiming to integrate them into society. The organizations observed here include some of the most widely respected and well-funded human rights organizations in Colombia. These groups also tend to have broad international networks. Their staff includes professional workers with college and advanced degrees from Colombia and elsewhere. These organizations pay clerical staff and supply them with office space and computers. They also hire translators to translate their reports into English and French. The staff at these organizations tend to be familiar with each other and organize joint events. They often attend professional meetings and conferences alongside government agencies. These organizations tend to have good access to media organizations. To the extent that private companies become involved in philanthropic forays into the human rights field, these are the organizations that companies tend to work with. They use non-confrontational tactics and focus on peacemaking efforts. Peacemaking tended to be uncontroversial, as the popularity of violent guerilla groups had been low. Their critiques of government wrongdoing are moderate in comparison to some of the smaller grassroots groups. These organizations document human rights abuses, investigate media reports of abuses, and also parse reports from other human rights organizations that venture into the countryside. They organize conferences and issue press releases. These groups do not knowingly engage in high-risk mobilization. Rather, they behave much more like a think tank or policy group.

Local, professionalized groups without access to international funding hire from the best universities in the country. But they often comment on their not having enough staff. They did, however, generally have one person to run each particular program or research area. They also usually hire trained specialists in advanced analytic techniques. They have reasonable access to the media. Their access to government varies depending on how much they deviate from the government's position. They share the same goal to achieve a peaceful resolution to the country's long-running civil war. But they also tend to work on addressing poverty and internal displacement. These groups lobby the government to compensate displaced people for their lost property. This sometimes puts them at odds with government policies. Their daily tasks also involve office work and running integration programs for former combatants. These integration programs include mentoring, help with obtaining social services, and a curriculum for successful integration into society. These groups sometimes receive private grants. But many of them are membership organizations that depend on small contributions. Such groups must provide content to their members while also running programs. Like membership organizations elsewhere, they tended to limit their risk-taking activities (Barkan et al., 1993).

Grassroots groups such as BOGDES do not have a large organizational capacity. With few resources and low-paid or volunteer staff, some of these groups rely on one or two paid staff and part-time volunteers. But many grassroots groups do not have any paid staff whatsoever. Their offices are small. They are membership-driven and their members tend to be of modest means. Some are able to support staff through small domestic grants. These funding streams can sometimes be sporadic. Grassroots leaders of small organizations have less time to network with each other. They are not always aware of other groups doing similar work. Their interactions in coalition meetings tend to illustrate a homogenous network of relationships with other grassroots organizations that resemble themselves. They have few connections to professional, state-funded organizations. Their media contacts are also few. The goals of these organizations are disparate, but their politics are radical. Their organizational goals are sometimes ideological in nature, and they blame the government for rampant poverty. They tend to envision a socialist Colombia with a robust welfare state. Their daily interactions tend to be chaotic and disorganized. Meetings and events do not start at the scheduled time. Procedures and plans are taken as informal suggestions. Many of them are themselves displaced. Their personal lives oftentimes interfere with their activism. But they are more connected to the communities they serve.

Ishmael, one such activist, kept me waiting for an hour on one occasion. He later explained that he was delivering a bag of clothes to a woman who had arrived to Bogotá having fled her home. These kinds of emergencies often interrupt regular business. Their work consists of meetings and delivering goods into the communities they serve. They also organize marches and help people navigate government bureaucracies. Displaced persons often have to register with the government to receive assistance. This often involves replacing lost documents and other details.

Their strength, such as it is, comes from their ability to mobilize large numbers of people. In 2007, a coalition of grassroots groups launched a campaign for "Land, Life, and Dignity." This included a series of marches and sleep-ins in and around downtown Bogotá. Less organized movements may

Table 5.2   Types of NGOs in Bogotá

	Member-Driven	Resource-Driven
Organized	N/A	State/IGOs
Decentralized	Grassroots NGOs	Professional NGOs

more effectively adopt high-risk tactics (Gamson 1975; Piven & Cloward 1977), but employing such tactics sometimes invites repression from government and non-state actors. Their lack of resources puts these organizations in constant crisis (table 5.2).

INTERNALLY DISPLACED PEOPLE'S MOVEMENTS

I stumbled upon a rally on my way to the Luis Ángel Arango Library in Bogotá in July 2007. I noticed more than the usual number of police as I arrived at the library entrance that morning. I had been making daily visits to the archives of *El Espectador*, spending my days leafing through fifty-year-old stories. But today, the doors had been sealed. Bewildered, I looked around me and noticed a small group of about ten people. Judging from their clothes, they appeared to me to be displaced *campesinos*. Having been denied my mid-twentieth-century metropolitan news, I instead watched on in curiosity as these activists milled around, preparing posters and banners. After a few minutes, they walked away from the library in a group. On impulse, I decided to follow them. ("After all, I am a student of social movements," I thought. Here before me was a budding movement campaign.) But I had incorrectly assumed that the group was about to begin a demonstration. Hurrying, I followed as the group walked to a nearby breakfast shop where they met another thirty or forty people. Having caught up as they stopped for breakfast, I was finally able to satisfy my curiosity. I addressed an elderly woman, asking her if they were about to hold a demonstration in support of internally displaced people. She and others in the group looked at me with suspicion but replied: "¿Si, porque?" (Yes, why?) I replied that I was a doctoral student from New York, writing about human rights in Colombia. They immediately became very friendly, even competing with each other for attention. They saw me as someone who might do them some good in the world. Activists who have little access to public opinion are anxious to tell their war stories. These activists believe that professionals can represent them and their cause to outsiders. (Auyero 2001) In the experience of Winifred Tate (2007), Colombian activists believe that U.S. citizens can bring them resources and attention.

After breakfast, the group marched with increasing numbers to a community center. Here, a mass meeting had already begun. At this point, the demonstration grew to include approximately five hundred people. Talking to those around me, I became friendly with a young man from the original group, Carlos. He took an interest in me and shepherded me around. Like William Whyte's (1993 [1955]) key informant, "Doc," Carlos was essential for entering and navigating this world. He told me who the important people were and introduced me to those he could. I became part of the advance guard for the march, despite myself. One demonstrator handed me one end of a banner, and another pushed me into the street from behind. I helped to block streets as the demonstrators confronted oncoming traffic. I marched with the demonstrators as they walked through the city to the Plaza de Bolívar, Colombia's political center. The Palace of Justice, National Cathedral, Mayor's office, and Capitol building surround the plaza. Here, the crowd had grown so much that it was impossible to see the end of the marchers.

There were no incidents at this event. But these kinds of actions can be dangerous for participants. There was widespread concern about being singled out. Some had their faces covered with bandanas. Others turned their backs to police or held posters up to their noses when passing them. Demonstrators responded the same way when I raised my camera to take a

Figure 5.1 Riot Police Corral Protesters in Bogotá. *Source*: Photograph taken by the author in 2008.

photograph of the scene. Several activists had participated in a "sleep-in" in the Plaza the night before. Riot police had removed some of the occupiers by force.

Activists who take part in illegal activities often obscure their identities. This is to impede the ability of police to identify them. The fear is that police will use their images to form dossiers. Police could combine images with other information to disrupt protest activity.[2] Many police forces around the world use these tactics. This ability is now enhanced with the increased use of security cameras and facial recognition technology. (Zalnieriute 2022) COINTELPRO in the United States leveraged vast resources to spy on grassroots activists. (Churchill and Vander Wall, 1990) In Colombia, grassroots activists also have paramilitary organizations to fear. Paramilitary organizations oppose the goals of grassroots organizations. But they also use intelligence information to levy death threats against activists.

Internally displaced people in Bogotá do not live in UN camps, as they do in many parts of the world. Displaced people in the country often fend for themselves, living in the foothills that ring the city. Much like the favelas of Rio de Janeiro, their dwellers number in the millions. There are at least hundreds of community groups and associations in these areas. Many of these join together for public demonstrations. One of their major events is a "March on Poverty," which begins in the neighboring city of Soacha. The march ends at the Plaza de Bolivar in Bogotá's center. I joined this march as it left Soacha for southern Bogotá. The march blocked several lanes of traffic, and it was not clear that they had a permit to march.[3]

For the uninitiated, the contrast between Soacha's and Bogotá's downtown city centers is remarkable to witness. Dozens of women and children begged along Soacha's pedestrian bridges.[4] I passed five such families on one pedestrian bridge alone. Each one of these families included at least one child with at least one missing limb. FARC and ELN have planted most of the landmines found in Colombia. Colombia's Ombudsman's office counts "4,289 landmine accidents" between 1990 and 2009. These devices killed or injured "7,428 people, 34 percent of which were civilian."[5] Colombia's vice president's office also found paramilitary groups responsible for planting landmines.[6]

Such conditions create a desperate environment for the displaced. People in poor situations often come from areas where there is poor infrastructure. These areas are not well-equipped to handle acute weather events. Colombia experiences routine floods and other natural disasters. Humanitarian relief after these events tends to make local politicians popular. (Gallego 2018) But this dynamic incentivizes political inaction. The debilitating impacts of disasters are often exacerbated by poverty and pre-existing inequalities (Klinenberg 2002). Soacha experiences mudslides and flooding due to poor or non-existent drainage systems. This is also true of many of the shanty-towns ringing Colombia's major cities.

BOGDES: INTERNALLY DISPLACED
PEOPLES COALITION

I followed up with Carlos in 2008 to meet other human rights organizations in his network. But these organizations needed to agree to provide such privileged access. A coalition of human rights organizations held a closed-door meeting. I waited outside for twenty minutes as activists debated my observation of their work. Then, Carlos emerged from the conference room. He said to me, "We are not in agreement."

Without saying much else, Carlos hurried back into the room. Those few seconds in which the door remained open revealed what seemed to be a robust conversation. I continued to sit in the foyer for another twenty minutes. I had now read every article in every newspaper strewn across the coffee table. I stared out of the window into the Bogotá skyline. Finally, they invited me into the room. As I entered, a man wearing a tie walked out of the meeting. I came in, shook a few hands, and sat down. Jairo, who was chairing the meeting, announced that they would be allowing me to observe. They also allowed me to record their deliberations. I felt a bit guilty that I had become the focus of an internal controversy. I made sure to communicate that I would stop if anyone felt uncomfortable. But the activists insisted that I stay.

I was never made privy to what took place behind those closed doors. No one explained who the man in the tie was or why he left as I walked in. I was not told why they seemed so ready to accept me after their discussion. What was unmistakable was that I had altered their normal operation. I was the cause of a tension that resulted in one of the members leaving the room. I could not be sure that the remaining members had used me as an excuse for a power play. But, I felt confident that activists themselves had made these decisions. I had not introduced any ideas or meaningful risk to their operations. They might have seen a potential benefit in my observation. Colombian activists often wish to spread their message and secure international partners (Tate 2007).

Death Threats

Those in my research networks were concerned about my safety. Research in conflict zones comes with some degree of risk. Those concerns were not unfounded. It is possible to conduct research even in active war zones (Goodhand 2000). But it is difficult, if not impossible, to remain neutral in these situations (Esparza 2012a). Conflict makes the research taxing and presents a host of problems (Wood 2006). There is still "great heterogeneity" in reviewing ethical guidelines in these environments (Mezinska 2016, 9). It would be important for me to protect the anonymity of activists. I tried to keep a low profile to protect their safety and mine.

One of those threats to safety would come in the form of death threats. These are commonplace for human rights activists in countries like Colombia (c.f. Monje 2018, 33; 36). These threats can range from mild harassment to real threats leading to murder. Regardless of the severity of the threat, these dampen activist efforts. Death threats mean to intimidate people into abandoning their work.

But Jairo revels in telling me about coolly dispatching harassing phone calls:

> There was one guy that said in the background, 'No man, that's not the guy, no. Not that guy.' So I said, 'Come, come, don't hang up on me. Come, who are you?' He said, 'That doesn't matter.' I said, 'Well tell me where you are, and I will go so that we can get to know each other. Yes? So that we can get to know each other, so we can, so we can see each other. Tell me where you are. Or I can tell you where I'll be coming out and we can meet there.' *Click*, he hung up. When I spoke to the other one later [in a subsequent phone call], the other one would say, 'See, that's not the guy. He is not the guy. He's not, not.' They stopped fucking with me. But in about another fifteen days, [he called] again. [He said,] 'So what's up, pal?' I said to him, 'How are you doing, sir? In the first place, I am not your pal. In the second place, you are a gentleman who deserves my respect, but I do not know who you are, I would like to know your name.' I said it just like that—calmly.

Jairo received three such calls in the few days between setting up our interview and the time we spoke. After our interview, Jairo brought the matter up with other activists during a meeting. Jairo and Susana defended this fearless approach to handling harassing phone calls:

Susana: One should not show fear.
Jairo: Nothing of that.
Susana: Never.
Jairo: So one guy he says to me, 'Oh, well you sure are smooth and fresh.' I told him, 'Well, in my land they taught me that one should be as fresh as lettuce and as smooth as a pomp.' [*Jairo clasps his hands*] So he says to me, 'What's a pomp?' I told him, imagine this, 'The pomp is when one is pompous, see? In a good sense?' So he tell me, 'Oh, okay, good, my brother, good.' *Click*, he hung up on me. So then that is when the threats started against me at the office.

Marta: They started calling me on 13 March. That night they called me at 7pm. Five times. From the FARC.

Jairo: Sometimes they call and they don't say anything.

Susana: Really?

This sharing of stories of harassment is a form of mutual support. It helps activists continue their work despite the intimidation. I asked Marta about her experience during a private interview after this exchange. She told me,

> [The FARC] had kidnapped my brother, his wife and their little girls. Exactly one month later they found my father. He was the one who organized the displaced people in that community. That was the profile of the type of people that they went after. And they started with me and they were going to do things to me. Well, then they guaranteed that they were not going to do anything to me, that they accepted me. That they accepted the organizations, that they accepted, so . . . I said, 'What is going to happen to my family?,' 'Don't worry,' they said, and then they started [the harassment]. And then, on the other side the AUC started. That they were going to assassinate me because I was funding the FARC. No! So they called my landline and then later they assassinated my brother. Then I decided that I had to be here in Bogotá to be more protected. A month after being here, I encountered one of these guys. Two blocks from the Ministry of Interior. That he worked there that he knew who I was and he says to me, 'That's your daughter, right?' And what was I supposed to say, he already knows that it is my daughter. I said, 'Yes.' Five days later they were sending me death threats here in Bogotá. What am I going to do to see if it is for real? But I sincerely doubt it.

Marta was being squeezed from both sides, from leftist guerrillas and right-wing paramilitaries. She fled her home to escape the violence that took her brother's life. Activists often receive these sorts of threats in the course of their work. But they often shrug them off once they are in Bogotá. The police often are not successful in following-up with these threats. Long-term fear can take a toll and may alter the way activists experience their adopted city.

Threats against Me

I, too, received death threats during the course of this fieldwork. Activists invited me to an event denouncing human rights violations by corporations. They called it a "Permanent People's Tribunal," and activists modeled it after the Bamako Appeal.[7] They formatted the event as a "trial." Participants would present evidence against multi-national corporations that violated their human rights. The National University in Bogotá hosted the Tribunal. They booked the event in an auditorium. But the number of attendees soared so high that they moved the event to a conch shell stadium. Thousands from around the country filled the soccer stadium for three days. Activists included a coalition of indigenous peoples, labor activists, and other non-profit groups.

Dozens of groups presented their testimony. Much of the testimony touched on familiar notes: harassment, intimidation, theft, and murder. This kind of widespread repression is difficult to prosecute in Latin America (Lessa 2021). Legal resistance against human rights violations, even against brutal dictatorships, is often stiff (Mignone et al., 1984).

Activists registered their names, state ID, email address, phone number, and organizational affiliation. Volunteers typed this information into a database held on a laptop. Only then could participants enter the stadium. The laptop went missing in the late afternoon on the first day of the Tribunal. This took place after nearly all participants had registered. An organizer commandeered the microphone. He announced over the loudspeaker that this laptop had gone missing. A shocked crowd speculated amongst themselves. The organizer surmised that either the police or paramilitary were responsible for the theft. He explained over the microphone that they would have an interest in having this list.[8]

In order for me to enter this activist space I had to register like everyone else. By doing so, I fell victim to the same risk as others. In the following weeks I received two death threats to my email address from the Black Eagles paramilitary group's Metropolitan Bogotá Bloc. The first one read, "They pass themselves off as displaced but are guerillas. For that reason, we declare you to be a military target of the Black Eagles." This text was accompanied by a picture of a pile of bones mixed with posters of the political party *Unión Patriótica*. One of the posters read, "I am a survivor of the genocide against the *Unión Patriótica*." A second one read, "The genocide against the *Unión Patriótica* is a state crime." The other posters were photographs of slain members of the *Unión Patriótica*. Below this picture appeared the words, "This is how you are going to end up, like these ex-guerilla bastard sons of bitches. You will be next."

The second death threat was titled "Death to the Leaders of the March for Peace, and the Guerrillas, and their auxiliaries." The first two lines were identical to those of the first death threat. What then followed was the following: "You used the march held on 6 March of this year to sink us more and to put the people against us. We will begin to kill you one by one. We will be implacable. We will leave no knot untied. We know that on 14 March you will carry out a march against us. We will be monitoring your activities. Beware, sons of bitches, because your days are numbered. We will begin to disappear Leftist leaders such as [. . .]." The death threat then listed 28 names and ended with, "and others who are on our list. We are still here. Black

Eagles, with one step toward the future!" I soon began to receive harassing phone calls to my home. These calls came in without cease until I disconnected the line. I moved out of that location to continue my fieldwork in Valle del Cauca a few months later.

It is impossible for ethnographers of high-risk activism to differentiate oneself from one's research respondents. One's lot is one with them; by being with them, one is also sharing and experiencing their risks. But this blurred boundary also helps to build trust with activists.

The level of risk being what it is, Bogotá's activists are less prone to risk than their rural counterparts. National government agencies and international organizations are not far away. Some of these are not embedded in communities, nor do they take part in public demonstrations. Movement scholars typically think of social movements as "collectivities acting with some degree of organization and continuity outside of institutional or organizational channels for the purpose of challenging or defending extant authority, whether it is institutionally or culturally based, in the group, organization, society, culture, or world order of which they are a part" (Snow et al., 2004). But groups vary in the degree to which they act outside of institutional channels. This variation is important when thinking about risk.

INTERNATIONAL INFLUENCE

This variation was also important for grassroots activists in Bogotá. Internally displaced people debated the extent of the influence of funding agencies. They believed that funding agencies steered community organizations away from disruptive tactics. UNHCR (United Nations High Commissioner for Human Rights) organized a series of workshops designed to support Bogotá IDPs. When Tomas, a representative from UNHCR, walked into the conference room on one of these occasions, one activist joked, "The money has arrived." The turn in the conversation from human rights issues to funding was quick. Nina admonished, "Organize yourselves and you will get money." Jairo said, "We might be better off without the money, actually, because over that money there could be people dead." The room roared with laughter. Jairo rejoined plainly, "I am serious!" Word spreads in poor communities when someone receives a windfall. This can lead to jockeying to hire certain individuals for specific projects. Some begin to propose initiatives that may be of benefit to a select few.

Jairo's organization receives funds from government and non-governmental sources. One day, an activist from another grassroots organization came into the office. With him was a woman whose husband, we soon learned, had been killed. Jairo lacks formal advanced education and training. But he demonstrated intimate knowledge about the laws pertaining to her case. Another activist in the room pointed out Jairo's unexpected expertise. Jairo retorted, "I did not dedicate myself to throwing rocks. I dedicated myself to defending myself. And up until today, it has served me well." Grassroots leaders are the local experts in their communities. They help others access resources and navigate government bureaucracies. Displaced people in need of help often seek out people like Jairo.

This coalition of organizations situated themselves in an office space paid for by an external grant. But they did not have the resources to furnish or maintain the space. Doors often did not have knobs or were otherwise difficult to lock or unlock. This sometimes interfered with meetings. At one of the meetings I observed, no one could figure out how to open the door. We had to sit on the floor outside of the conference room for our meeting. They rented any technological equipment that they needed. What passed for a projection screen was in fact the backside of a framed canvas. A motley collection of furniture sat stacked along the back of the conference room. Participants often fussed with the office environment to conduct meetings. This contrasted with the spectacular view of Monseratte from the wrap-around corner-office windows. A piece of quartz, one square-foot in diameter, sat on the floor as a doorstop. Bullet holes decorated the office façade window. According to activists, the previous tenant had been a jewel dealer. Presumably, he had experienced a robbery attempt.

At one meeting, activists discussed then-U.S. presidential candidate Barack Obama. Carlos called him "Paracobama," "paraco" being derogatory slang for paramilitary. Carlos used this term to equate Obama's politics with that of the paramilitary. Carlos was the president of UNIAFRO [pseudonym]. This Bogotá-based group focuses on Afro-Colombian human rights issues. I asked Carlos about his use of this term, and he seemed thrilled that I took an interest in this. Others in the office seemed uneasy as he spoke to me, "Paracobama is basically the same as Bush, is he not? Nothing is going to change on U.S. policy towards Colombia. Why should I support a black *paraco* over a white *paraco*? They're all bad. I haven't heard anything new." Carlos is expressing his lack of trust in U.S. leadership. He justifies this by appealing to past experience with previous U.S. administrations. Internally displaced activists often expressed skepticism about the role of the U.S. government. This skepticism also applied to pro-U.S. Colombian officials.

Community leaders are often invited to governmental and NGO events. Some were invited to the opening of a new branch of a social services office for displaced people. Mayor Samuel Moreno and other city officials were in attendance. Mayor Moreno belonged to the liberal party, *Polo Democratico*. But Carlos and other activists attending this event were critical of his administration. This despite the fact that their organizations receive funding from the Mayor's office.

One grassroots activist spoke at a meeting about how he feels that non-profits exploit displaced persons: "I went to [HESDOC] and they said, oh, can you collect this information for me? So we do, and they don't pay us anything. But they get paid, so why shouldn't we if we are doing their work? But we are not even working ourselves." HESDOC [pseudonym] is a Colombian non-profit that collects demographic data. They asked him to go into his community to collect data via a questionnaire. It often will make sense for many non-profits to work with displaced activists in this way. Internally displaced activists have the trust of local communities. But this activist expresses resentment. Payment poses its own set of problems, as Jairo illustrated earlier.

ACTIVIST KNOWLEDGES

The relationship between Nina and internally displaced activists was not always smooth. My field notes on one day bear this out: "I went to the BOG-DES offices today. Jairo announced that he had canceled the workshop that was to take place. Nina is sick from her recent trip near Valledupar [along the border region with Venezuela], visiting with an indigenous group. Jairo said he thought it was malaria." This illustrates how dependent BOGDES was on Nina, even refusing to meet on their own. Jairo did not have enough buy-in from these different groups to hold a meeting without Nina. Each activist in the coalition had their own community groups and agendas to manage. If the groups were not going to receive training from Nina, then they felt that they had no need to be there. Some members complained that they were not told about the cancellation in advance. But on a similar occasion, weeks earlier, Jairo had not cancelled the meeting. He even managed to convince activists to stay. But the meeting produced infighting about having to meet rather than meaningful results.

Nina admonished IDP activists upon her return. She recited the importance of having a clear vision and mission statement. She also emphasized the importance of organizing across their groups. The meeting was particularly well attended after Nina's hiatus. Nina gales:

> Millions of pesos are given to Colombia to deal with the displaced problem and what have we got? The government is afraid of organized people, in particular organized displaced people. If you do not organize and if you do not organize well, then you will not get what it is that you want. The skills are simply not here. I would never approve your project because it is not realistic, it is too

expensive, the objectives are not the objectives that we have for displaced people, and you don't even justify them or even make them clear, for that matter.

One problem is that activists may become cozy with government officials and non-profits. Some prefer receiving funds rather than being in the communities. Nina argues that the government is monopolizing the grant money. She wants displaced activists to compete for poverty alleviation funds. "We cannot own the problem because we are not organized," Nina insists. "Let's change that."

But Nina also encouraged activists to demand funds from the government. Nina argued that their goal is not to improve the community, but to force the state to improve the community. This seems to contrast with the strategy that Nina and the Doves advocated in Valle del Cauca.

But several activists appreciated what they viewed as a professionalizing process. Nina, and Tomás from UNHCR during his brief visits, delivered informative workshop presentations. They emphasized the need to make objectives measurable, attainable, specific, and appropriate. They encouraged activists to provide a realistic timeline to attract more funding. Winifred Tate also describes an emphasis on professionalization in Colombian human rights organizations. This has been the case since the 1990's. Tate (2007, 109) describes what this means for grassroots activism:

> The transformation of solidarity organizations linked to social movements into professionalized NGOs was the most important institutional shift of the 1990's. This shift involved myriad changes on multiple levels. The organizational structure changed as new resources allowed for paid staff rather than volunteers. Increasing staff specialization meant organizational hierarchies, including salary differentiation, which exacerbated class tensions. Some groups received more international funding than others, setting up rivalries, competition, and class tensions between organizations. The need for accountability to donors led to new institutional practices involving staff supervision, fund-raising and proposal development, evaluation and accounting procedures, and operational changes. Groups were required to submit work plans outlining objectives and delineating measurable outcomes (with specific indicators) and schedules. The availability of international funding allowed some groups to expand their focus in certain areas but forced cutbacks in others and in some cases brought about the redirection of mandates and work.

Grassroots activists often ignore these trends—or are not aware of them. International funding instead goes into expanding professionalized, hierarchical non-profits. But even non-profit activists confront an imposed logic of being representatives from a "developing country" when attending international conferences (Rajão and Duarte 2018).

HUMAN RIGHTS ORGANIZATIONS

The weekly meetings of the Coalition for Social Justice (CSJ) are a class-segregated admixture. This is an accomplishment in Bogotá, a city that is itself class-segregated. Between twelve and thirty members shuffle in on Wednesday mornings. They take turns as they announce their group's events for the week. CSJ was a coalition of about 160 organizations at the time. Some of these groups file reports with state officials or to foreign ambassadors. Others file their minutes with judges or international agencies. And still others announce their marches or food distribution programs. This part of the meeting is usually devoid of substantive discussion. There was but one notable exception during months of fieldwork.

During that meeting, a grassroots activist from outside of Bogotá detailed the plight of an Afro-Colombian community in the north of the country. The presenter explained that this community was in need of help. This announcement received no feedback. The presenter became impatient and sharp. He asked CSJ members why they even bother to make these announcements. He admonished them for not supporting each other. The others became defensive. Many of them run their own organizations, one explained. Another said that it is difficult to find free time to go to other people's events. A third added that it is difficult for people to make it to events outside of Bogotá.

This kind of frustration is usually reserved for the funders. But sometimes, smaller groups will chide the larger organizations for their perceived inaction. At another meeting, a grassroots activist from the Afro-Colombian Choco region pleaded for CSJ to use their organizational power to attract media attention to their large regional event. She also requested that the organization send delegates. She feared that paramilitaries might try to harass local activists if there were no outsiders present. Members retreated to the coalition's usual promotional role: producing press releases. One explained that they work on policy, organize workshops, and meet with government officials. They do not confront armed actors.

This kind of response is understandable. But it can also be frustrating for grassroots activists, one of which accused members of turning CSJ into nothing more than an "ornament." Like so many arguments, this one ran much deeper than the subject under discussion. This was not so much about NGO attendance at grassroots events. Rather, this was an expression of ongoing tensions between NGOs and grassroots groups. A heterodox space was important for generating a consensus on human rights. But competing organizational interests and varied individual experiences and backgrounds can lead to difficult communication. As a result, the coalition offers a great deal of autonomy to the various groups and individuals. Member organizations work alone or in concert with a small network of others. The result is that the larger, better organized NGOs build influential relationships. NGOs have more time and resources to influence the development of CSJ meeting agendas. They also make disproportionate use of CSJ resources.

Indeed, the NGOs and CSJ always sent the morning's agenda by email in the afternoon on the day before the meeting. CSJ has paid staff members that are responsible for this, among other coordinating tasks. CSJ hires staff according to designated job descriptions. The organization specifies the finite responsibilities of staff. This is one mechanism by which NGOs prevent CSJ staff from fulfilling some of the requests of grassroots groups.

CSJ tasked a dedicated staff person to run the meetings. The group made regular use of projection, Wi-Fi, and computer technology. During a typical meeting, it was not uncommon to see up to a third of the room working in front of their laptops. Meetings were also catered, with a waitstaff that distributed the morning's breakfast.

Most members appeared aesthetically indistinguishable from their government and international counterparts. This only added to the conflict with grassroots groups who come from limited means. But they also shared important grievances against the government. For example, one common point of conflict between CSJ and the government was about how to frame human rights issues. Julio raised the issue of the use of the term "armed conflict" as a cause of displacement. Armed actors are the main drivers of emigration from the countryside. But the government wanted to use the word "violence" instead. This more general term diverts attention from the culpability of paramilitary forces. It is also more consistent with how the government generally frames the discussion. Julio felt that this term did not reflect the true reality of what is taking place—the eviction of *campesinos*. "Violence" is vague, he argued, and its use makes it more difficult to identify solutions. Julio felt that the government did not want to admit to the real problem, joking, "They might as well say that people are displaced by violence of their own invention! Where else is this violence coming from if not the armed conflict?"

CSJ members were also sometimes disappointed with their interactions with the United Nations (UN). They complained that the UN would often co-opt their community development plans. The UN would task CSJ to develop a program to distribute goods in the community. The CSJ would then use their grassroots networks to develop a detailed distribution plan. The UN would then put the program into place. Afterward, the UN opens the program up for NGOs to comment. But many CSJ members complained that they would rather have the UN treat them as an equal partner. Since they were the ones responsible for developing the program, they argued, they should also be the ones to run it. NGOs compete to win contracts to carry out parts of the program. By opening up the program for comment after implementation, CSJ members now had to compete to run programs that they had designed.

CSJ activists find the UN to be inefficient. One CSJ activist described that a particular UN program had divided its office work according to "regions." But these regions did not correspond to the political divisions in the country. "That is not how the government, or the cultures, or civil society is organized! This does not make any sense for how to help people," she said.

Sometimes the discussions drifted into the minutia of Colombian human rights law. This involved the use of specific legal language. Several NGO representatives around the table were themselves lawyers or were otherwise well-versed. But these discussions tended to exclude grassroots activists. Grassroots activists often remained silent during such discussions. When they did speak, they would often preface their comments, qualifying their statements and pointing to their limited knowledge of the law.

Yet, some activists do use CSJ to their advantage. One grassroots activist from Choco was working on reducing poverty in Afro-Colombian regions. She said to those gathered, "I am afraid that the government will say that they have already paid reparations and that they therefore won't give us anything else. You know how agile the government is." Julio also noted the same problem. The government can and often does water down the language in draft documents, he agreed.

There was near-universal agreement among CSJ activists about the paramilitary. Most believed that the paramilitary are not honest actors in the conflict. In their view, the government is not aggressive enough in prosecuting known crimes. One activist asked at a meeting, while complaining of government inaction, "Why did some paramilitary group dissolve in some area? Because they genuinely believe in peace and justice and demobilization? Or because they have achieved their objectives of displacing the *campesinos* from that area?" Demobilizing paramilitary combatants receive government funds and administrative support. But some activists are suspicious of government motives. Funds to incentivize demobilizing actors are disproportionate to that available to displaced persons. This was a common complaint of grassroots activists for displaced people. Another activist added, "The reason why the paramilitaries demobilize and the guerrilla do not is because the paramilitaries have achieved power. They control half the country. The guerrillas do not. That is why the paramilitaries have demobilized and the guerillas are still in the jungle."

This analysis brings up an important cleavage between human rights and peace movements. Both sides advocate for the demobilization of all non-state forces. But human rights activists link this issue with issues of injustice and inequality. Human rights groups tend to advocate for humanitarian re-settlement and social reforms. These would address some of the FARC's concerns. But many peace groups do not place such conditions on achieving peace.

Not all CSJ activists were critical of the government. Once, one member admonished the others about the "inflammatory tone" of the conversation. "We should mention what the government has done so that we are not always asking and demanding, but also assessing," she said. Some CSJ staff complained about the quality of human rights data in rural areas of Colombia. NGOs collect much of this data. Some areas of the country have large concentrations of NGOs, while other areas have few. This makes it difficult to create and assess comparative data across regions.

CSJ activists were deliberate about the language and framing of human rights issues. This is especially true when negotiating with the government. Ahead of a meeting with one government agency, a CSJ sub-committee debated the contents of a report. Addressing the issue of poverty, one activist argued that the proposed document states that Colombians are not "poor," but rather are "impoverished." This individual wanted to draw attention to the determinants of poverty and not to "the poor" as a political identity. There was also tension around economic development projects. One Choco activist argued, "What multinationals do is displace people in order to put development into effect." For her, the government's drive to develop is the cause of the displacement. The presence of paramilitary is a symptom of this drive for development.

The process of approving reports is a contentious one. Tensions arise between committee recommendations and the CSJ body as a whole. Some organizations have little staff or resources to commit to CSJ matters. These groups often have reservations about the language produced in committee. Andreo, a representative from a *campesino* organization, was one such individual. He interrupted one meeting, prefacing his critique with, "I would like to throw some meat on the table, since this conversation seems a little anemic." Although Andreo went on to raise several important issues, the group backed the committee's document. This was often the outcome, as committee members were also among the most active CSJ members. But this also contributed to mistrust from smaller, grassroots organizations.

This was so much so that Andreo began to challenge the committee structure itself. This time, others also backed his intervention. Most, though not all, of his backers were other grassroots activists. "Even though we do not have resources, we produce," said Andreo about his organization. "Our organizations are not isolated. They are embedded in communities." Andreo solicited a response from a professor from Bogotá University [pseudonym]. She represented a women's NGO and was a CSJ trustee. "Our documents are not created solely in the organization's committees," she said, "we are opening it up here in this space for you to comment on." The professor then attempted to steer the conversation back toward the agenda. But Nadia, the representative from a grassroots Afro-Colombian organization, intervened. She said, "In the whole year, I think this is the most useful conversation we have had, so let's not rush. I don't think it is so bad if we go over time today."

This tension has implications for the production of human rights knowledge. NGOs represent few people when compared to grassroots organizations. But their influence is disproportionate. NGOs also make disproportionate use of the organization's resources. This is due to the organization's structure, which privileges meeting attendance.

CSJ generally uses parliamentary procedure. But they become more flexible when grassroots organizations question this process. This occurs because CSJ derives its legitimacy from its members. Creating "buy-in" can be difficult, even in organizations that use a consensus process (Polletta 2002). This democratic tension is necessary for participants to feel that they have some agency.

GRASSROOTS GROUPS AND NON-GOVERNMENTAL ORGANIZATIONS

The conversation is often dominated by the voices of those representing larger NGOs. Even the topics of conversations were often accessible only to NGO representatives. Just about every meeting featured ample speculation and gossip about the interactions between NGO representatives and government officials. Grassroots groups have little access to government and do not take part in these exchanges. On one particular day, an NGO representative said to the room, "Akiko [pseudonym] at the Japanese embassy was curt with me last night," sparking a conversation about tact and negotiating strategies with embassy staff. Social capital seemed to play some role in excluding people from these spaces. Modesty and decorum can have a place in the activist repertoire. But grassroots activists attended these meetings to provide their perspectives rather than to be genteel. Grassroots activists are more used to taking an adversarial stance, using protest and disruption to achieve their movement's aims. These are sometimes at odds with more conciliatory approaches. But sometimes these exchanges provide useful context for grassroots groups. A subsequent meeting provides the example of Cecilia recalling a discussion with government officials in Sierra Nevada. She said that the government representative called NGOs "enemies of the state." Cecila pushed back, saying, "These are the kinds of comments that put us at risk."

International NGOs often pressure Colombian NGOs to work on their international priorities. One CSJ staff person explained that he was being lobbied to work on the banning of landmines. An international NGO had offered to provide funding for a CSJ member organization to dedicate itself to this task. "The problem," this staff person said, "is that there are no organizations in Colombia that work only on the issue of landmines." NGOs making up the international human rights regime often have their own priorities. This means that their agenda does not always reflect local priorities.

Landmine injuries and deaths in Colombia are a problem worth working to address. Many Colombian landmines are the result of left-wing guerrilla activity. Landmines make inexpensive munitions, making them a common weapon. The Colombian military benefits the most from the banning of landmines. They must navigate guerrilla landmines in dense jungle forests. Many local human rights groups are ambivalent about helping the Colombian military. Their priorities are in ending paramilitary violence against *campesinos*, re-settlement, and poverty alleviation. The banning of landmines is a complimentary but peripheral issue from their perspective.

Another example of a topic mainly of interest to larger, more organized NGOs was the World Social Forum. Lacho brought up the topic, the 2007 World Social Forum meetings in Nairobi having recently taken place. Only the academics in the room seemed to show interest in the discussion. Few others knew many details about it, grassroots activists least of all. Grassroots organizations concerned themselves with immediate needs in their local communities. At the next meeting, Lacho came into the room wearing a 2006 World Social Forum t-shirt that he purchased in Caracas. Walden Bello (2007) captures the tensions that led to the eventual demise of the Forum. Among the tensions was a kind of "travel activist" culture that is found among some middle-class activists (Esparza & Price 2015; Esparza 2023b). Santos (2006), however, saw the Forum as having great potential for the translation of different knowledges.

On occasion, CSJ would host an outside speaker at their regular meeting. These events usually took place at the insistence of a member NGO. One of these speakers was a representative from a prominent British NGO who had recently published a book. Four staff assistants flanked him as he entered the room to deliver his talk. The room was full beyond capacity and was by far the most popular meeting during my fieldwork. Activists and NGO representatives had anticipated the talk for weeks. The author focused his remarks on the Group of Eight and the international political order. "The goal," he said, "is not to fight against the government or against multinational corporations, but to develop public responsibility and demand transparency and democratic processes."

Only the academics and a handful of NGO representatives in the room engaged the speaker. His message seemed not to resonate with most, least of all the representatives from grassroots organizations. Many remained silent, even distracted. This had been a much-anticipated event. But no one said a word after the author's departure. The agenda marched along to the next item as if the speech had never taken place.

CSJ sometimes organizes and hosts workshops in Bogotá. These become important spaces for grassroots theorizing about social movement strategy. At one such event, a grassroots activist presented his views on movement strategy. He argued that international organizations put pressure on Colombian activists to make unwanted compromises. He outlined several risks associated with acquiescing to the government's position:

1) *The government can use the negotiations as evidence that they are receptive to human rights concerns.* This is enough to delay progress nearly indefinitely, allowing the government continue its current practices;
2) *Social movement mobilization becomes stalled.* Because issues will become fragmented and worked upon separately, social movements will find it harder to crystallize around specific points since the government can always effectively sidestep concerns by stating that they are being addressed in negotiations with the NGOs;
3) *The government wins the public debate.* The government is adept at spinning human rights rhetoric in their favor to reflect policies that they support or can at least tolerate. They may be able to do this successfully before social movements are able to frame the public debate. Since the government has superior access to the media and to other organizations, they are better able to implement a proactive strategy here;
4) *A plan that is bad for human rights could be implemented, and worse, with our consent.* This could deflate the movement, which would have put an enormous amount of time, hope, and creative energy into the process. NGOs are inadequately accountable to grassroots movements, and they should not monopolize the process;
5) *A plan that is good for human rights could pass but may not be implemented.* Although this can be used as a rallying point by movements, it further delays the implementation of human rights and it also puts social movements in danger because they have to mobilize against the government in order to force implementation;
6) *Participation could result in divisions between social movements that support and those that do not support the negotiations.* Clearly, this would complicate both the movement and the process to attain human rights;
7) *Negotiations are hijacked by elites.* Once the appearance of legitimacy is established in the negotiations, social movements could be crowded out by NGOs and other elites. They may then dictate the terms of an agreement on our behalf.

This list is a strategic outline for grassroots movements. Such sentiments were often expressed by grassroots organizations in CSJ. But this is the first time that one of the activists had organized and packaged them. The NGO representatives challenged many of the points on this list. After several verbal exchanges, the NGOs remained unpersuaded. But many grassroots organizations were supportive of this outline.

Human rights activists often complain that paramilitaries attend these workshops. They fear that paramilitaries will single people out for their outspokenness. One of the speakers during this workshop stated this from the stage: "There were national as well as regional threats made by the Black Eagles against organizations, including organizations present here today. This means we have to be deliberate about safety of people involved in these organizations. We must be very conscious of safety. The government needs to give guarantees about our safety in this process. Not just police presence, but political guarantees that give us explicit legitimacy and expressions of faith. The president, one minute is pro-human rights, when it suits him, and the next minute he is not. In a couple of weeks, he will be anti-human rights again."

Both NGOs and grassroots groups were skeptical of the government's commitment to human rights. The government does sometimes take policy positions in favor of human rights reforms. But they also accuse NGOs and grassroots organizations of supporting the FARC. Many activists feared that some of the president's statements give paramilitaries license to attack them.

Both CSJ and Koronos [pseudonym] are important fixtures in Colombian human rights networks. They provide important interventions that improve people's lives. Their tension with grassroots movements is a tension about differing views on representation. Each believes that they are the true guardians of the public interest. For NGO actors, "civil society" is composed nearly entirely of themselves. Leading human rights scholars also tend to equate "civil society" with the population of NGOs (Jordan and van Tuijl 2006). But grassroots activists define civil society as the grassroots. They believe that NGOs are, at best, imperfect conduits of public interest. Grassroots activists tend to use NGOs to extend their reach and to secure funding. NGOs tend to value the legislature's deliberative process as the pinnacle of Colombian democracy. For grassroots activists, democracy is a process that is *disarticulated* (Touraine 1985, 754) from the state.[9] Both agree that strengthening the role of civil society enhances the democratic process in the country. But they disagree on what exactly that is supposed to mean. What is "civil society" and what is "democracy?" Movements in Bolivia and Mexico illustrate that "it is not only desirable to build power beyond the state, but also possible" (Zibechi 2010, 1).

INTERNATIONAL HUMAN RIGHTS COMMUNITY

International human rights organizations are an important source of reliable information on human rights in Colombia. Working with their domestic partners, Amnesty International, Human Rights Watch, and others create data that informs policy. International agencies such as the Organization of American States (OAS) and the United Nations High Commissioner for Human Rights (UNHCHR) also work with domestic partners to generate insightful human rights data. These above actors and their networks interface with the "international human rights regime" to expand individual rights (Nowak 2003). This regime references a large body of international law and human rights conventions. Governments, domestic NGOs, and academics consume and analyze the data that these networks produce. This work is important for the monitoring of human rights conditions. Many of these organizations have offices or some staff in Bogotá. Staff members put themselves at some risk there, but especially when traveling to certain rural areas.

The U.S. State Department and other organizations sometimes prohibited their staff from traveling outside of Bogotá. This is particularly true where political violence has recently taken place. Fewer international NGOs have permanent field offices outside of the capital. But short fact-finding trips to different regions are common when conditions permit. Even so, there are limitations to the quality of data that one can gather using these methods. More robust approaches, including ethnographic ones, can be dangerous or impractical. But there are some foreign organizations, such as Peace Brigades International, that do embed their team into a community (Coy 2001). There are also examples of foreign journalists who have been successful at bringing attention to local human rights abuses (Molano 2005). But the price of this work can be high. The character of this work sometimes leads the interlocutor to have to leave the country. Having to endure assassination attempts or death threats is not uncommon (IDMC 2006; Robben and Nordstrom 1995; Sluka 1995).

President Uribe often painted human rights and national security objectives as mutually opposed and exclusive categories. But Uribe's vice president, Francisco Santos had been supportive of human rights initiatives. In an incident chronicled by Gabriel García Márquez (1997), Santos had been kidnapped by Pablo Escobar in 1990 while Santos served as editor-in-chief of *El Tiempo*, one of Colombia's largest-circulation newspapers. This division sometimes sends mixed messages to human rights defenders. Uribe's rhetoric at times became quite heated, accusing human rights organizations of siding with guerillas. Broadly speaking of related dynamics in Bolivia, Zibechi (2007, 82) discloses that "[i]t is very likely that the implicit project of the popular movements [. . .] is the dispersion of the neocolonial and neoliberal state." There do exist counterexamples in Colombia, however. To take one example, the International Campaign to Ban Landmines criticizes all sides in the Colombian dispute for their use of anti-personnel landmines. But this criticism affects guerilla organizations more than it does the state or paramilitary groups. Guerilla forces relied on landmines more than others in the conflict.

ANARCHISTS

There is a vibrant punk and anarchist culture among many student youth in Bogotá. According to some activists, student social movement organizations are becoming increasingly anarchist (Red Revuelta 2008). More recent protests in Colombia also show organizational styles and demographics consistent with decentralized student movements (Observatorio-semillero En Movimiento et al., 2023). In addition to campus student groups, however, there are also music venues and cultural centers that host punk groups, anarchist cultural performances and events, and other spaces around the city. Raul owned and operated one of the main anarchist spaces in the city, the Markhor Center. Raul was in his mid-forties and had been running the center since he first opened it over five years prior.

Raul told me that his motivation to open the center was to honor his son. He said his son, Abraham, was killed by riot police during May Day protests in Bogotá in 2003. According to Raul's account, Abraham and his friends had been unarmed, and was only fifteen years old at the time of his death. After many years of pursuing his son's case through the courts, Raul has not succeeded in bringing the police officers involved in the attack to justice. There are many activist deaths and injuries that result from police contact. Police sometimes can overreact to civil disobedience, causing injuries and deaths to activists, to the young as well as the old. A movement against police impunity gained momentum in Bogotá after Abraham's death, and Raul put all of his energy and resources into founding the Markhor Center as a home for anarchists in the city. Raul wished to institutionalize the movement against police impunity and against the unbridled capitalism that has made them possible, according to his analysis.

The Markhor Center has an all-volunteer staff and raises most of its money through beer and food sales at weekend parties that they host. This not only benefits the Center but also local bands who charge an entrance fee to their shows and sell merchandise. Local artists also showcase their work at the Center and are able to sell wares during these shows. The Center hosts events during the week, often popular progressive films or independent films made by local youth. Other times, they host workshops and teach-ins on issues of importance to surrounding communities. Occasionally, Latin American activists who travel through Bogotá stop at the Center and give talks on popular mobilizations in their local communities. Sometimes the Center would host a professor from a local university to provide expert advice or information on a particular issue that is important to people who frequent the Center. It is also a place where youth can and do smoke cigarettes without worrying about parental supervision, Raul explained. Some, however, come to the Center because they feel safe, he said.

The interior walls are artfully decorated. Murals and other wall art change with some frequency. The only wall that remained static during my fieldwork was a memorial wall, a painted portrait in honor of Abraham. The Center also sometimes housed banners and placards for protests, or hosted people on the eve of large or important protests before venturing out into the streets.

The March on Poverty was an event that brought together the Markhor Center, BOGDES, and the Coalition for Social Justice (CSJ). An activist announced the event at a CSJ meeting. She explained that a constellation of activist, indigenous, and community groups had agreed to participate in the march to downtown Bogotá. Two others at the meeting expressed strong support for the march and the issues of poverty being raised. CSJ decided not to take a position, however, and it was not clear that any organization present would be sending delegates.

The march itself saw skirmishes with police along the march route. Police followed the march, occasionally trying to prevent it from turning down certain roads. The march continued through Bogotá's major commercial centers before settling in a park by mid-afternoon. Waiting at the park were local activists, including others from BOGDES and the Markhor Center, as well as a more sizable delegation of the Association of Indigenous Councils of Northern Cauca (ACIN) Indigenous Guard.[10] Police presence was relatively high in the park. Activists began to express concern about the police having blocked off the main exit roads from the park, effectively blockading the rally into the park. Police had set up loose checkpoints at the park's four corners, looking through belongings as pedestrians traversed the park.

Most of the event was calm, featuring cultural dances and performances from indigenous groups, pop performers, and hip-hop artists. But police presence increased as twilight drew near. Those who took the stage became more vocal in their criticisms of the police and of the government. When Carlos from BOGDES took the stage, the crowd began to rush away. A confrontation between police and activists had taken place opposite the stage. One activist bled from a head wound, complaining about having been pistol whipped by an officer.

When activists began to realize what had taken place, they began to shove the police back toward the edge of the park. A hail of debris rained down on police from the crowd: pieces of bread, plastic bottles, cans, and the contents of nearby trash containers. The police held their formation for about five or ten minutes. Then they turned around and retreated behind a line of ESMAD that had, in the meantime, formed along one side of the park. These riot police banged on their shields with clubs, as if to intimidate. The crowd stood across from the ESMAD for about ten minutes, after which people began to disperse on their own accord.

From the time the activist was injured until people began to disperse, Raul circulated through the crowd, collecting information on what eyewitnesses had seen in an attempt to identify the officer who had allegedly struck the activist. The activist explained that he had seen a plain-clothes officer taking pictures of activists in the park. He confronted the plainclothes officer about his behavior, and that is when the officer allegedly removed a gun from his hip holster and struck him across the crown with the butt of the gun. The activist began to bleed, and then others, seeing what had happened, began to shove and throw debris at police. The activist claimed that the plainclothes officer who had allegedly struck him ran into a nearby bus station, located behind police lines. A few activists gave chase, but police prevented them from chasing after him.

After most of the crowd had dispersed, Raul and the ACIN Indigenous Guard began to prepare to leave the park. They were concerned that as darkness fell and without the protection of numbers, individuals could be exposed to police abuse. The Indigenous Guard had set up a perimeter to protect pregnant women, children, and a few others. Activists were concerned that police may try to follow certain individuals on their way home. Raul claimed to have observed one officer single out individuals for another officer, though I did not observe this myself. Raul recruited eight other activists to chaperone a group, including myself, to the Markhor Center. They routed this retreat down a major boulevard where a festival was underway. As we navigated through the merry crowd, Raul explained that we were attempting to lose any police that may be following. We arrived safely at the Markhor Center some distance away, on foot.

We remained there for several hours, "until things calm down," Raul said. Someone bought a round of beers for the group. I spoke with a circle of about a half-dozen anarchists standing next to the bar. I shared with them who I was, and they began to interrogate my politics. They were particularly interested in my opinion of then-U.S. president George W. Bush. Having apparently passed their test, they decided aloud that I was not a spy. After some relieved banter among themselves, one of them decided to make a toast. They raised their bottles of Aguila beer towards the center of the room.

"To 9/11," said one.

I put my bottle down. One of them noticed.

"Wait, we have a New Yorker here," he offered.

They paused to study my face. I was incredulous. Then they turned to look toward the individual who offered the toast.

"No matter. To 9/11!"

They cheered, clinked their bottles together, and took generous swigs.

Bogotá is home to several small, radical, grassroots social movement groups which are today receiving somewhat more attention. Their movements and confrontations with police, at least as they appeared in the final years of the Uribe government, do not seem to receive the support of larger NGOs that receive national and international funding. Even grassroots NGOs in Bogotá seem to be steered toward less disruptive tactics. Anarchist-oriented and student groups have a long tradition of engaging police. While there is some interaction between these groups through the CSJ, it operates as a forum of separate actors rather than as an *emancipatory network* for coordinated action. There appears to be some hesitancy among some NGOs to work too closely with radical organizations that may jeopardize their funding sources. But while anarchist groups may have felt freer to select the tactics of their choice, they were also less able to direct efforts toward coalition-building. Freeman (1972, 161) notes that "[t]he more unstructured a movement is, the less control it has over the directions in which it develops." Community organizations, NGOs, and grassroots organizations were linked. But groups that engage in more disruptive tactics were somewhat isolated from the larger NGOs.

NOTES

1. Some local activists refer to movement groups of many types as "human rights" groups. I use the term here in the somewhat narrower sense to refer to groups that the UN Office of the High Commissioner for Human Rights (UNOHCR 2011) refers to as "human rights defenders" (UN General Assembly 1999).

2. Scholars have written about images that social movements take themselves (Atton 2002) or about media depictions (McCurdy 2012). Less is known about the effects of police taking images of activists. Police surveillance is less understood area of social movement studies (Marx 1974). Surveillance studies theorizes that surveillance promotes self-regulatory behavior (Foucault 1977). But surveillance also "threatens the solidarity between organizations in networks" and "[s]urveilled organizations are often abandoned by their allies" (Starr et al., 2008, 259). Others also find that covert action dampens activism (Davenport 2005; Cunningham and Noakes 2008). One study found that surveillance of drivers in the United States reduces traffic infractions (Rothengatter 1982). These studies suggest that police surveillance intimidates activists into obeying the law. For an overview, consult Starr et al. (2008, 266).

3. Many well-planned, but seemingly spontaneous marches occur in the city without a permit.

4. In Bosnia and Herzegovina, displaced women and children have been found to suffer disproportionate levels of psychological harm (Dybdahl 2001).

5. See Republic of Colombia Ombudsman's Office (2007) "Informe de Riesgo No. 004-07."

6. See Republic of Colombia Vice-president's Office (2009) "Situación Nacional de Minas Antipersonal."

7. "The Bamako Appeal" was presented in Mali in 2006 at the start of the World Social Forum. It was the 50th anniversary of the Bandung Conference and echoed many of its themes. Chief among these were opposition to neocolonialism, communism, and capitalism (Amin 2008, 107; Foster et al., 2006).

8. I was not able to verify these claims. It is not inconceivable that the culprit intended to sell the laptop for money or to have it for personal use. But I often carried around expensive equipment during my fieldwork. I have also observed others in activist spaces with expensive equipment. I never saw or heard of theft being a problem. The fear that activists in the audience expressed was palpable. Repression in Colombia is not an abstraction.

9. Even Colombian social movement scholars tend to view the democratic project as fundamentally a statist process: "constructing democracy, in the Colombian case, means widening the public sphere. This process necessitates an underwriter, ideally in the form of the state" (Archila 2001, 39). This orientation prioritizes a process of state reform. But others theorize democratic processes outside of the state (Dussel 2008, 131). These more radical activists pursue a strategy more akin to Trotsky's elaboration of "dual power" (Rockefeller 2007). Speaking of Bolivia, Linera (2021, 134) concludes that, "[c]itizenship entails an uninterrupted ritual of seduction and connection between the State and 'civil society.' Moreover, this involves mutable agreements and commitments."

10. The Indigenous Guard (IG) is the security arm of the ACIN, Association of Indigenous Councils of Northern Cauca. They serve to protect the indigenous peoples belonging to one of the councils of the association in Northern Cauca and are often deployed when the ACIN mobilize their people in support of or against certain issues or government policies. They also are deployed when the ACIN accompany other movements.

Conclusion

The Valle del Cauca and Bogotá cases illustrate how activist network arrangements can impact movement outcomes. In Valle del Cauca, thousands of black and mestizo men seized hundreds of acres of arable land in Valle del Cauca. Hundreds of black and mestizo women organized their neighbors. Dozens of white and mestizo professionals battled in the media and in the courts. Using structural leverage and heterogenous networks, sugarcane workers extracted concessions from national agricultural interests. Bogotá's activists, in contrast, were stymied by their differences and distracted by international funding.

The growth of cases from less developed nations under study has begun to complicate our understanding of how activists engage in risky forms of activism. *Emancipatory networks* become important when considering how large protest networks organize themselves in repressive environments. The sugarcane strike illustrates the texture of political risk-taking in rural Colombia. Workers and their families, human rights workers, politicians, and union leaders coordinated their efforts to oppose large sugarcane plantations in the country. Their strategy, including their own motives, leadership structures, resources, and audacity, proved effective in sustaining the strike over nearly two months. Their case also illustrates findings in the literature that security forces tend to respond more acutely to more organized and effective activists (Chamberlain and Yanus 2022). Sugarcane workers felt responsible for the wellbeing of their families. Their inability to fulfil their traditional role as breadwinners led to widespread feelings of humiliation. These emotions motivated them to take action when the opportunity to strike presented itself.

Human rights leaders, drawing from their experiences in other social movements, brought important insight to bear on the sugarcane workers strike. Experienced activists may have cooler heads when presented with emotionally taxing protest events. Understanding different forms of "knowing" from experience and from learning—*conocer* and *saber*—can help us understand why groups that have both kinds of knowledge might have an edge in solving *strategic dilemmas* (Jasper 2004).

Internally displaced people's movements in Bogotá illustrate the problem that financial backing can pose. Social movement leaders were less coordinated, even if better funded, as they competed for influence with funding agencies and displaced communities. These agencies sought domestic partners through which they could distribute resources to the public. Not wanting to risk their privileged relationships, larger non-profits resisted government policies selectively, and kept some distance from smaller groups that pushed hard against the government. Frustrated with these moderating dynamics, anarchist groups constitute a break from these relations. But anarchist groups also attracted the most police repression, received little or no outside funding, and were more isolated from non-profit and activist community organizations and agencies.

CATNETS

In the collective action model outlined by Tilly (1978), *catnets* operate in the context of organization. The movement literature has largely limited itself to Tilly's interpretation of *catnets* to explain why some traits become salient for mobilization while others do not. Individual traits on their own do explain contentious organizations. Rather, these need to be coupled, at least, with networks. As Tilly (1978, 63) explains, "a set of individuals is a group to the extent that it comprises both a category and a network."

As is often the case with work strikes, negotiations surrounding labor contract renewal created the opportunity for workers to strike to increase their bargaining leverage. One factor in the innovation of this networked style of organization may have been the immense threat created by the prospect of leading a labor strike in a country that has seen so much repression against labor movements. Sugarcane workers struck against their employers in order to gain concessions. Plantation owners benefited from a sympathetic conservative government under President Uribe, willing to use force to repel striking workers.

Sugarcane workers were largely black, working class, and mistreated. But their motives for mobilization have more to do with the emotional trauma emerging from overwhelming conditions. Taking advantage of opportunities for collective action and making strategic choices, sugarcane workers transmuted individual experiences of humiliation into the fuel that propelled a radical picket for eight weeks.

Catnets, instead, help us to understand how the tight-knit Doves became involved. But how do discrete movement groups, such as sugarcane workers and human rights activists, mobilize as a coalition? Scholars studying the organization of Diasporic networks have identified the importance of human rights networks (Harrison 2012). Even within large organizations, personal networks seem more consequential than status hierarchies in understanding influence and outcomes (March and Simon, 1958). If *catnets* have to do with how a group mobilizes, then *emancipatory networks* have to do with how groups mobilize (as a coalition). Because there is a second layer of abstraction, *emancipatory networks* have different properties. The Doves hang together as a *catnet*, for example, because of their cohesive, tight, concentrated relationships. The *emancipatory network*, in contrast, does so because of the coordination of loose, discrete, and differentiated actors. *Catnets* and *emancipatory networks* address different questions and different levels of analysis (figure 6.1).

The concept of the *emancipatory network* is distilled from the Latin American literature on social movements (Linera 2021, 133; Uribe 2004, 82–3; Zibechi 2010, 13). Because they are tied to personal identity or specific cultural contexts, postcolonial ideas are suited to *relational* (White, 2008a) approaches to the study of movements. Postcolonialists tell stories about how inequality impacts the subaltern poor. The telling of these stories is empirically significant as their telling changes the reality from which we analyze the societies we inhabit. Yet, as much as postcolonialists wish to "de-colonize" Western intellectual traditions, they are also influenced by these ideas (c.f. Esparza 2023a; Gordon 2017, 113). For example, Antillean scholars including Aime Césaire "went back [. . .] to his own sources, to his "Bambara ancestors," to Negro-African poetry" (Senghor 1948, as cited in Hale, 1976, 163). He also integrated those ideas with Western anti-establishment writers such as the Situationist Comte de Lautréamont (Larrier 2010, 40). Such creative fusions of universalist and particularist ideas are necessary, and exemplified by critical theorists such as Horkheimer (1934, as cited in Outhwaite 1987, 77–8), who would fuse "truth" and "ethics" (Melucci 1989, 160) in the service of analysis and critique.

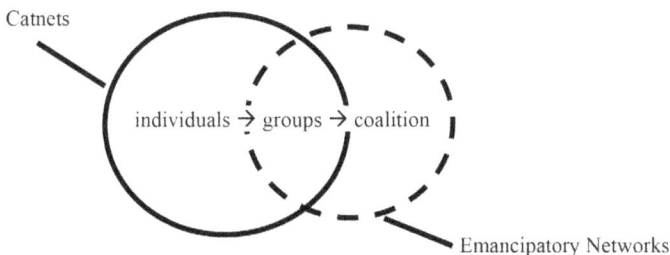

Figure 6.1 Catnets and Emancipatory Networks. *Source*: Figure created by author.

White's discussion of the constituents of social structure (White 2008b [1965]) similarly influences the inductive approach I chose in categorizing activists. That a network arrangement of workers, communities, human rights activists, unions, and politicians emerged as consequential stems from a close study of activist behavior. White insists that networks are local structures operating wholly within a culture. But ethnographers, too, illustrate inductive, micro-sociological approaches to theorizing about movements (Auyero 2001; Burawoy 1991; Zibechi 2010, 112). This approach can lead to important insights as social movements are themselves often the source of important sociological theories (de Sousa Santos 2009; Esparza 2023a).

Despite the looseness of an *emancipatory network* vis-à-vis the tightness of the *catnet*, there still exists a degree of cohesiveness. This cohesiveness is defined according to White's (2008b [1965]) parameters for the constituent elements of a social structure. The extent to which indirect relations impact a given actor, for instance, depends on the extent to which the given actor is familiar with the intermediaries. This concept has been commonly applied as "the strength of weak ties" (Granovetter 1973). In the context of the *emancipatory network*, the worker's movement organization served as the primary intermediary between disparate actors. This also illustrates another facet of White's *catnet*, which is that direct network connections are distinct from influence. Community members have direct network ties to their leaders. But no matter how well this relationship goes, achieving community aims relies on other coalition ties rather than a singular community-leader tie.

Neither attributional nor attitudinal networks are composed of identities (Schwartz 2008, 1). Even where organizations explicitly define activists according to their identity, activists themselves often embed themselves in broad networks. Fontana & Grugel (2016, 6) explain in the Bolivian case that "ethnic-based parties did not pursue an ethnocentric and exclusionary program. Instead, they tended to articulate ethnic claims along with classic populist electoral strategies that appealed to diverse sectors of the electorate." Even though identities and networks are not entirely mutually exclusive, as networks begin to take on some definition, they can sometimes coalesce into new categories (White 2008b [1965]). Thinking of identities as networks sidesteps identarian concerns about "when a shared characteristic becomes relevant" (Cohen 1985, 685). It also addresses ethnic minority populations in states where their low numbers make it difficult for them to address their needs solely through identarian political movements (Busdiecker 2009). While blurring this conceptual boundary between categories and networks somewhat, White does not cast himself as a deconstructionist (White, Fuhse, Thiemann, and Buchholz 2018). Put another way, the fundamental theory of network analysis is that networks create content (Schwartz 2008, 2). While the implications of this for explaining the mutability of identity is beyond our scope here, I hope at least to have illustrated that the relationship between networks and identities can be dynamic.

STRATEGY

Organizations are one vehicle through which individuals collectively express power. At least also the agents of change, networks, and individuals may sometimes be more consequential in this regard. Albert Einstein observed that large organizations may not be well equipped to handle the task of moral protest. Referencing the international peace movements of the interwar years, Einstein (1934, 44) wrote,

> [T]he formation of large organizations with a large membership can in itself bring us very little nearer to our goal. In my opinion, the best method in this case is the violent one--conscientious objection, which must be aided by organizations that give moral and material support to the courageous conscientious objectors in each country. In this way we may succeed in making the problem of pacifism an acute one, a real struggle to which forceful spirits will be attracted. It is an illegal struggle, but a struggle for the true rights of the people against their governments as far as they demand criminal acts of their citizens.

In Colombia, the Doves connected national and international organizations to local sugarcane workers. Involved in activism of the conscious, sugarcane workers organized for what Einstein calls "true rights." This activity sometimes involves illegality. Even explicitly non-violent movements, of the type seen in the U.S. Civil Rights Movement, for instance, set out to break unjust state laws in favor of higher ethical principles. These sorts of movement tasks seem to be more effectively undertaken by networks.

Decentralization might be suited to the task of squaring up against particularly oligarchic authorities. As economic inequality, electronic surveillance, and state-corporate partnerships spread, they threaten individual and collective civil and political rights (Esparza 2022). But such challenges can be effectively met by an organizing style that prioritizes networks of small, nimble, low-cost, and independent entities. Especially as activists become more tolerant of ideological and tactical differences between themselves, their networks can attract the heterogeneous resources necessary to create leverage over sclerotic authorities. The differences between activists and oligarchical elites are far greater and more consequential than those among activists.

A NOTE ON SEXUALITY AND GENDER

I did not ask anyone about their sexual orientation during my fieldwork. This subject does not have universal acceptance in the rural valleys of the Cauca River. Even the Doves, as cosmopolitan as they may seem, expressed mostly derisive attitudes toward queer groups. A group of "Pink Cutters" posted a statement of solidarity to an online blog during the sugarcane workers' strike. I was unable to make contact with this group, but the Doves and worker leadership committee did discuss them at a meeting in Palmira. Some of the Doves and the sugarcane worker leadership openly ridiculed this group. Juana teased one particular worker by jokingly accusing him of being a "pink cutter." Only Nina came to the defense of the Pink Cutters. Nina explained that the Pink Cutters had made a public statement in support of the strike and that the workers should be more accepting of them. Nina scolded Javier, who was most brutal, for his disparaging comments. Almost certainly, workers who might have been discovered to have male partners, or were even suspected of having such, could be the subject of open mockery and harassment.

This may be because sugarcane cutters place a great deal of importance on manual labor as an expression of masculinity. This strong gender identity may make it difficult for sugarcane cutters to adapt to other lines of work, especially after injury (Castro Muñoz 2016). But it may also be a way of insulating oneself from the effects of long and difficult labor. Latin American workers have some of the longest working hours among OECD (2023a) countries. This work ethic is exploited by extractive industries today (Vergara 2013). But even in the colonial period, Colombians endured hard labor. Dussel (2013, 11–3) theorizes that this work ethic may originate in Inca-Quechua culture. Dussel (1981, 132) quotes the sixteenth-century Spanish Bishop Juan Valle writing of Cauca: "It would seem that this land is more like that of Babylon than of Carlos I. . . . What is certain is that the Indians are more exhausted than were the Israelites in Egypt." [ellipsis in original]

Workers did show great respect and gratitude for Adriana's work as a member of the Doves. However, I found most women that supported the strike among the spouses of sugarcane workers in the strike kitchens.[1] This is consistent with the practice of insurgent revolutionary camps in Colombia (de Greiff 2023) and elsewhere in Latin America (Reif 1986). There were some exceptions to this, with some men taking over cooking duties when no women were available. Women also organized and conducted support rallies and marches. The availability of food to support striking workers was a necessary condition for the strike's success. This is so much so that some movements organize their entire campaigns around feeding their activists (Potorti 2017).

CONCLUSION

In the years since this study, Colombian politics has seen a new openness to political inclusion. The 2022 Presidential election of Gustavo Petro signals increasing openness to the integration of former guerilla fighters into normal politics. Large, student-led protests in 2021 against austerity measures signal that movements continue to play an important role in challenging state authority. To the extent that Colombian society continues to progress toward peace and reconciliation, it will be up to its networks of social movements to ensure a stable reality for those living at the margins.

NOTE

1. Colombian police and plantations seemed to target strike kitchens. The water supply at the plantations was turned off, necessitating the importation of cooking and drinking water from elsewhere. In the case of the death of FARC leader Manuel Marulanda, Colombian forces may have found a way of tainting the food supply (LADB Staff 2008). There was no evidence of the use of this tactic in the sugarcane workers' strike, however.

Appendix A

Interviews

Summer 2007, Bogotá

1. Human rights activists

Summer 2008, Bogotá

2. Human rights activists
3. International human rights activists
4. Anarchists

Fall 2008, Valle del Cauca

5. Sugarcane workers
6. Human rights activists
7. International human rights activists
8. Indigenous activists
9. Labor union organizers
10. Elected officials

References

Acosta García, Nicolás and Katharine N. Farrell. 2019. "Crafting Electricity through Social Protest: Afro-Descendant and Indigenous Embera Communities Protesting for Hydroelectric Infrastructure in Utría National Park, Colombia." *Environment and Planning D: Society and Space* 37(2):236–54.

AFP. 2014. "Militares Colombianos Espiaron Conversaciones Entre FARC y periodistas, según Univisión." New York: *Agence France Presse*. 13 February.

Alinsky, Saul. 1971. *Rules for radicals*. New York: Vintage.

Álvarez, Eleonora Dávalos. 2007. "La caña de azúcar: ¿una amarga externalidad?" *Desarrollo y Sociedad* 59(1):85–113.

Álvarez, Sonia E., Evelina Dagnino, and Arturo Escobar. 1998. *Cultures of politics/ politics of cultures: re-visioning Latin American social movements*. Boulder: Westview Press.

Amin, Samir. 2008. *The world we wish to see: revolutionary objectives in the twenty-first century*. New York: Monthly Review Press.

Anderson, Patrick D. 2022. *Cypherpunk ethics: radical ethics for the digital age*. New York: Routledge.

Andrews, Kenneth T. 2004. *Freedom is a constant struggle: the Mississippi civil rights movement and its legacy*. Chicago: University of Chicago Press.

Archila, Mauricio. 2001. "Vida, passión y . . .: De los movimientos sociales en Colombia." In *Movimentos Sociales, Estado y Democracia*, edited by Mauricio Archila and Maurcio Pardo. Bogotá: Universidad Nacional de Colombia.

Arias, Enrique Desmond. 2006. *Drugs & democracy in Rio de Janeiro: trafficking, social networks, & public security*. Chapel Hill: University of North Carolina Press.

Arias Mendoza, Jhon Jairo, Tito Morales Pinzón, and Andrés Suarez Agudelo. 2016. "Aspectos socioeconómicos y percepciones de los corteros de caña sobre la mecanización en Risaralda, Colombia." *Scientia et Technica* 21(1):69–74.

Arocha, Jamie. 2008. "Cuerpos inmunes al dolor." *El Espectador*. Opinion. Bogotá. 8 October.

Arroyave, Jesus and Marta Milena Barrios. 2012. "Journalists in Colombia." In *The Global Journalist in the 21st Century*, edited by David H. Weaver and Lars Willnat. London: Taylor & Francis.

Associated Press. 2008. "Colombia bitterly divided on anti-rebel march." Bogotá: Associated Press International. 3 Feb.

———. 2008. "Colombia police tear-gas pyramid scheme clients." Bogotá: Associated Press International. 20 Nov.

Asocaña. 2008. *Informe anual de Asocaña 2007-2008*. Cali: Asocaña. www.asocana .org.

———. 2009a. "Balance azucarero colombiano Asocaña 2008 (toneladas)." Cali: Asocaña. www.asocana.org.

———. 2009b. *Informe anual de Asocaña 2008-2009*. Cali: Asocaña. www.asocana .org.

———. 2009c. "Sector Azucarero Colombiano 2009-2010: Una agroindustria que jalona el crecimiento regional y nacional." Cali: Asocaña. www.asocana.org.

———. 2020. "Reporte de Sostenibilidad del Sector Azucarero Colombiano (Ajuste #7)." Communication on Engagement Asocaña. UN Global Compact.

———. 2022. "Balance azucarero colombiano Asocaña 2020-2022 (toneladas)" (dataset) Cali: Asocaña. www.asocana.org

———. 2023a. "Precio máximo del etanol en Colombia de acuerdo con resoluciones del Mininsterio de Minas y Energía." (dataset) Cali: Asocaña. www.asocana .org.

———. 2023b. "Precio promedio mensual azúcar crudo primera posición - Nueva York Contrato N° 11 - USDcents/lb." (dataset) Cali: Asocaña. www.asocana.org.

Atton, Chris. 2002. "News Cultures and New Social Movements: Radical Journalism and the Mainstream Media." *Journalism Studies* 3(4):491–505. https://doi.org/10 .1080/1461670022000019209.

Auyero, Javier. 2001. *Poor people's politics: Peronist survival networks and the legacy of Evita*. Durham, NC: Duke University Press.

———. 2003. *Contentious lives: two Argentine women, two protests, and the quest for recognition*. Durham, NC: Duke University Press.

———. 2007. *Routine politics and violence in Argentina: the gray zone of state power*. Cambridge; New York: Cambridge University Press.

Avruch, Kevin. 2001. "Notes Toward Ethnographies of Conflict and Violence." *Journal of Contemporary Ethnography* 30:637–48.

Baird, Adam. 2017. "Dancing with Danger: Ethnographic Safety, Male Bravado and Gang Research in Colombia." *Qualitative Research* 18(3):342–60.

Barkan, Steven E., Steven F. Cohn, and William H. Whitaker. 1993. "Commitment across the Miles: Ideological and Microstructural Sources of Membership Support in a National Antihunger Organization." *Social Problems* 40(3):362–73. https://doi .org/10.2307/3096885

Barnes, Nicholas. 2022. "The Logic of Criminal Territorial Control: Military Intervention in Rio de Janeiro." *Comparative Political Studies* 55(5):789–831.

Barnes, Samuel H. and Max Kaase. 1979. *Political action: mass participation in five Western democracies*. Beverly Hills: Sage Publications.

Beck, Ulrich. 2000. "The Cosmopolitan Perspective: Sociology of the Second Age of Modernity." *British Journal of Sociology* 51:79–105.

Beck, Ulrich and Natan Sznaider. 2006. "Unpacking Cosmopolitanism for the Social Sciences: A Research Agenda." *British Journal of Sociology* 57:1–23.

Becker, Howard S. 1967. "Whose Side Are We On?" *Social Problems* 14(3):239–47.

Becker, Marc. 2021. *The CIA in Ecuador*. Durham, NC: Duke University Press.

Bedoya, Yuri. 2000. *"Estan Quemando La Caña"* [Lyrics]. Mercury (France).

Beissinger, Mark R., Amaney A. Jamal, and Kevin Mazur. 2015. "Explaining Divergent Revolutionary Coalitions: Regime Strategies and the Structuring of Participation in the Tunisian and Egyptian Revolutions." *Comparative Politics* 48(1):1–24.

Bello, Walden. 2007. "World Social Forum at the Crossroads." *Foreign Policy in Focus* 5.

Blee, Kathleen and Verta Taylor. 2002. "Semi-Structured Interviewing in Social Movements Research." In *Methods of social movement research, Social movements, protest, and contention*, edited by Bert Klandermans and Suzanne Staggenborg. Minneapolis: University of Minnesota Press.

Bob, Clifford. 2005. *The marketing of rebellion: insurgents, media, and international activism*. New York: Cambridge University Press.

Bonhoeffer, Dietrich. 1995[1948]. *The cost of discipleship*. New York: Touchstone.

Bookchin, Murray. 2007. *Social ecology and communalism*. Oakland, CA: AK Press.

Brass, Paul. 2005. *Forms of collective violence: riots, pogroms, and genocide in modern India*. New Delhi: Three Essays Collective.

Breines, Wini. 1980. "Community and Organization: The New Left and Michels' "Iron Law"." *Social Problems* 27:419–29.

Bumsted, J. M. 1968. "A Well-Bounded Toleration: Church and State in the Plymouth Colony." *Journal of Church and State* 10(2):265–79.

Burawoy, Michael. 1991. "Reconstructing Social Theories." In *Ethnography unbound: Power and resistance in the modern metropolis*, edited by Michael Burawoy, Alice Burton, Ann Arnett Ferguson, and Kathryn J. Fox. Berkeley: University of California Press.

Busdiecker, Sara. 2009. "The Emergence and Evolving Character of Contemporary Afro-Bolivian Mobilization." In *New Social Movements in the African Diaspora: Challenging Global Apartheid*, edited by Leith Mullings. New York: Palgrave Macmillan.

Calhoun, Craig. 2002. "The Class Consciousness of Frequent Travelers: Towards a Critique of Actually Existing Cosmopolitanism." *The South Atlantic Quarterly* 101:869–97.

Cárdenas Lesmes, Rosa María. 2008. "La conspiración." *Portafolio*. Bogotá. 28 October.

Carroll, Leah Anne. 1999. "Palm Workers, Patrons, and Political Violence in Colombia: A Window of Opportunity for the Left Despite Trade Liberalization." *Political Power and Social Theory* 13:149–200.

———. 2011. *Violent democratization: social movements, elites, and politics in Colombia's rural war zones, 1984-2008*. Notre Dame: University of Notre Dame Press.

Cartagena, Laura Catalina. 2016. "Los estudios de la violencia en Colombia antes de la violentología." *Diálogos Revista Electrónica* 17(1):63–88.

Castaño, Alen and Mónica Castillo-Cubillos. 2021. "Lo dulce y amargo del azúcar: el caso de las condiciones laborales de los trabajadores de caña de azúcar de Valle del Cauca (Colombia)." *Boletín de Antropología Universidad de Antioquia* 36(61):118–35.

Castro Muñoz, Betsy Johana. 2016. "Construcción y transformación de masculinidades de los corteros de caña de azúcar del Valle del Cauca." *Revista Colombiana de Sociología* 39(1):79–102.

Cepeda, Iván. 2006. "Genocidio político: el caso de la Unión Patriótica en Colombia." *Revista Cetil* 1(2):101–12.

Chamberlain, Adam and Alixandra B. Yanus. 2022. "The Southern Farmers' Alliance, Populists, and Lynching." *Social Science History* 47(1):121–44.

Child, Curtis D., and Kirsten A. Grønbjerg. 2007. "Nonprofit Advocacy Organizations: Their Characteristics and Activities." *Social science quarterly* 88(1):259–81.

Churchill, Ward and Jim Vander Wall. 1990. *The COINTELPRO papers: documents from the FBI's secret wars against domestic dissent*. Boston: South End Press.

CINEP. 2008. *Noche y Niebla: Panorama de Derechos Humanos y Violencia Política en Colombia*. Banco de Datos de Violencia Política (38). Bogotá: Editorial Códice.

Cloward, Richard A. and Frances Fox Piven. 1984. "Disruption and Organization: A Rejoinder [to William A. Gamson and Emilie Schmeidler]." *Theory and Society* 13:587–99.

CODHES. 2006. "Número de Personas Desplazadas por Municipio de Llegada." Consultoría Para Los Derechos Humanos y El Desplazamiento.

Cohen, Jean. 1985. "Strategy or Identity: New Theoretical Paradigms and Contemporary Social Movements." *Social Research* 52(4):663–716.

Cohen, Robert. 2009. *Freedom's orator: Mario Savio and the radical legacy of the 1960s*. New York: Oxford University Press.

Collins, Charles David. 1983. "Formación de una sector de clase social: la burguesía azucarera en el Valle de Cauca durante los años treinta y cuarenta." *Historia y Espacio* 3(9):44–112.

Collins, Randall. 2004. *Interaction ritual chains*. Princeton: Princeton University Press.

Corporación Nuevo Arco Iris. 2007. Base de Datos Municipal (database). Bogotá.

Correa, Guillermo and Diana Patricia Cárdenas Quintero. 2008. "Documento de Trabajo No. 330." In *Cronología del conflicto social: Colombia*, edited by Consejo Latinoamericano de Ciencias Sociales. October. http://biblioteca.clacso.edu.ar/clacso/osal/20190430041644/Colombia_2008.pdf

Coy, Patrick G. 2001. "Shared Risks and Research Dilemmas on a Peace Brigades International Team in Sri Lanka." *Journal of Contemporary Ethnography* 30:575–606.

Cuéllar, Martha Elisa Monsalve and Camilo Piedrahita Vargas. 2018. "El Contrato Sindical en Colombia: ¿Un Mecanismo de Promoción de la Sindicalización o de Violación de Derechos Laborales?" *Revue Européenne du Droit Social* 39(2):17–24.

Cruz Salas, Luis. 2019. *Las Izquierdas en los ochenta: Notas Criticas*. Santiago: Omnia Sunt Communia.

Cunningham, David. 2003. "The Patterning of Repression: FBI Counterintelligence and the New Left*." *Social Forces* 82(1):209–40. https://doi.org/10.1353/sof.2003.0079. https://doi.org/10.1353/sof.2003.0079.

Cunningham, D. and Noakes, J. 2008. ""What if she's from the FBI?" The Effects of Covert Forms of Social Control on Social Movements." In *Surveillance and Governance: Crime Control and Beyond*, edited by Mathieu Deflem and Jeffrey T. Ulmer. Bingley: Emerald.

Curtis Jr., Russell L. and Louis A. Zurcher Jr. 1973. "Stable Resources of Protest Movements: The Multi-Organizational Field." *Social Forces* 52:53–61.

CUT. 2020. "Informe del Departamento de Derechos Humanos y Solidaridad LXVI (66)." CUT National Board. 1 April.

DANE. 2007. "Censo General 2005: Resultados Área Metropolitana de Bogotá." Bogotá: Departamento Administrativo Nacional de Estadística.

Davenport, Christian. 2007. "State Repression and Political Order." *Annual Review of Political Science* 10(1):1–23. https://doi.org/10.1146/annurev.polisci.10.101405.143216.

Dawsey, John Cowart. 2005. "O teatro dos 'bóias-frias': repensando a antropologia da performance." *Horizontes Antropológicos* 11(24):15–34.

de Greiff, Alexis. 2023. "Artifacts, Actions, Knowledge and Irregular Warfare in Latin America." Science Diplomacy and Science in Times of War. Berlin: Max Planck Institut für Wissenschaftsgeschichte. 14 Feb.

Delanty, Gerard. 2006. "The Cosmopolitan Imagination: Critical Cosmopolitanism and Social Theory." *British Journal of Sociology* 57:25–47.

Delgadillo-Vargas, Olga, Roberto Garcia-Ruiz, and Jaime Forero-Álvarez. 2016. "Fertilising Techniques and Nutrient Balances in the Agriculture Industrialization Transition: The Case of Sugarcane in the Cauca River Valley (Colombia), 1943–2010." *Agriculture, Ecosystems & Environment* 218:150–62.

della Porta, Donatella. 2006. *Social movements, political violence, and the state: a comparative analysis*. Cambridge University Press. Cambridge.

Des Forges, Alison Liebhafsky. 1999. *"Leave none to tell the story": genocide in Rwanda*. New York: Human Rights Watch.

Desmond, Matthew. 2007. *On the fireline: living and dying with wildland firefighters*. Chicago: University of Chicago Press.

Diani, Mario. 2012. "Attributes, Relations, or Both? Exploring the Relational Side of Collective Action." *Contributions to Nepalese Studies* 39:21–44.

Díaz Jaramillo and José Abelardo. 2019. "Los trabajos de la memoria: la masacre de las bananeras y los sectores subalternos en Colombia, 1929-2008." *Trashumante: Revista Americana de Historia Social* 13:30–54.

Dube, Oeindrila and Suresh Naidu. 2015. "Bases, Bullets, and Ballots: The Effect of Us Military Aid on Political Conflict in Colombia." *The Journal of Politics* 77(1):249–67. https://doi.org/10.1086/679021.

Dudley, Steven S. 2004. *Walking ghosts: murder and guerrilla politics in Colombia*. New York: Routledge.

Dussel, 1981. *A history of the church in Latin America: colonialism to liberation (1492-1979)*. Grand Rapids, MI: Eerdmans.

———. 2008. *Twenty theses on politics*. Durham: Duke University Press.

———. Enrique D. 2013. *Ethics of liberation in the age of globalization and exclusion*. Durham: Duke University Press.

Dybdahl, Ragnhild. 2001. "Children and Mothers in War: An Outcome Study of a Psychosocial Intervention Program." *Child Development* 72:1214–30.

Earl, Jennifer. 2003. "Tanks, Tear Gas, and Taxes: Toward a Theory of Movement Repression." *Sociological Theory* 21(1): 44–68. https://doi.org/10.1111/1467-9558 .00175.

Echeverri, Lina María, Eduardo Rosker, and Martha Lucía Restrepo. 2010. "Los orígenes de la marca país Colombia es pasión." *Estudios y perspectivas en turismo* 19(3):409–21.

Eckstein, Susan. 1989. *Power and popular protest: Latin American social movements*. Berkeley: University of California Press.

Einstein, Albert. 1934. *The World as I See It*, edited and translated by Alan Harris. New York: Covici, Friede.

Einwohner, R. L. 2006. "Identity Work and Collective Action in a Repressive Context: Jewish Resistance on the "Aryan side" of the Warsaw Ghetto." *Social Problems* 53:38–56.

El Espectador. 1960a. *Archive and Microfilm*. Bogotá: Biblioteca Luís Angel Arango.

———. 1960b. "Fue Asesinado el Alcalde de Obando en el Valle, Anoche." Bogotá. 4 May.

———. 2008. "El paro de los corteros de caña." Editorial. Bogotá. 25 September.

El País. 2023. "Asocaña rechazó nuevo ataque que dejó heridos a trabajadores del Ingenio La Cabaña." Cali. 2 May.

Emirbayer, Mustafa, and Jeff Goodwin. 1994. "Network Analysis, Culture, and the Problem of Agency." *American Journal of Sociology* 99(6):1411–54.

Esparza, Louis Edgar. 2009. "Global Movement Coalitions: The Global South and the World Trade Organization in Cancun." Societies Without Borders 4(2):226–47.

———. 2011. "Ensuring Economic & Social Rights in the US Constitution." In *Sociology and Human Rights: A Bill of Rights for the Twenty-first Century*, edited by Judith Blau and Mark Frezzo. Pine Forge.

———. 2012a. "Only a Monster: Neutrality and Ethics." *Societies Without Borders* 7(2):229–33.

———. 2012b. "Time to Strike: Cross-Europe Solidarity Forging a Path Out of Austerity." *In These Times*. 16 November.

———. 2013. "Power and Authority in Social Movements: A Political Philosophy of Prefigurative Politics." *Partecipazione e Conflitto* 6(2):40–67.

———. 2022. "Contemporary First Amendment Politics." *Contexts* 21(3):22–27.

———. 2023a. "Social Justice & Sociological Theory: Césaire, Mills, & de Beauvoir." *Journal of Social Encounters* 7(1): 186–207.

———. 2023b. "Occupy Los Angeles: democracy, space, and loss at City Hall Park." *Interface* 14(1): 101–121.

Esparza, Louis Edgar, and Rhiannan Price. 2015. "Convergence Repertoires: Anti-Capitalist Protest at the 2010 Vancouver Winter Olympics." *Contemporary Justice Review* 18(1):22–41.

Fals-Borda, Orlando and Luis E. Mora-Osejo. 2003. "Context and Diffusion of Knowledge: A Critique of Eurocentrism." *Action Research* 1(1):29–37.

Fantasia, Rick. 1988. *Cultures of solidarity: consciousness, action, and contemporary American workers*. Berkeley: University of California Press.

Farer, Tom. 2020. *Migration and integration: the case for liberalism with borders*. Cambridge: Cambridge University Press.

Farnsworth-Alvear, Ann, Marco Palacios, and Ana María Gómez López. 2017. *The Colombia reader: history, culture, politics*. Durham: Duke University Press.

Felbab-Brown, Vanda. 2006. "The Intersection of Terrorism and the Drug Trade." In *The Making of a Terrorist: Recruitment, Training, and Root Causes, vol. III*, edited by J. J. F. Forest. Westport, Connecticut: Praeger.

Fernandez, Roberto M. and Doug McAdam. 1988. "Social Networks and Social Movements: Multiorganizational Fields and Recruitment to Mississippi Freedom Summer." *Sociological Forum* 3:357–82.

Flacks, Richard. 2004. "Knowledge for What? Thoughts on the State of Social Movement Studies." In *Rethinking social movements: structure, meaning, and emotion*, edited by Jeff Goodwin and James M. Jasper. Lanham: Rowman & Littlefield.

Fleming, Sean. 2022. "The Unabomber and the Origins of Anti-Tech Radicalism." *Journal of Political Ideologies* 27(2):207–25. https://doi.org/10.1080/13569317 .2021.1921940.

Fontana, Lorenza B., and Jean Grugel. 2016. "The Politics of Indigenous Participation Through 'Free Prior Informed Consent': Reflections from the Bolivian Case." *World Development* 77:249–61.

Foster, John Bellamy, et. al. 2006. "The Bamako Appeal." *Monthly Review Online*. https://mronline.org/2006/01/17/the-bamako-appeal/.

Foucault, Michel. 1977. *Discipline and punish: the birth of the prison*. New York: Pantheon.

Foweraker, Joe. 2020. *Oligarchy in the Americas: Comparing oligarchic rule in Latin America and the United States*. New York: Springer International Publishing.

———. 2001. "Grassroots Movements and Political Activism in Latin America: A Critical Comparison of Chile and Brazil." *Journal of Latin American Studies* 33(4):839–65.

Freeman, Jo. 1972. "The Tyranny of Structurelessness." *Berkeley Journal of Sociology* 17:151–164.

Fried Amilivia, Gabriela. 2016. "Trauma social, memoria colectiva y paradojas de las políticas de Olvido en el Uruguay tras el terror de Estado (1973-1985): memoria generacional de la post-dictadura (1985-2015)." *ILCEA: Revue de l'Institut des langues et cultures d'Europe, Amérique, Afrique, Asie et Australie* (26). https://doi .org/10.4000/ilcea.3938

Gallego, Jorge. 2018. "Natural Disasters and Clientelism: The Case of Floods and Landslides in Colombia." *Electoral Studies* 55:73–88. https://doi.org/10.1016/j .electstud.2018.08.001

Gamson, William A. 1975. *The strategy of social protest*. Homewood, Ill.: Dorsey Press.

Gandhi, L. 2019[1998]. *Postcolonial theory: a critical introduction: Second Edition*: Columbia University Press.

Gates, Henry Louis. 1986. *"Race," writing, and difference*. Chicago: University of Chicago Press.

Gayles, Prisca. 2021. "¿De dónde sos?: (Black) Argentina and the Mechanisms of Maintaining Racial Myths." *Ethnic and Racial Studies* 44(11):2093–112.

Geertz, Clifford. 1973. *The interpretation of cultures: selected essays*. New York: Basic Books.

Gelderloos, Peter. 2006. *Consensus: a new handbook for grassroots social, political, and environmental groups*. Tucson: See Sharp Press.

Glen, John M. 1988. *Highlander, no ordinary school, 1932-1962*. Lexington, KY: University Press of Kentucky.

Goffman, Erving. 1967. *Interaction ritual: essays in face-to-face behavior*. Chicago: Aldine Pub. Co.

Gómez Nieto, Libia Esperanza, Jorge Luis Vallejo, and Reinaldo Giraldo Díaz. 2016. "La huelga de corteros de caña de 2008 en la agroindustria de la caña de azúcar." In *El cambio de paisaje y la agroecología como alternativa a la crisis ambiental comtemporanea*, edited by Julialba Ángel Osorio. Bogotá: Libros Universidad Nacional Abierta y a Distancia.

Gómez Trujillo, Olmedo, Luis Delio Cruz Álvarez, and Esaud Urrutia Noel. 2007. *La Violencia en el Centro del Valle del Cauca: 1948-1965*. Cali: Unidad Central del Valle del Cauca, Institución Universitaria Publica de Formación profesional.

González Arana, Roberto and Ivonne Molinares Guerrero. 2013. "Movimiento obrero y protesta social en Colombia. 1920-1950." *Historia Caribe* 8(22):167–93.

Goodhand, Jonathan. 2000. "Research in Conflict Zones: Ethics and Accountability." *Forced Migration Review* 8(4):12–16.

Goodwin, Jeff. 1997. "The Libidinal Constitution of a High-Risk Social Movement: Affectual Ties and Solidarity in the Huk Rebellion, 1946 to 1954." *American Sociological Review* 62:53–69.

———. 2001. *No other way out: states and revolutionary movements, 1945-1991*. New York: Cambridge University Press.

Goodwin, Jeff, and James M. Jasper. 2003. *The social movements reader: cases and concepts*. Malden, MA: Blackwell Pub.

———. 2004. *Rethinking social movements: structure, meaning, and emotion*. Lanham: Rowman & Littlefield.

Goodwin, Jeff, James M. Jasper, and Francesca Polletta. 2000. "The Return of the Repressed: The Fall and Rise of Emotions in Social Movement Theory." *Mobilization* 5:65–84.

Goodwin, Jeff and Steven Pfaff. 2001. "Emotion Work in High-Risk Social Movements: Managing Fear in the US and East German Civil Rights Movements." In *Passionate politics: emotions and social movements*, edited by Jeff Goodwin, James M. Jasper, and Francesca Polletta. Chicago: University of Chicago Press.

Gordon, D. 2017. "'Civilization' and the Self-Critical Tradition." *Society* 54(2):106–23. doi:10.1007/s12115-017-0110-4

Gould, Jeffrey. 2011. "Response to Anthony Pereira." In *Contention in context: political opportunities and the emergence of protest*, edited by Jeffrey Goodwin and James M. Jasper. Stanford: Stanford University Press.

Grande, Edgar. 2006. "Cosmopolitan Political Science." *British Journal of Sociology* 57(1).

Graeber, David. 2007a. *Lost people: magic and the legacy of slavery in Madagascar*. Bloomington: Indiana University Press.

———. 2007b. *Possibilities: essays on hierarchy, rebellion and desire*. Edinburgh: AK.

Gramsci, Antonio. 1971[1935]. *Selections from the Prison Notebooks*. New York: International Publishers.

Grande, Edgar. 2006. "Cosmopolitan Political Science." *British Journal of Sociology* 57.

Granovetter, Mark S. 1973. "The Strength of Weak Ties." *American Journal of Sociology* 78(6):1360–80.

———. 1978. "Threshold Models of Collective Behavior." *American Journal of Sociology* 83(6):1420–43.

Greca, Verónica. 2009. "Un proceso de rebelión indígena: los mocovíes de San Javier en 1904." *Avá* 15.

Guerrero-Velasco, Rodrigo, et. al. 2021. "Homicide Epidemic in Cali, Colombia: A Surveillance System Data Analysis, 1993–2018." *American Journal of Public Health* 111(7):1292–99.

Gundelach, Peter and Jonas Toubøl. 2019. "High- and Low-Risk Activism: Differential Participation in a Refugee Solidarity Movement." *Mobilization* 24(2):199–220. https://doi.org/10.17813/1086-671X-24-2-199

Gutman, Herbert George. 1977. *Work, culture, and society in industrializing America: essays in American working-class and social history*. New York: Vintage Books.

Guzmán Campos, Germán, Orlando Fals-Borda, and Eduardo Umaña Luna. 1962. *La Violencia En Colombia: Estudio De Un Proceso Social*. Bogotá: Ediciones Tercer Mundo.

Guzmán, Daniel, Tamy Guberek, and Megan Price. 2012. "Unobserved Union Violence: Statistical Estimates of the Total Number of Trade Unionists Killed in Colombia, 1999-2008." Palo Alto, CA: Benetech Human Rights Program.

Haerpfer, C., Inglehart, R., Moreno, A., Welzel, C., Kizilova, K., Diez-Medrano J., M. Lagos, P. Norris, E. Ponarin & B. Puranen (eds.). 2022. *World values survey: round seven - country-pooled datafile version 4.0*. Madrid, Spain & Vienna, Austria: JD Systems Institute & WVSA Secretariat. doi:10.14281/18241.18

Hale, T. A. 1976. "Structural Dynamics in a Third World Classic: Aimé Césaire's Cahier d'un retour au pays natal." *Yale French Studies* 53:163–74.

Harrison, Faye V. 2012. "Building Black Diaspora Networks and Meshworks for Knowledge, Justice, Peace, and Human Rights." In *Afrodescendants, identity, and the struggle for development in the Americas*, edited by Bernd Reiter and Kimberly Eison Simmons. East Lansing: Michigan State University Press.

Hinton, William. 1983. *Shenfan*. New York: Random House.

Hobbes, Thomas. 2021[1651]. *Leviathan*. New York: W.W. Norton & Company.

Hochschild, Arlie Russell. 1983. *The managed heart: commercialization of human feeling*. Berkeley: University of California Press.

Hoffman, Abbie. 1971. *Steal This Book*. New York: Pirate.

Hofstetter, Marc, Daniel Mejía, José Nicolás Rosas, and Miguel Urrutia. 2018. "Ponzi Schemes and the Financial Sector: DMG and DRFE in Colombia." *Journal of Banking & Finance* 96:18–33.

Holloway, John and Eloína Peláez. 1998. *Zapatista!: reinventing revolution in Mexico*. Sterling, VA: Pluto Press.

Hope, E.C., R. Gugwor, K.N. Riddick, and K.N. Pender. 2019. "Engaged Against the Machine: Institutional and Cultural Racial Discrimination and Racial Identity as Predictors of Activism Orientation among Black Youth." *American Journal of Community Psychology* 63:61–72. https://doi.org/10.1002/ajcp.12303

Horton, Myles, Judith Kohl, and Herbert R. Kohl. 1990. *The long haul: an autobiography*. New York: Doubleday.

Hostetler, John A. 1993. *Amish Society*. Baltimore: John Hopkins University Press.

Human Rights Watch. 2007. "Maiming the People: Guerrilla Use of Antipersonnel Landmines and other Indiscriminate Weapons in Colombia." New York: Human Rights Watch.

Hylton, Forrest. 2006. *Evil hour in Colombia*. New York: Verso.

ICLR. 2004. "ICLR Summary and Recommendations." New York: International Commission for Labor Rights.

ICTUR. 2009. "Colombia Bulletin." London: International Centre for Trade Union Rights. January.

IDMC. 2006. "Colombia: Government "peace process" Cements Injustice for IDPs." Internal Displacement Monitoring Centre. Oslo: Norwegian Refugee Council.

Independent. 2011. "How Corny comedians Are Laughing All the Way to the Bank." 23 Oct. London: Independent Ltd.

Irons, Jenny. 1998. "The Shaping of Activist Recruitment and Participation: A Study of Women in the Mississippi Civil Rights Movement." *Gender and Society* 12:692–709.

Jaramillo Ferro, Jhon Edier. 2017. "Movilización de los corteros de caña de azúcar en el Valle del Cauca, huellas y despliegues de una acción colectiva." *Revista de Antropología y Sociología: Virajes* 19(2):93–114.

Jasper, James M. 1997. *The art of moral protest: culture, biography, and creativity in social movements*. Chicago: University of Chicago Press.

———. 1998. "The Emotions of Protest: Affective and Reactive Emotions In and Around Social Movements." *Sociological Forum* 13:397–424. https://doi.org/10.1023/A:1022175308081

———. 2004. "A Strategic Approach to Collective Action: Looking for Agency in Social-Movement Choices." *Mobilization* 9(1):1–16. https://doi.org/10.17813/maiq.9.1.m112677546p63361.

———. 2011. "Emotions and Social Movements: Twenty Years of Theory and Research." *Annual Review of Sociology* 37:285–303.

Jelin, Elizabeth. 2003. "Mas allá de la nación: las escalas múltiples de los movimientos sociales." Buenos Aires: Zorzal.

Jenkins, J Craig, and Craig M Eckert. 1986. "Channeling Black Insurgency: Elite Patronage and Professional Social Movement Organizations in the Development of the Black Movement." *American Sociological Review* 51(6):812–29.

Jenss, Alke. 2023. *Selective security in the war on drugs: the coloniality of state power in Colombia and Mexico.* Lanham: Rowman & Littlefield.

Jiménez, Leonardo Reales. 2012. "Ethnic Identity and Political Mobilization: The Afro-Colombian Case." In *Afrodescendants, Identity, and the Struggle for Development in the Americas,* edited by Bernd Reiter and Kimberly Eison Simmons. East Lansing: Michigan State University Press.

Johnston, Hank and Bert Klandermans. 1995. *Social movements and culture.* Minneapolis, Minn.: University of Minnesota Press.

Jones, Oliver R. 2008. "Implausible Deniability: State Responsibility for the Actions of Private Military Firms." *Connecticut Journal of International Law* 24(2):239–90.

Jones, Terry-Ann. 2020. *Sugarcane Labor Migration in Brazil.* Cham, Switzerland: Springer International Publishing.

Jordan, Lisa, and Peter van Tuijl. 2006. *NGO accountability: politics, principles and innovations.* Sterling, VA: Earthscan.

Jung, Moon-Ho. 2006. *Coolies and cane: race, labor, and sugar in the age of emancipation.* Baltimore: Johns Hopkins University Press.

Jung, Moon-Kie. 2006. *Reworking race: the making of Hawaii's interracial labor movement.* New York: Columbia University Press.

Kaldor, Mary. 2002. "Cosmopolitanism and Organized Violence." In *Conceiving Cosmopolitanism,* edited by S. Vertovec and R. Cohen. Oxford: Oxford University Press.

Kearney, Colin. 2011. "International Human Rights Corporate Liability Claims not Actionable under the Alien Tort Statute: Kiobel v. Royal Dutch Petroleum Co., 621 f.3d 111 (2d cir. 2010)." *Suffolk Transnational Law Review* 34(1):263–72.

Keck, Margaret E., and Kathryn Sikkink. 1998. *Activists beyond borders: advocacy networks in international politics.* Ithaca, N.Y.: Cornell University Press.

Kelley, Robin D. G. 1990. *Hammer and hoe: Alabama Communists during the Great Depression.* Chapel Hill: University of North Carolina Press.

Kiernan, Ben. 2008. *The pol pot regime: race, power, and genocide in Cambodia under the Khmer rouge, 1975-79.* Yale: New Haven.

Klandermans, Bert. 1992. "The Social Construction of Protest and Multiorganizational Fields." In *Frontiers in social movement theory,* edited by Aldon D. Morris and Carol McClurg Mueller. New Haven, Conn.: Yale University Press.

Klinenberg, Eric. 2002. *Heat wave: a social autopsy of disaster in Chicago.* Chicago: University of Chicago Press.

Kolben, Kevin. 2010. "Labor Rights as Human Rights." *Virginia Journal of International Law* 50(2):449–84.

Kropotkin, Petr Alekseevich. 1987 [1902]. *Mutual aid: a factor of evolution.* London: Freedom Press.

LADB Staff. *2008.* "Leader of Colombian Rebel Group FARC Confirmed Dead." Latin America Digital Beat. 6 June. https://digitalrepository.unm.edu/notisur/13696.

Lareau, Annette, and Erin McNamara Horvat. 1999. "Moments of Social Inclusion and Exclusion: Race, Class, and Cultural Capital in Family-School Relationships." *Sociology of Education* 72(1):37–53.

Larrier, R. 2010. "A Tradition of Literacy: Césaire in and out of the Classroom." *Research in African Literatures* 41(1):33–45. https://doi.org/10.2979/ral.2010.41 .1.33.

Latinobarómetro Corporation. 2007. "Latinobarómetro 2007" (database). Providencia, Chile.

———. 2008. "Latinobarómetro 2008" (database). Providencia, Chile.

———. 2009. "Latinobarómetro 2009" (database). Providencia, Chile.

———. 2010. "Latinobarómetro 2010" (database). Providencia, Chile.

———. 2017. "Latinobarómetro 2017" (database). Providencia, Chile.

LeGrand, Catherine. 1988. *Colonización y protesta campesina en Colombia (1850-1950).* Bogotá: Universidad de los Andes.

Leistner, Alexander. 2022. "'Die Friedensbewegung ist eine sehr deutsche, sehr weiße, eine sehr alte Bewegung': Perspektiven aus der Friedensbewegung im Gespräch mit Alexander Leistner (FJSB)." *Forschungsjournal Soziale Bewegungen* 35(4):639–52. https://doi.org/10.1515/fjsb-2022-0054.

Lenin, Vladimir Ilích. 1988[1902]. *What is to be done? Burning Questions of Our Movement.* Penguin classics. New York: Penguin Books. Translated by Robert Service.

Leondar-Wright, Betsy. 2014. *Missing class: strengthening social movement groups by seeing class cultures.* Ithaca: ILR Press.

Lessa, Francesca. 2021. "Remnants of Truth: The Role of Archives in Human Rights Trials for Operation Condor." *Latin American Research Review* 56(1):183–99.

Lévinas, Emmanuel. 1998[1991]. *Entre nous: on thinking-of-the-other.* New York: Columbia University Press.

Levine, Daniel H. 2011. "Camilo Torres: Fe, Política y Violencia." *Sociedad y religión* 21(34–35).

Levy, Daniel, and Natan Sznaider. 2006. "Sovereignty Transformed: A Sociology of Human Rights." *The British Journal of Sociology* 57(4):657–76.

Linera, Álvaro García. 2021. *La Potencia Plebeya: Acción colectiva e identidades indígenas, obreras y populares en Bolivia*: Buenos Aires: CLACSO.

Ling, Peter. 1995. "Local Leadership in the Early Civil Rights Movement: The South Carolina Citizenship Education Program of the Highlander Folk School." *Journal of American Studies* 29(3):399–422. http://www.jstor.org/stable/27556015.

Longtin, David. 2019. "Entre vie nue et projets de mort: l'imaginaire de la violence dans le discours du Conseil civique des organisations populaires et indigènes du Honduras (2009–2015)." *Canadian Journal of Latin American and Caribbean Studies* 44(2):139–68. HTTPS://DOI.ORG/10.1080/08263663.2019.1602370.

López-Pedreros, A. Ricardo. 2019. "Forward." In *Social Protests in Colombia: A History, 1958–1990,* edited by Mauricio Archila Neira. Lanham, MD: Lexington Books.

Lorde, Audre. 1984. *Sister outsider: essays and speeches.* Trumansburg, NY: Crossing Press.

Loveman, Mara. 1998. "High-Risk Collective Action: Defending Human Rights in Chile, Uruguay, and Argentina." *The American Journal of Sociology* 104:477–525.

Luna, Rohnal José Rada. 2022. "Percepción que tienen los trabajadores rurales respecto a la seguridad y salud en el trabajo." *Revista Colombiana de Salud Ocupacional* 12(1).

Luna-Cortés, Gonzalo. 2018. "Differences among Generations of USA Tourists Regarding the Positive Content Created about Colombia in Social Media." *Journal of Hospitality and Tourism Management* 36:31–39. https://doi.org/10.1016/j.jhtm .2018.07.002

Lyle, Fay. 2006. *The struggle for worker rights in Colombia.* Justice for All Series. Washington, DC: American Center for International Labor Solidarity (Solidarity Center).

Mahmood, Cynthia Keppley. 2001. "Terrorism, Myth, and the Power of Ethnographic Praxis." *Journal of Contemporary Ethnography* 30:520–45.

Maldonado, Etelvina [Singer]. 2002. "¿Porque me pega?" *Cantaoras.* Composed by Leonardo Gómez Jattín. Alé Kumá Recordings. Compact Disc.

Mandela, Nelson. 1994. *Long walk to freedom: the autobiography of Nelson Mandela.* Boston: Little, Brown and Company.

Marable, Manning. 2011. *Malcolm X: a life of reinvention.* New York: Viking.

March, James G., and Herbert A. Simon. 1958. *Organizations.* New York: Wiley.

Marchetti, Raffaele. 2006. "Global Governance or World Federalism? A Cosmopolitan Dispute on Institutional Models." *Global Society* 20(3):287–305. HTTPS://DOI.ORG/10.1080/13600820600816282

Marcos. 2001. *Our word is our weapon: selected writings*, edited by J. Ponce de Leon. New York: Seven Stories Press.

Marks, Tom. 1994. "Making Revolution with Shining Path." In *The Shining Path of Peru*, edited by D. S. Palmer. New York: Palgrave Macmillan.

García Márquez, Gabriel. 1997. *News of a kidnapping.* New York: Knopf.

Marx, G. T. 1974. "Thoughts on a Neglected Category of Social Movement Participant: The Agent Provocateur and the Informant." *American Journal of Sociology* 80(2):402–42.

McAdam, Doug. 1986. "Recruitment to High-Risk Activism: The Case of Freedom Summer." *The American Journal of Sociology* 92:64–90.

———. 1988. *Freedom summer.* New York: Oxford University Press.

———. 1989. "The Biographical Consequences of Activism." *American Sociological Review* 54:744–60.

———. 1996. "The Framing Function of Movement Tactics: Strategic Dramaturgy in the American Civil Rights Movement." In *Comparative Perspectives on Social Movements: Political Opportunities, Mobilizing Structures, and Cultural Framings*, edited by Doug McAdam, John D. McCarthy, and Mayer N. Zald. Cambridge: Cambridge University Press.

McAdam, Doug and Ronnelle Paulsen. 1993. "Specifying the Relationship Between Social Ties and Activism." *The American Journal of Sociology* 99:640–67.

McAdam, Doug, Sidney G. Tarrow, and Charles Tilly. 2001. *Dynamics of contention*. New York: Cambridge University Press.

McCarthy, John D. and Mayer N. Zald. 1977. "Resource Mobilization and Social Movements: A Partial Theory." *The American Journal of Sociology* 82:1212–41.

McCurdy, Patrick. 2012. "Social Movements, Protest and Mainstream Media." *Sociology Compass* 6:244–55. https://doi.org/10.1111/j.1751-9020.2011.00448.x

Mead, Margaret. 1928. *Coming of age in Samoa: a psychological study of primitive youth for western civilisation*. New York: W. Morrow & Company.

Meijering, et. al. 2007. "Intentional Communities in Rural Spaces." *Journal of Economic and Human Geography* 98(1):42–52.

Melucci, Alberto. 1989. *Nomads of the present*. Philadelphia: Temple.

Menchu, Rigoberta. 1984. *I... Rigoberta Menchu: An Indian woman in Guatemala*. London: Verso.

Mezinska, Signe, Péter Kakuk, Goran Mijaljica, Marcin Waligóra, and Dónal P. O'Mathúna. 2016. "Research in Disaster Settings: A Systematic Qualitative Review of Ethical Guidelines." *BMC Medical Ethics* 17(62). https://doi.org/10.1186/s12910-016-0148-7

Michels, Robert. 1915. *Political parties; a sociological study of the oligarchical tendencies of modern democracy*. New York: Hearst's International Library Co.

Mignone, Emilio Fermin, Cynthia L. Estlund, and Samuel Issacharoff. 1984. "Dictatorship on Trial: Prosecution of Human Rights Violations in Argentina." *Yale Journal of International Law* 10(1):118–50.

Mills, C. W. 1956. *The power elite*. New York: Oxford University Press.

Ministerio de Defensa Nacional. 2011. *Política Nacional de Defensa de la Libertad Personal 2011-2014*. Bogotá: Imprenta Nacional de Colombia.

Mische, Ann. 2008. *Partisan publics: communication and contention across Brazilian youth activist networks*. Princeton: Princeton University Press.

———. 2011. "Relational Sociology, Culture, and Agency." In *The Sage handbook of social network analysis*, edited by John Scott and Peter J. Carrington. Thousand Oaks, Calif.: Sage.

Mockus, Antanas. 1999. "Armonizar Ley, Moral Y Cultura: Cultura Ciudadana Prioridad De Gobierno Con Resultados En Prevención Y Control De Violencia En Bogotá, 1995-1997." Washington, DC: Inter-American Development Bank.

Molano, Alfredo. 2005. *The dispossessed: chronicles of the Desterrados of Colombia*. Chicago, Ill.: Haymarket Books.

Molina Fernando and Antonio Miguez. 2008. "The Origins of Mondragon: Catholic Co-Operativism and Social Movement in a Basque Valley (1941–59)." *Social History* 33(3):284–98.

Moncada, Alberto. 1995. *España americanizada*. Madrid: Temas de Hoy.

Monje, Juanita Barreto. 2018. "Liminality and Third Spaces as Negotiation Sites: Identity and Diasporic Social Movements." *Ethnographic Encounters* 9(1):32–38.

Montoya Duque, Gloria Inés. 2011. "El paro de corteros de caña en el Valle del Cauca - Colombia: Una acción colectiva de cara al modelo económico." *Entramado* 7:104–13.

Morris, Aldon. 1986. *Origins of the civil rights movement*. Free Press.

Morris, Aldon D. and Suzanne Staggenborg. 2004. "Leadership in Social Movements." In *The Blackwell companion to social movements*, edited by David A. Snow, Sarah A. Soule, and Hanspeter Kriesi. Malden, MA: Blackwell Pub.

Observatorio-semillero En Movimiento; Instituto de Estudios Políticos de la Universidad de Antioquia, Lolita Moreno, Nicolás Daniel Yepes, Maritza Quiroz, Víctor Calle, Karen Daniela Vidal, Yaritza García, Sebastián Flórez, Yuly Jiménez, Jorge Andrés Gallego, and María Andrea Canchila. 2023. "Reencuentros en movimiento: Un acercamiento académico-político a los procesos organizativos y las redes de activistas juveniles populares y estudiantiles durante y después del estallido social de 2021 en el Valle de Aburrá, Colombia." In *Derechos humanos y paz: Dimensiones para el fortalecimiento de la democracia*, edited by Pablo Vommaro. Buenos Aires: CLACSO.

Munson, Ziad W. 2008. *The making of pro-life activists: how social movement mobilization works*. Chicago: University of Chicago Press.

Murillo, Mario. 2008. "Weaving a Communication Quilt in Colombia: Civil Conflict, Indigenous Resistance and Community Radio in Northern Cauca." In *Global indigenous media: cultures, poetics, and politics*, edited by P. Wilson and M. Stewart. Durham: Duke University Press.

Naimark, Norman. 2006. "Totalitarian States and the History of Genocide." *Telos* 136:10–25.

Neira, Mauricio Archila. 2019. *Social Protests in Colombia: A History, 1958–1990*. Lanham, MD: Lexington Books.

Nepstad, Sharon Erickson. 2008. *Religion and war resistance in the plowshares movement*. Cambridge: Cambridge University Press.

Nepstad, Sharon Erickson and Christian Smith. 1999. "Rethinking Recruitment to High-Risk/Cost Activism: The Case of Nicaragua Exchange." *Mobilization* 4:25–40.

Nicolato, Giulia. 2022. "The Case of Giulio Regeni: Between Commercial Relations and Human Rights." MA Thesis. Venice: Ca' Foscari University of Venice.

Nowak, Manfred. 2003. *Introduction to the International human rights regime*. Boston: Brill.

O'Donnell, Guillermo. 1993. "On the State, Democratization and Some Conceptual Problems: A Latin American View with Glances at Some Postcommunist Countries." *World Development* 21(8):1355–69.

OAS. 2006. "Séptimo Informe Trimestral del Secretario General al Consejo Permanente Sobre la Misión de Apoyo al Proceso de Paz en Colombia." Bogotá: MAPP/Organization of American States.

Ochoa, Laura Correa. 2019. "Introduction: Afro-Latin America Rising." *Transition* 127:1–29. https://doi.org/10.2979/transition.127.1.01.

OECD. 2023a. "Hours Worked: Average Annual Hours Actually Worked." *OECD employment and labour market statistics* (database). Paris. https://doi.org/10.1787/data-00303-en.

———. 2023b. "Inflation (CPI)" (dataset). https://doi.org/10.1787/eee82e6e-en.

Olesen, Thomas. 2005. *International Zapatismo: the construction of solidarity in the age of globalization*. New York: Zed Books.

Oliver, Pamela, Gerald Marwell, and Ruy Teixeira. 1985. "A Theory of the Critical Mass. I. Interdependence, Group Heterogeneity, and the Production of Collective Action." *American Journal of Sociology* 91(3):522–56.

Ortega y Gasset, José. (1959[1934]). *Ideas y creencias y otros ensayos de filosofía.*

Ostrander, Susan A. 2004. "Democracy, Civic Participation, and the University: A Comparative Study of Civic Engagement on Five Campuses." *Nonprofit and Voluntary Sector Quarterly* 33(1):74–93. https://doi.org/10.1177/0899764003260588.

Outhwaite, William. 1987. *New philosophies of social science: Realism, hermeneutics and critical theory.* London: MacMillan.

Pacini, Deborah. 1995. *Bachata: a social history of a Dominican popular music.* Philadelphia: Temple University Press.

Paige, Jeffery M. 1975. *Agrarian revolution: social movements and export agriculture in the underdeveloped world.* New York: Free Press.

Palacios, Paulo César León. 2012. "El espectacular lanzamiento de la guerrilla urbana en Colombia, el M-19 en 1974." *Historias: Revista de la dirección de Estudios Históricos INAH* 83:103–11.

Pappas, Takis S. 2008. "Political Leadership and the Emergence of Radical Mass Movements in Democracy." *Comparative Political Studies* 41:1117–40.

Paschel, Tianna S. 2018. "Rethinking Black Mobilization in Latin America." In *Afro-Latin American studies: an introduction*, edited by Alejandro de la Fuente and George Reid Andrews. New York: Cambridge University Press.

Paternostro, Silvana. 1995. "Mexico as a Narco-Democracy." *World Policy Journal* 12(1):41.

Paul, Shuva, Sarah J. Mahler, and Michael Schwartz. 1997. "Mass Action and Social Structure." *Political Power and Social Theory* 11:45–99.

Pécaut, Daniel. 1987. *L'ordre Et La Violence: Évolution Socio-Politique De La Colombie Entre 1930 Et 1953.* Paris: Éditions de l'École des hautes études en sciences sociales.

Peña, Alejandro M., Larissa Meier, and Alice M. Nah. 2023. "Exhaustion, Adversity, and Repression: Emotional Attrition in High-Risk Activism." *Perspectives on Politics* 21(1):27–42.

Pereria Novales, José Roberto. 2007. "Champions of Productivity: Pains and Fevers in São Paulo's Sugarcane Plantations." *Estudios Avançados* 21(59):167–78.

Pérez Prieto, Victorino. 2016. "Los Orígenes de la Teología de la Liberación en Colombia: Richard Shaull, Camilo Torres, Rafael Ávila, 'Golcanda,' Sacerdotes para América Latina, Cristianos por el Socialismo y Comunidades Eclesiales de Base." *Cuestiones Teológicas* 43:73–108.

Pérez Rincón, Mario Alejandro and Paula Alvarez Roa. 2009. *Deuda Social y Ambiental del Negocio de la Caña de Azúcar en Colombia.* Bogotá: ARFO Editores e Impresores, Ltda.

Perrow, Charles. 2002. *Organizing America: wealth, power, and the origins of corporate capitalism.* Princeton: Princeton University Press.

Petras, James, and Henry Veltmeyer. 2003. "Dynamics of Peasant Organizing in Latin America." *Social Policy* 33(4):33–39.

Phajan, Teerasak, Kessarawan Nilvarangkul, Dariwan Settheetham, and Wongsa Laohasiriwong. 2014. "Work-Related Musculoskeletal Disorders among Sugarcane Farmers in North-Eastern Thailand." *Asia Pacific Journal of Public Health* 26(3):320–27.

Pierson, Paul. 2000. "Not Just What, But When: Timing and Sequence in Political Processes." *Studies in American Political Development* 14(1):72–92.

Pineda Duque, Javier. 2015. "Colombia: el sesgo antilaboral del modelo de desarrollo y las políticas de formalización." *Cuadernos del CENDES* 32(89):103–40.

Piven, Frances Fox. 2006. *Challenging authority: how ordinary people change America.* Lanham: Rowman & Littlefield.

Piven, Frances Fox and Richard A. Cloward. 1977. *Poor people's movements: why they succeed, how they fail.* New York: Pantheon Books.

Polanía, Laura, Catalina Guzmán, and Diana Cristina Cruz Gómez. 2019. "Enfermedades y accidentes laborales generados por factores de riesgo en la actividad agrícola." *Mente Joven* 8:89–105.

Polletta, Francesca. 2002. *Freedom is an endless meeting: democracy in American social movements.* Chicago: University of Chicago Press.

———. 2006. *It was like a fever: storytelling in protest and politics.* Chicago: University of Chicago Press.

Potorti, Mary. 2017. "'Feeding the Revolution': the Black Panther Party, Hunger, and Community Survival." *Journal of African American Studies* 21(1):85–110. https://doi.org/10.1007/s12111-017-9345-9.

Prado, Mario Fernando. 2008. "Que protesten, pero que no bloqueen." Opinion. *El Espectador.* Bogotá. 25 September.

Rajah, Colin. 2000. "Globalism and Race at A16 in DC." *Colorlines* 3(3).

Rajão, Raoni, and Tiago Duarte. 2018. "Performing Postcolonial Identities at the United Nations' Climate Negotiations." *Postcolonial Studies* 21(3):364–78.

Ralchev, P. 2018. "Non-State Agents in Contentious Politics: Transnational Networks of Soros' Open Society and Gulen's Hizmet Movement." *Journal of the University of National and World Economy* 1(1):95–107.

Ramos, Howard. 2008. "Opportunity for Whom?: Political Opportunity and Critical Events in Canadian Aboriginal Mobilization, 1951-2000." *Social Forces* 87:795–823.

Red Revuelta. 2008. "The Students are Preoccupied, and the Campus is Too: Shutting Down/Opening Up the National University of Colombia." *Rolling Thunder* 6:57–64.

Reed, Jean-Pierre. 2002. "Culture in Action: Nicaragua's Revolutionary Identities Reconsidered." *New Political Science* 24(2):235–63.

Reif, Linda L. 1986. "Women in Latin American Guerrilla Movements: A Comparative Perspective." *Comparative Politics* 18(2):147–69. https://doi.org/10.2307/421841.

Republic of Colombia Ombudsman's Office. 2007. "Informe de Riesgo No. 004-07." Early Warning System. May 23. Bogotá.

Republic of Colombia Vice-president's Office. 2009. "Situación Nacional de Minas Antipersonal." Programa Presidencial para la Acción Integral contra Minas Antipersonal. 30 June. Bogotá.

Richani, Nazih. 2002. *Systems of violence: the political economy of war and peace in Colombia*. Albany: State University of New York Press.

Robben, Antonius C. G. M. and Carolyn Nordstrom. 1995. "The Anthropology and Ethnography of Violence and Sociopolitical Conflict." In *Fieldwork under fire: contemporary studies of violence and survival*, edited by C. Nordstrom and A. C. G. M. Robben. Berkeley: University of California Press.

Robnett, Belinda. 1996. "African-American Women in the Civil Rights Movement, 1954-1965: Gender, Leadership, and Micromobilization." *American Journal of Sociology* 101:1661.

———. 1997. *How long? How long? : African-American women in the struggle for civil rights*. New York: Oxford University Press.

Rockefeller, Stuart Alexander. 2007. "Dual Power in Bolivia: Movement and Government Since the Election of 2005." *Urban Anthropology and Studies of Cultural Systems and World Economic Development* 36(3):161–93.

Romanos, Eduardo. 2014. "Emotions, Moral Batteries and High-Risk Activism: Understanding the Emotional Practices of the Spanish Anarchists under Franco's Dictatorship." *Contemporary European History* 23(4):545–64.

Romero Leal, Karen Lorena. 2017. "Condiciones de producción de un boom de literatura testimonial del secuestro en Colombia." *Revista Colombiana de Sociología* 40(1):161–86.

Rooksby, J., and I. Sommerville. 2012. "The Management and Use of Social Network Sites in a Government Department." *Computer Supported Cooperative Work* 21:397–415. https://doi.org/10.1007/s10606-011-9150-2

Rosenthal, Naomi, Meryl Fingrutd, Michele Ethier, Roberta Karant, and David McDonald. 1985. "Social Movements and Network Analysis: A Case Study of Nineteenth-Century Women's Reform in New York State." *The American Journal of Sociology* 90:1022–54.

Rothengatter, Talib. 1982. "The Effects of Police Surveillance and Law Enforcement on Driver Behaviour." *Current Psychological Reviews* 2:349–358. https://doi.org/10.1007/BF02684467

Ruiz, Bert. 2001. *The Colombian civil war*. Jefferson, N.C.: McFarland.

Russell, Bertrand. 1997[1912]. *The problems of philosophy*. New York: Oxford University Press.

Rutten, Rosanne. 2000. "High-Cost Activism and the Worker Household: Interests, Commitment, and the Costs of Revolutionary Activism in a Philippine Plantation Region." *Theory and Society* 29:215–52.

Salgado, María Mercedes. 2018. "High Risk Activism: The Sandinista National Liberation Front (FSLN) ¡Patria libre o morir!" *Anuario de Estudios Centroamericanos* 44:367–98.

Sánchez, Alejandro. 2014. "COHA Report: Drones in Latin America." *Council on Hemispheric Affairs*. Policy Memo #4: 1 Dec. Washington, D.C.

Sánchez Mejía, Hugues R. and Adriana Santos Delgado. 2014. "Estado, innovación y expansión de la agroindustria azucarera en el valle del río Cauca (Colombia), 1910-1945." *América Latina en la historia económica* 21(3):201–30.

Santos, Boaventura de Sousa. 2006. *The rise of the global left: the world social forum and beyond*. New York: Zed Books.

———. 2009. "Para além do Pensamento Abissal: das linhas globais a uma ecologia de saberes." In *Epistemologias do Sul*, edited by Boaventura de Sousa Santos and Maria Paula Meneses. Coimbra: Edições Almedina S.A.

Scheper-Hughes, Nancy. 1992. *Death without weeping: the violence of everyday life in Brazil*. Berkeley: University of California Press.

Schneider, Cathy Lisa. 1995. *Shantytown protest in Pinochet's Chile*. Philadelphia: Temple University Press.

Schneider Marques, Teresa Cristina. 2017. "O Exílio e as Transformações de Repertórios de Ação Coletiva: A Esquerda Brasileira no Chile e na França (1968-1978)." *Dados: Revista de Ciências Sociais* 60(1):239–79.

Schussman and Soule. 2005. "Process and Protest: Accounting for Individual Protest Participation." *Social Forces* 84(2):1083–108. https://doi.org/10.1353/sof.2006.0034

Schwartz, Michael. 1976. *Radical protest and social structure: the Southern Farmers' Alliance and cotton tenancy, 1880-1890*. New York: Academic Press.

———. 2007. "Author-Meets-Critic." *Social Movement Studies* 6:195 - 205.

———. 2008. "A postscript to 'Catnets'." *Sociologica* 2(1).

Schwarzbach, N. and B. Richardson. 2014. "Bitter Harvest: Child Labour in Sugarcane Agriculture and the Role of Certification Systems." *U.C. Davis Journal of International Law & Policy* 21(1):99–130.

Scott, James C. 2009. *The art of not being governed: an anarchist history of upland Southeast Asia*. New Haven: Yale University Press.

Scussolini, Mirco. 2011. *Drugspot: analisi e critica degli spot audiovisivi sociali sulle droghe*. Milan Polytechnic. Master's Thesis. http://hdl.handle.net/10589/19331

Semana. 2008. "Que no les piquen más caña." Bogotá. 23 September.

Sharp, Gene. 1973. *The politics of non-violent action*. Boston: Porter Sargent.

Shaw, Rosalind. 2007. "Displacing Violence: Making Pentecostal Memory in Postwar Sierra Leone." *Cultural Anthropology* 22(1):66–93.

Sitrin, Marina. 2006. *Horizontalism: voices of popular power in Argentina*. Edinburgh: AK Press.

Skocpol, Theda. 1979. *States and social revolutions: a comparative analysis of France, Russia, and China*. New York: Cambridge University Press.

Slovo, Gillian. 1997. *Every secret thing: my family, my country*. Boston: Little, Brown.

Sluka, Jeffrey A. 1995. "Domination, Resistance and Political Culture in Northern Ireland's Catholic-Nationalist Ghettos." *Critique of Anthropology* 15(1):71–102.

Snow, David A. and Robert D. Benford. 1988. "Ideology, Frame Resonance, and Participant Mobilization." *International Social Movement Research* 1:217.

Snow, David A., Sarah Anne Soule, and Hanspeter Kriesi. 2004. "Introduction." In *The Blackwell companion to social movements*, edited by David A. Snow, Sarah A. Soule, and Hanspeter Kriesi. Malden, MA: Blackwell.

Snow, David A., Louis A. Zurcher, Jr., and Sheldon Ekland-Olson. 1980. "Social Networks and Social Movements: A Microstructural Approach to Differential Recruitment." *American Sociological Review* 45:787–801.

Sobottka, Emil A. 2002. "Organizações civis buscando uma definição para além de ONGs e terceiro setor." *Civitas: Revista de Ciências Sociais* 2(1):81–95.

Souza, Renato, Thomaz Wood, and Brad Jackson. 2021. "What Favelas Can Teach Us about Leadership: The Importance of Shared-Purpose and Place-Based Leadership." In *Reimagining leadership on the commons: shifting the paradigm for a more ethical, equitable, and just world*, edited by D.P. Singh, R.J. Thompson, and K.A. Curran. Bingley: Emerald.

Sriram, Chandra Lekha. 2009. "Maintenance of Standards of Protection during Writeup and Publication." In *Surviving field research: working in violent and difficult situations*, edited by Chandra Lekha Sriram, John C. King, Julie A. Mertus, Olga Martin-Ortega, and Johanna Herman. New York: Routledge.

Starr, Amory, Luis A. Fernandez, Randall Amster, Lesley J. Wood, and Manuel J. Caro. 2008. "The Impacts of State Surveillance on Political Assembly and Association: A Socio-Legal Analysis." *Qualitative Sociology* 31:251–70. https://doi.org/10.1007/s11133-008-9107-z

Storrs, K. L. and Veillette, C. 2003. *Andean Regional Initiative (ARI): FY2002 supplemental and FY2003 assistance for Colombia and neighbors.* Congressional Research Service. Library of Congress. 25 July.

Tarde, G. 1890. *Les Lois de Limitation: Etude Sociologique.* Paris: Felix Alcan.

Tarrow, Sidney. 1995. "Fishnets, Internets and Catnets: Globalization and Social Movements." In *conference on" Structure, Identity and Power: The Past and Future of Collective Action*," Amsterdam.

Tate, Winifred. 2007. *Counting the dead: the culture and politics of human rights activism in Colombia.* Berkeley: University of California Press.

Taylor, Verta. 1989. "Social Movement Continuity: The Women's Movement in Abeyance." *American Sociological Review* 54(5):761–75.

Thalhammer, Kristina E. 2001. "I'll Take the High Road: Two Pathways to Altruistic Political Mobilization Against Regime Repression in Argentina." *Political Psychology* 22(3):493–519.

Thompson, E. P. 1971. "The Moral Economy of the English Crowd in the Eighteenth Century." *Past and Present* 50:76–136.

Tilly, Charles. 1964. *The Vendee.* Cambridge, Mass.: Harvard University Press.

———. 1978. *From mobilization to revolution.* New York: Random House.

———. 1985. "War Making and State Making as Organized Crime." In *Bringing the state back in*, edited by Peter B. Evans, Dietrich Rueschemeyer, and Theda Skocpol. Social Science Research Council. New York: Cambridge University Press.

———. 1986. *The contentious French.* Cambridge, Mass.: Belknap Press.

———. 1993. *European revolutions, 1492-1992.* Cambridge, Mass.: Blackwell.

———. 1995. "Contentious Repertoires in Great Britain." In *Repertoires and cycles of collective action*, edited by M. Traugott. Durham: Duke University Press.

———. 1996. "Invisible Elbow." *Sociological Forum* 11(4):589–601.

———. 2005. "Repression, Mobilization, and Explanation." In *Repression and Mobilization: Social Movements, Protest, and Contention*, edited by Christian Davenport, Hank Johnston and Carol McClurg Mueller. Minneapolis: University of Minnesota Press.

————. 2008. "Describing, Measuring, and Explaining Struggle." *Qualitative Sociology* 31:1–13.

Tilly, Charles, and Sidney G. Tarrow. 2007. *Contentious politics*. Boulder, Colo.: Paradigm Publishers.

Torres, Camilo. 1969. *Revolutionary writings*. New York: Herder and Herder.

Touraine, Alain. 1985. "An Introduction to the Study of Social Movements." *Social Research* 52(4):749–87.

Turner, Brian. 2006. "Classical Sociology and Cosmopolitanism: A Critical Defense of the Social." *British Journal of Sociology* 57:133–51.

Turner, Ralph H., and Lewis M. Killian. 1957. *Collective behavior*. Englewood Cliffs, N.J.: Prentice-Hall.

Turner, Scott. 1998. "Global Civil Society, Anarchy and Governance: Assessing an Emerging Paradigm." *Journal of Peace Research* 35:25–42.

Tversky, Amos, and Daniel Kahneman. 1974. "Judgment under Uncertainty: Heuristics and Biases: Biases in Judgments Reveal Some Heuristics of Thinking under Uncertainty." *Science* 185(4157):1124–31.

Tyagi, Juhi. 2018. "Individual–Territory–Movement Nexus in Armed Movement Resilience: Case of the Maoist Movement in Warangal, Telangana." In *Intractable Conflicts in Contemporary India*, edited by Savyasaachi. New York: Routledge.

Uhl-Bien, Mary, and Sonia Ospina. 2012. *Advancing relational leadership research: a dialogue among perspectives*. Charlotte, NC: Information Age.

UN General Assembly. 1999. "Declaration on the Right and Responsibility of Individuals, Groups and Organs of Society to Promote and Protect Universally Recognized Human Rights and Fundamental Freedoms." A/RES/53/144. United Nations: New York. 8 March.

UNOHCR. 2007. "Report of the United Nations High Commissioner for Human Rights on the situation of human rights in Colombia." Office of the High Commissioner for Human Rights. Geneva: United Nations.

————. 2011. "Commentary to the Declaration on the Right and Responsibility of Individuals, Groups and Organs of Society to Promote and Protect Universally Recognized Human Rights and Fundamental Freedoms." UN Special Rapporteur on the situation of human rights defenders. Office of the High Commissioner for Human Rights. Geneva: United Nations. July.

University of Georgia; Esri 3.x; Landsat; UNODC-SIMCI. 2007. Data Repository: GIS Support Team. Athens. Made using QGIS by Louis Edgar Esparza.

Uribe, María Teresa. 2004. "Emancipación Social en un Contexto de Guerra Prolongada: El Caso de la Comunidad de Paz de San Jose de Apartado." In *Emancipación social y violencia en Colombia*, edited by Boaventura de Sousa Santos and Mauricio García Villegas. Bogotá: Grupo Editorial Norma.

Uribe-Castro, Hernando. 2014. "Expansión Cañera en el Valle del Cauca y Resistencias Comunitarias (Colombia)." *Ambiente y Sostenibilidad* 4(1):16–30.

U.S. State Department. 2022. *Colombia 2021 human rights report*. Washington, DC: Bureau of Democracy, Human Rights, and Labor.

————. 2021. "Revocation of the Terrorist Designations of the Revolutionary Armed Forces of Colombia (FARC) and Additional Terrorist Designations" [press release]. 30 Nov. Washington, D.C.

Van Cott, Donna Lee. 2009. *Radical democracy in the Andes*. New York: Cambridge University Press.

Vergara, Ángela. 2013. "Paternalismo industrial, empresa extranjera y campamentos mineros en América Latina: un esfuerzo de historia laboral y transnacional." *Avances del Cesor* 10:113–28.

Vergara-Camus, Leandro. 2009. "The Politics of the MST: Autonomous Rural Communities, the State, and Electoral Politics." *Latin American Perspectives* 36(4):178–91. https://doi.org/10.1177/0094582x09338608.

Vergara-Camus, Leandro and Cristóbal Kay. 2017. "Agribusiness, Peasants, Left-Wing Governments, and the State in Latin America: An Overview and Theoretical Reflections." *Journal of Agrarian Change* 17(2):239–57. https://doi.org/10.1111/joac.12215.

Villoro, Luis. 2002[1982]. *Creer, saber, conocer*. Coyoacán, México: Siglo Veintiuno.

Viterna, Jocelyn S. 2006. "Pulled, Pushed, and Persuaded: Explaining Women's Mobilization into the Salvadoran Guerrilla Army." *American Journal of Sociology* 112:1–45.

Vlastos, Stephen. 1986. *Peasant protests and uprisings in Tokugawa Japan*. Berkeley: University of California Press.

Wada, Takeshi. 2006. "Event Analysis of Claim Making in Mexico: How are Social Protests Transformed into Political Protests?" *Mobilization: An International Quarterly* 9(3):241–57.

Warhurst, Christopher. 1996. "High Society in a Workers' Society: Work, Community and Kibbutz" *Sociology* 30(1):1–19.

Warren, Kay B. 1998. *Indigenous movements and their critics: Pan-Maya activism in Guatemala*. Princeton, NJ: Princeton University Press.

Weinstein, Jeremy M. 2007. *Inside rebellion: the politics of insurgent violence*. New York: Cambridge University Press.

White, Harrison. 2008a. *Identity & control: how social formations emerge*. Princeton: Princeton University Press.

————. 2008b [1965]. "Notes on the Constituents of Social Structure. Soc. Rel. 10 – Spring '65. " *Sociologica* (1). https://doi.org/10.2383/26576. Transcribed by Michael Schwartz.

White, Harrison, Jan Fuhse, Matthias Thiemann, and Larissa Buchholz. 2018. "Networks and Meaning: Styles and Switchings." In *Zehn Jahre danach. Niklas Luhmanns "Die Gesellschaft der Gesellschaft,"* edited by Dirk Baecker, Michael Hutter, Gaetano Romano and Rudolf Stichweh. Boston: De Gruyter Oldenbourg.

White, Robert. 2007. ""I'm not too sure what I told you the last time": Methodological Notes on Accounts from High-Risk Activists in the Irish Republican Movement." *Mobilization* 12(3):287–305.

Whyte, William Foote. 1993 [1955]. *Street corner society: the social structure of an Italian slum*. Chicago: University of Chicago Press.

Wilkinson, Daniel. 2002. *Silence on the mountain: stories of terror, betrayal, and forgetting in Guatemala*. Boston: Houghton Mifflin.

Wiltfang, Gregory L. and Doug McAdam. 1991. "The Costs and Risks of Social Activism: A Study of Sanctuary Movement Activism." *Social Forces* 69(4):987–1010.

WOLA. 2007. "The Captive State: Organized Crime and Human Rights in Latin America." Washington, D.C.: Washington Office on Latin America.

———. 2010. "Workers without Rights: Labor Activists in Valle del Cauca's Sugar Sector under Fire." Washington, DC: Washington Office on Latin America.

———. 2021. *A long way to go: implementing Colombia's peace accord after five years*. Washington, DC: Washington Office on Latin America.

Wood, Elisabeth Jean. 2003. *Insurgent collective action and civil war in El Salvador*. New York: Cambridge University Press.

———. 2006. "The Ethical Challenges of Field Research in Conflict Zones." *Qualitative Sociology* 29(3):373–86. http://dx.doi.org/10.1007/s11133-006-9027-8.

World Bank. 2022. Poverty and Equity Database (database). Washington, DC.

X, Malcolm. 1992 [1970]. *By any means necessary*. New York: Pathfinder.

Xe Currency Data API. 2023. http://www.xe.com.

Yohanani, L. 2022. "High-Risk Transnationalism: Why Do Israeli-Americans Volunteer in the Israeli Military?" *Sociological Forum* 37:533–56. https://doi.org/10.1111/socf.12806.

Young, Kevin A. 2022. "Our Social Conquests Will Be Respected: Peasants and Military Dictatorship in Cochabamba, Bolivia." *Hispanic American Historical Review* 102(3):481–512. https://doi.org/10.1215/00182168-9798304.

Zalnieriute, M. 2022. "How Public Space Surveillance is Eroding Political Protests in Australia." In *Überwachung im öffentlichen Raum*, edited by Marlene Straub. Berlin: Verfassungsbooks.

Zibechi, Raúl. 2005. "The Other Colombia, the One of Hope: Militarism and Social Movements." *Counterpunch*, 5–6 March, Weekend Edition.

———. 2007. *Autonomías y emancipaciones: América Latina en movimiento*. Lima: Universidad Nacional Mayor de San Marcos.

———. 2010. *Dispersing power: social movements as anti-state forces*. Oakland, CA: AK Press.

Zulaika, Joseba. 1988. *Basque violence: metaphor and sacrament*. Reno: University of Nevada Press.

Zwerman, Gilda. 1994. "Mothering on the Lam: Politics, Gender Fantasies and Maternal Thinking in women Associated with Armed, Clandestine Organization in the United States." *Feminist Review*:33–56.

Zwerman, Gilda and Patricia Steinhoff. 2005. "When Activists Ask for Trouble: State-Dissident Interactions and the New Left Cycle of Resistance in the United States and Japan." In *Repression and mobilization, social movements, protest, and contention*, edited by Christian Davenport, Hank Johnston, and Carol Mueller. Minneapolis: University of Minnesota Press.

Index

Page references for figures are italicized.

About the Author

Louis Edgar Esparza is Professor of Sociology at California State University-Los Angeles. He was Fulbright Distinguished Scholar in Democracy, Human Rights and Violence Prevention at the University of Brasília in 2022 and a National Endowment for the Humanities Summer Scholar at the University of Tampa in 2023. His research has appeared in *Contexts, Global Labor Journal, Contemporary Justice Review, Society & Natural Resources, Interface, Partecipazione e Conflitto,* and elsewhere. Louis is co-author of *Human Rights: A Primer* (2016) and co-editor of *Human Rights Of, By, and For the People* (2017). He served as Co-Chair of the Task Force on Contingent Faculty for the American Sociological Association and is a founding member of the Human Rights section.

www.ingramcontent.com/pod-product-compliance
Lightning Source LLC
Chambersburg PA
CBHW022314280326
41932CB00010B/1099